D1065206

GREAT FOODS OF THE WORLD

Regional Italian, Mexican and Asian Cooking

Evan Kleiman
Susan Feniger and Mary Sue Milliken
Joyce Jue

FOG CITY PRESS

First published in the U.S.A. in 1996 by
Sunset Publishing Corporation

Originally published as
Pizzeria (© 1996 Weldon Owen Inc.)
Cantina (© 1996 Weldon Owen Inc.)
Far East Cafe (© 1996 Weldon Owen Inc.)

Produced by
FOG CITY PRESS
Chief Executive Officer: John Owen
President: Terry Newell
Chief Operating Officer: Larry Partington
Publisher: Lynn Humphries
Project Manager/Editor: Julie Stillman
Sales Manager: Emily Jahn
Vice President International Sales: Stuart Laurence
Copy Editor: Sharon Silva
Indexer: Michael D. Loo
Design: Patty Hill
Production Manager: Chris Hemesath
Digital Production: Joan Olson
Food Photography: Peter Johnson, Joyce Oudkerk Pool
Assistant Food Photography: Dal Harper, Mil Truscott
Food Stylist: Janice Baker, Stephanie Greenleigh
Prop Stylist: Carol Hacker
Assistant Food Stylists: Liz Nolan, Claudia Breault
Chapter Opener Illustrations: Faranak, Miriam Fabbri,
   Mick Armson
Glossary Illustrations: Alice Harth

A Weldon Owen Production
Copyright © 2002 Weldon Owen Inc.

10 9 8 7 6 5 4 3 2 1

Library of Congress Cataloging-in-Publication Data is
available.

ISBN 1-892374-61-7

Printed in Singapore by Kyodo Printing Co. (S'pore)
   Pte Ltd

Photography Credits:
Jason Lowe pages 1, 4 (top), 6–7, 8 (bottom), and
10–11; Steven Rothfeld pages 8 (top) and 9 (top);
Ignacio Urquiza pages 2–3, 4 (middle), 9 (bottom),
and 120–121; Via eStock Photo Agency: Steve Vidler
pages 4 (bottom) and 230–231.

A Note on Weights and Measures:
All recipes include customary U.S., U.K., and metric measure-
ments. Conversions are based on a standard developed for these
books and have been rounded off. Actual weights may vary.

GREAT FOODS OF THE WORLD

Regional Italian, Mexican and Asian Cooking

Contents

INTRODUCTION

"**D**o you feel like Italian, Mexican or Chinese tonight?" These words echo around the house at dinnertime, because whether it's pizza, tacos or sweet-and-sour chicken, these three cuisines seem to be the perennial favorites. Now you can re-create the ethnic specialties you love, in your own kitchen. *Regional Italian, Mexican and Asian Cooking* brings home the best food from casual dining spots around the globe.

This volume was inspired by the unpretentious fare you find at Italian pizzerias, Mexican cantinas and Asian street cafes—everything from appetizers to desserts. Over the years, these foods have evolved and been reinterpreted for the changing tastes of today's global palate, and we bring you 165 recipes that feature traditional home-style dishes as well as their contemporary counterparts.

Italian Foods

The recipes in the Italian section have their origins in the simple fare of the pizzeria—from its humble beginnings in the alleyways of Naples to the more sophisticated establishments found in our major cities today. There are plenty of recipes for the cherished pizza, ranging from the classic *pizza Margherita* to a twenty-first-century version featuring smoked salmon and smoked mozzarella. Other Italian specialties share the stage with the array of pizzas: antipasti and salads; calzones; simple pasta dishes; savory focaccias; roasted chicken and other rustic main dishes; and, of course, a selection of classic Italian desserts.

Mexican Foods

In Mexico, the cantina is the place that working folk gather to relax and enjoy good food. From the first sip of a margarita with salsa and chips, through the main course with mandatory rice and beans, to the last soothing spoonful of flan, a cantina meal awakens the senses with vibrant tastes and textures. This cantina approach to cooking has found its way north of the border, where many American restaurants serve their own traditional and contemporary interpretations in the form of New Mexican, Tex-Mex and Cal-Mex food.

The recipes in this section reflect Mexico's diverse regional specialties—grilled lobster from the seaside cantinas of Baja California,

exotic Mayan-style tamales wrapped in banana leaves from the Yucatán, grilled or dried beef dishes from the taco stands of the north, or chicken simmered in the legendary mole sauce of Oaxaca.

Asian Foods

Throughout Asia, people are accustomed to eating many little meals during the day, so the street-food stall—a portable kitchen run by street vendors offering family recipes—is a way of life. This "street food" may be found at a roadside stand, a bustling sidewalk cafe, or an air-conditioned food court in a department store. Whatever the location, the sound of a sizzling wok and the pungent and savory aromas that fill the air signal that good food awaits.

Paying homage to this simple Asian dining tradition, this section of the book offers a sampling of dishes from the diverse ethnic and regional styles around the continent—spring rolls from Vietnam, Chinese dim sum, Indonesian fritters and satays, and the steaming noodle dishes and soups that play a major role in all Asian cuisine

Bringing It Home

Throughout this book are features designed to make it simple to enjoy the great foods of the world in your own home. Basic recipes for tomato sauce and pizza dough, tortillas and salsas, and Asian sauces enable you to prepare dishes easily from scratch. In addition, an illustrated glossary (pages 340–348) defines common ingredients, cooking procedures and equipment. Full color photographs show you exactly how each finished dish should look.

So whether you're in the mood for Sausage and Mushroom Pizza (page 47), Chiles Rellenos (page 188) or Thai Coconut Chicken Soup (page 284), there's no need to leave the house—you hold the recipes in your hand.

ITALIAN

The roots of the modern pizza may be traced back to the first century A.D., but it wasn't until sometime in the sixteenth century—after the arrival of the tomato in Naples from the New World—that pizzas began to resemble the food we know today. Soon after tomatoes joined the dough, the modern pizzeria had its humble beginning in the streets of Naples. Small rooms were cut into the city's venerable stone walls to house beehive-shaped ovens in which *pizzaioli* or "pizza makers" would bake disks of dough topped simply with tomatoes, a drizzle of olive oil and some oregano.

The late nineteenth and early twentieth centuries saw many workers leave Naples in search of better lives in America, and the *pizzaioli* brought their talent and recipes with them. But it wasn't until the return of GIs from Europe after World War II that pizza began to develop the extraordinary following it has today. In the 1970s, an explosion of interest in cooking influenced by fresh ingredients and the traditions of different European and Asian cuisines brought more variety to the pizzeria, as pizzas were served with ever-more-creative combinations of sauces, toppings and cheeses. As cooking and eating habits change, so does the pizzeria change with them—today offering a wide range of dishes as evidenced in the following recipes.

Antipasti

The contemporary sit-down pizzeria would not be complete without an abundant display of antipasti to whet customers' appetites. Tender eggplant crosshatched with grill marks, strips of scarlet roasted bell peppers, delicate slices or balls of fresh mozzarella cheese and creamy white beans flecked with the herbs from a marinade are among the classic Italian antipasti on the menu.

An innovative pizzeria chef will often reinterpret favorite antipasti in new ways, perhaps rolling eggplant slices around fresh goat cheese or wrapping mozzarella in marinated grape leaves and searing them on a grill. A few salads enlivened with artichokes or sautéed mushrooms cater to today's interest in light, fresh foods. Or an unusual new dish such as bite-sized sandwiches made with polenta might appear among the antipasti selections.

Such creations underscore that few courses of a meal hold the potential to inspire both chef and appetite as do the antipasti. Because portions are meant to be small, flavors can be big and bold to make the maximum first impression. Abundant herbs and sharp, piquant condiments are joined with the freshest of market vegetables or the finest cheeses. Every trip to the market can yield new and delicious combinations for cook and hungry diner alike.

Deep-Fried Polenta–Gorgonzola Sandwiches

In Italy, pizza vendors sometimes offer bite-sized rectangles of deep-fried polenta in addition to a regular assortment of simply prepared pizzas. In this upscale version of the crispy Italian snack, creamy, pungent Gorgonzola is sandwiched between thin slices of golden polenta, then deep-fried.

FILLING

1¼ lb (625 g) spinach, tough stems removed

¼ lb (125 g) Gorgonzola cheese, crumbled

Pinch of freshly grated nutmeg

Salt and freshly ground pepper

POLENTA

2 cups (16 fl oz/500 ml) water

2 cups (16 fl oz/500 ml) chicken stock

1 teaspoon salt

1 cup (5 oz/155 g) polenta or coarsely ground yellow cornmeal

2 tablespoons unsalted butter

⅓ cup (1½ oz/45 g) freshly grated Italian Parmesan cheese

1 ball fresh mozzarella, ½ lb (250 g), cut into slices ½ inch (12 mm) thick, then torn into quarters

Vegetable oil for deep-frying

1 cup (5 oz/155 g) all-purpose (plain) flour

1 egg

½ cup (4 fl oz/125 ml) water

1 cup (4 oz/125 g) fine dried bread crumbs

Tomato-basil sauce *(recipe on page 118)*, warmed

◾ To make the filling, rinse the spinach, but do not dry. Place in a saucepan over medium-low heat, cover and cook, turning occasionally, until wilted, 2–4 minutes. Drain the spinach and squeeze to remove the liquid. Chop coarsely and place in a bowl. Add the Gorgonzola, nutmeg and salt and pepper to taste. Toss to mix well.

◾ To make the polenta, in a large, heavy saucepan, combine the water, stock and salt. Bring to a simmer. Sprinkle in the polenta or cornmeal in a slow, thin stream, whisking constantly. Reduce the heat to very low and cook, stirring every 1–2 minutes, until the mixture comes away from the sides of the pan and the grains have begun to soften, 15–20 minutes total. Stir in the butter and Parmesan and remove from the heat.

◾ Rinse a 6-by-9-inch (15-by-23-cm) roasting pan with water and shake out the excess. Working quickly and using a spatula repeatedly dipped in very hot water, evenly spread half of the polenta into the pan. Spread the filling over the polenta and distribute the mozzarella evenly over the filling. Spread the remaining polenta over the filling. Cover with a kitchen towel and let rest for at least 2 hours at room temperature or for up to 24 hours in the refrigerator.

◾ To serve, cut the polenta into eighteen 1-by-3-inch (2.5-by-7.5-cm) "sandwiches." In a large, heavy saucepan, pour in vegetable oil to a depth of about 4 inches (10 cm) and heat to 375°F (190°C) on a deep-frying thermometer. Place the flour in a shallow bowl. In a second bowl, whisk together the egg and water. Place the bread crumbs in a third bowl. Ease the sandwiches out of the pan and gently dredge in the flour, coating evenly. Carefully shake off the excess, dip both sides in the egg mixture, then coat with the bread crumbs. When the oil is hot, carefully slip 6 sandwiches into the hot oil and deep-fry until deeply golden, 4–5 minutes. Nudge occasionally with a slotted spoon to ensure they brown evenly. Transfer to paper towels to drain. Repeat with the remaining sandwiches in 2 batches.

◾ Spoon a small pool of the tomato-basil sauce on each plate, place the sandwiches on top and serve at once.

Makes 18 small sandwiches; serves 6

Tuna Salad with Peppers, Green Beans and Zucchini

Most casual Italian dining spots offer a rendition of the ubiquitous tuna salad among their antipasti. Although it is common for Italian cooks to rely on canned tuna for these creations, here grilled fresh tuna is used. The salad is delicious eaten right away or marinated for up to 24 hours.

2   large, firm yellow bell peppers
    (capsicums)

DRESSING
⅔   cup (5 fl oz/160 ml) extra-virgin
    olive oil
    Juice of 2 lemons
¼   cup (⅓ oz/10 g) chopped fresh
    oregano or 2 teaspoons dried
    oregano, crumbled
2   cloves garlic, minced
    Salt and freshly ground pepper

SALAD
    Ice water
¼   lb (125 g) small, tender green
    beans, ends trimmed
2   tablespoons extra-virgin olive oil
2   small, firm zucchini (courgettes),
    cut in half crosswise, then cut
    lengthwise into thin strips
½   lb (250 g) tuna fillet, cut into
    thin slices
    Olive oil for brushing
10 round or pear-shaped cherry
    tomatoes, halved
¼   cup (⅓ oz/10 g) thinly sliced
    fresh basil leaves
2   teaspoons capers, rinsed and
    drained

▣ Preheat a broiler (griller) or preheat an oven to 450°F (230°C). Arrange the peppers on a baking sheet and place in the broiler or oven. Broil (grill) or bake, turning as necessary, until the skin is charred and blistered on all sides. Alternatively, one at a time, using tongs or a fork, hold the peppers over a gas flame until charred and blistered. Immediately place the peppers in a bowl and cover tightly with plastic wrap. Let steam until cool, about 15 minutes. Using your fingers, peel off the charred skin, then pull out and discard the stem and seeds. Cut in half lengthwise and trim away any seeds and tough white ribs. Cut each pepper lengthwise into thin strips.

▣ Prepare a fire in a charcoal grill or preheat a ridged stove-top griddle until very hot.

▣ To make the dressing, in a small bowl, whisk together the olive oil, lemon juice, oregano, garlic and salt and pepper to taste. Set aside.

▣ Bring a saucepan three-fourths full of lightly salted water to a boil. Have ready a large bowl three-fourths full of ice water. Add the green beans to the boiling water, blanch for 1 minute, then drain and plunge them into the ice water to stop the cooking and preserve the color. Transfer to a colander to drain well. Set aside.

▣ In a sauté pan over medium heat, warm the 2 tablespoons extra-virgin olive oil. Add the zucchini and sauté, stirring occasionally and regulating the heat so that the strips do not burn, until tender and golden brown, about 5 minutes. Using a slotted spoon, transfer to paper towels to drain briefly.

▣ Lightly brush the tuna slices with olive oil and season to taste with salt and pepper. Place the tuna on the grill rack about 8 inches (20 cm) above the fire or on the griddle and cook, turning once, until firm and cooked through, 3–5 minutes total. Remove from the rack or griddle and, when cool enough to handle, gently break into large pieces.

▣ In a large bowl, combine the bell peppers, green beans, zucchini, tomatoes, basil and capers. Whisk the dressing briefly, then drizzle over all. Toss gently to coat the vegetables evenly. Add the tuna and toss again gently to mix. Serve immediately, or cover and refrigerate for up to 24 hours.

Serves 6–8

Artichoke and Mushroom Salad

One of Rome's venerable salads is a rustic combination of raw artichoke hearts and curls of Parmesan cheese. In this updated version of that classic, the artichokes are cooked together with shiitake mushrooms and served on tender greens.

½ cup (4 fl oz/125 ml) plus 1 tablespoon extra-virgin olive oil

16 baby artichokes, about 1 lb (500 g), trimmed *(see glossary, page 340)* and halved lengthwise

4 cloves garlic, minced

4 tablespoons (⅓ oz/10 g) coarsely chopped fresh flat-leaf (Italian) parsley

2 tablespoons coarsely chopped fresh basil
  Juice of 1 lemon

½ cup (4 fl oz/125 ml) water
  Salt and freshly ground pepper

½ lb (250 g) fresh shiitake mushrooms, stems removed, sliced

¼ lb (125 g) mixed baby greens (about 4 cups/4 oz/125 g loosely packed)
  Extra-virgin olive oil for drizzling, optional

¼ lb (125 g) wedge Italian Parmesan cheese
  Lemon wedges

◻ In a sauté pan just large enough to hold all the artichokes in a single layer, heat the ½ cup (4 fl oz/125 ml) olive oil over medium-high heat. Add the artichokes and sauté, turning occasionally with tongs and regulating the heat so that the artichoke halves do not burn, until golden brown and slightly crusty, about 10 minutes.

◻ Add half of the garlic, parsley and basil and sauté for another several seconds until the aroma of the garlic is released. Add the lemon juice and water and deglaze the pan by stirring to loosen any browned bits stuck to the pan bottom. Reduce the heat to low, cover and braise the artichokes until the bases are tender when pierced with a sharp knife, about 5 minutes longer. Using a slotted spoon, remove the artichokes from the pan and set aside; keep warm. Raise the heat to high and boil the braising liquid until reduced by half, 3–5 minutes. Remove from the heat and set aside.

◻ In another sauté pan over medium-low heat, warm the remaining 1 tablespoon olive oil. Add the shiitakes and the remaining garlic, parsley and basil. Sauté, stirring occasionally, until tender, 6–8 minutes. Remove from the heat.

◻ Place the mixed greens in a large, shallow salad bowl. Top with the warm artichokes and shiitakes. Drizzle with a little olive oil, if desired, and the reserved braising liquid. Using a vegetable peeler, shave long curls of cheese over the top. Serve with lemon wedges.

Serves 4–6

Sweet Pepper Pinwheels with Olive Salad

Many pizzerias offer menu specials comprising a creative assortment of ingredients already on hand for pizza making. In these appetizers, roasted red peppers are the centerpiece. For convenience, you may prefer to use one of the excellent brands of firm, meaty roasted peppers packed in jars.

SALAD

10   large green olives, pitted and coarsely chopped

20   Kalamata olives or other brine-cured black olives, pitted and coarsely chopped

1   tender celery stalk from the heart of the bunch, trimmed and minced

¼   cup (⅓ oz/10 g) coarsely chopped fresh flat-leaf (Italian) parsley

1   clove garlic, minced

2   tablespoons extra-virgin olive oil

1   tablespoon red wine vinegar
    Freshly ground pepper

PINWHEELS

4   large, smooth red bell peppers (capsicums)
    Juice of 1 lemon

4   cloves garlic, crushed

⅓   cup (½ oz/15 g) chopped fresh basil
    Salt and freshly ground pepper

8   thin slices Black Forest ham

8   thin slices provolone cheese
    Extra-virgin olive oil for drizzling

    Lemon wedges

◨ To make the olive salad, in a bowl, combine the green olives, Kalamata or other black olives, celery, parsley, garlic, olive oil, vinegar and pepper to taste. Toss to mix well. Cover and refrigerate for at least 2 hours or for up to 24 hours to blend the flavors.

◨ To make the pepper pinwheels, preheat a broiler (griller) or preheat an oven to 450°F (230°C). Arrange the peppers on a baking sheet and place in the broiler or oven. Broil (grill) or bake, turning with tongs as necessary, until the skin is charred and blistered on all sides. Alternatively, one at a time, using tongs or a fork, hold the peppers over a gas flame until charred and blistered. Immediately place the peppers in a bowl and cover tightly with plastic wrap. Let steam until cool, about 15 minutes. Using your fingers, peel off the charred skin, then pull out and discard the stem and seeds. Cut each pepper in half and trim away any tough white ribs. Trim each half into a neat rectangle for easy rolling. Gather together all of the trimmings, mince them and add to the olive salad.

◨ Place the peppers in a bowl, sprinkle with the lemon juice and mix with the garlic cloves, basil and salt and pepper to taste. Cover and let marinate at room temperature for 1–2 hours.

◨ Discard the garlic cloves from the pepper mixture. Lay each pepper piece, smooth side down, on a work surface. Trim the ham and provolone slices into shapes similar to the pepper pieces. Lay a slice of ham atop each pepper piece and top with a slice of provolone. Starting from a short end, roll up each pepper stack tightly. Cover and refrigerate until ready to serve.

◨ Just before serving, using a sharp knife, cut each roll crosswise into 4 pinwheels. Arrange the pinwheels on a platter or on individual plates and drizzle with a little olive oil. Garnish with spoonfuls of the olive salad and lemon wedges. Serve immediately.

Serves 4–6

Grilled Mozzarella in Grape Leaves

Anywhere grapes grow and fresh mozzarella is made, one sees these rustic little bundles rushed to tables while the wrappers are still piping hot and the cheese is creamy soft. If you have a lemon or orange tree in your yard, tuck a leaf from it inside each bundle for additional flavor and aroma.

3　balls fresh mozzarella, ½ lb (250 g) each, drained

1　jar (16 oz/500 g) grape leaves

　Salt and freshly ground pepper

　Vegetable oil for grilling

　Tomato-basil sauce *(recipe on page 118),* warmed

　Lemon wedges

◩ Soak enough raffia or kitchen string (4 yards/4 meters) or enough wooden toothpicks (20–25) to secure each mozzarella slice in a grape leaf for at least 30 minutes, then drain.

◩ Prepare a fire in a charcoal grill or preheat a ridged stove-top griddle until it is very hot. Meanwhile, cut the mozzarella into slices ½ inch (12 mm) thick. Lay them on paper towels to drain briefly.

◩ Remove the grape leaves from the jar, leaving the brine in the jar so any unused grape leaves can be returned to it. Rinse the leaves under running cold water and drain well. Using a small, sharp knife, trim away any long or tough stems from the leaves. Place 1 large leaf (or 2 overlapping smaller ones), shiny side down, on a work surface. Place 1 mozzarella slice in the center of the leaf and sprinkle to taste with salt and pepper. Bring up the sides of the leaf and wrap them around the cheese to enclose it completely. Tie the packets with raffia or

kitchen string or secure with a toothpick. Repeat the process until all the mozzarella slices are wrapped.

◩ Brush some vegetable oil onto the rack of the grill or the surface of the griddle. Place the mozzarella packets on the grill rack about 6 inches (15 cm) above the fire or on the griddle and cook, turning once, until there are grill marks on the outside and the cheese has softened, 3–5 minutes total on a charcoal grill or about 5 minutes on a stove-top griddle.

◩ As soon as the cheese packets are softened and well marked from the grill, spoon some of the tomato-basil sauce onto a warmed platter or individual plates. Place the hot packets atop the sauce and garnish with the lemon wedges. Serve immediately.

Serves 4–6

Sweet-and-Sour Eggplant with Crostini

This is the queen of the Italian tradition of agrodolce, or sweet-and-sour dishes. Commonly served as an antipasto, the savory combination of eggplant, zucchini and red onion with the mild, pale yellow innermost stalks of a celery bunch is set off by the piquant flavors of capers and green olives.

1   eggplant (aubergine), unpeeled, ends trimmed and cut into ½-inch (12-mm) dice
      Salt
      Olive oil for frying, plus 2 tablespoons olive oil

2   zucchini (courgettes), ends trimmed and cut into ½-inch (12-mm) dice

1   small red (Spanish) onion, cut into ½-inch (12-mm) dice

1   celery heart, trimmed and cut crosswise into slices ½ inch (12 mm) thick

1   cup (8 fl oz/250 ml) tomato-basil sauce *(recipe on page 118)*

1   cup (5 oz/155 g) small green olives, pitted

2   cloves garlic, minced

2   tablespoons capers, rinsed and drained

¼–½ cup (2–4 oz/60–125 g) sugar

¼–½ cup (2–4 fl oz/60–125 ml) red wine vinegar
      Salt and freshly ground pepper

CROSTINI

1   small, slender baguette, cut on the diagonal into slices ¼ inch (6 mm) thick
      Extra-virgin olive oil for drizzling

◙ In a colander, toss the diced eggplant with a generous amount of salt. Place the colander in a sink or over another bowl and let drain for 1 hour. Rinse the eggplant with cold running water to remove the salt and bitter juices, then pat dry with paper towels or roll up in a kitchen towel.

◙ In a small frying pan over medium-high heat, pour in olive oil to a depth of ½ inch (12 mm). When hot but not smoking, add the eggplant in several batches; do not crowd the pan. Fry, stirring occasionally, until tender and golden brown, 6–8 minutes. Using a slotted spoon, transfer the eggplant to a double thickness of paper towels to drain. Fry the zucchini in the same pan in the same manner, adding more oil as needed to measure ½ inch (12 mm) deep; transfer the zucchini to paper towels to drain. In a nonaluminum bowl, combine the eggplant and zucchini and set aside.

◙ In a frying pan over medium heat, warm the 2 tablespoons olive oil. Add the onion and celery and sauté until tender, 5–7 minutes. Add the tomato-basil sauce, olives, garlic and capers and cook, stirring occasionally, until the sauce thickens slightly, 5–8 minutes. Stir in ¼ cup (2 oz/60 g)

sugar and ¼ cup (2 fl oz/60 ml) vinegar and simmer, stirring constantly, until the sugar dissolves completely. Stir in salt and pepper to taste. Taste and add more sugar and vinegar as necessary to achieve a good sweet-sour balance. Add the sauce mixture to the eggplant and zucchini and toss together gently. Cover and refrigerate for at least 12 hours or for up to 3 days before serving.

◙ When ready to serve, bring the eggplant mixture to room temperature.

◙ To make the crostini, preheat an oven to 400°F (200°C). Place the baguette slices in a large bowl and drizzle with a bit of olive oil. Toss the slices until the oil is evenly distributed (they should be slightly moistened, not coated). Lay the slices in a single layer on a large baking sheet. Bake, turning once, until lightly golden and crisp, 5–7 minutes. Watch carefully, as they burn easily.

◙ Spoon the eggplant mixture onto individual plates or a platter and surround with the warm crostini.

Serves 10–12

White Beans in Tomato-Sage Sauce

In this traditional recipe from Tuscany, white beans are served all'uccelletto, *seasoned with tomato sauce scented with earthy sage. The secret to perfect white beans is to cook them at the barest simmer. The less they move around in the pot, the better they retain their shape.*

1½ cups (10 oz/315 g) dried cannellini or Great Northern beans
Salt

½ cup (4 fl oz/125 ml) extra-virgin olive oil, plus olive oil for serving

8 plum (Roma) tomatoes, peeled, seeded and coarsely chopped, or 1 can (16 oz/500 g) plum (Roma) tomatoes with their juices, coarsely chopped

8 large fresh sage leaves or 1 tablespoon dried sage, crumbled

2 cloves garlic, minced
Freshly ground pepper

◾ Sort through the beans, discarding any misshapen beans or stones. Rinse the beans well by swishing them around in a large bowl with plenty of water. Drain and transfer to a large, heavy cooking pot, preferably of flameproof earthenware. Add water to cover by about 3 inches (7.5 cm) and bring to a rolling boil. Immediately reduce the heat to low so that the water is barely simmering, cover and cook until the beans are very soft yet still hold their shape, about 1¼ hours. As the beans cook, check the water level occasionally and add another cup or so of hot water if the level drops. When the beans are done, add salt to taste and remove from the heat. Leave the beans in their cooking liquid until ready to mix with the tomato sauce.

◾ In a large frying pan over medium heat, warm the ½ cup (4 fl oz/ 125 ml) olive oil. Add the tomatoes and cook, stirring frequently, until they begin to break down and form a sauce, about 10 minutes. Add the sage and garlic and season to taste with salt and pepper. Continue cooking, stirring occasionally, until the sauce has thickened and most of the liquid has evaporated, about 10 minutes.

◾ Drain the beans, reserving 1 cup (8 fl oz/250 ml) of the cooking liquid. Add the beans to the sauce and toss gently to mix. Add the reserved cooking liquid, 1 tablespoon at a time, as needed to moisten the dish. It should be thick and saucelike in consistency. Transfer to a serving dish and let cool until barely warm or to room temperature. Drizzle with a little olive oil before serving.

Serves 4–6

Tomato, Mozzarella and Basil Salad

With this colorful dish, the island of Capri, off Italy's southern coast, has given the world a fresh and delicate gift. Few ingredients are more perfectly suited than ripe summer tomatoes, fresh mozzarella and fragrant basil. Try to find the tiny balls of mozzarella called bocconcini, *and Sweet 100s, a recent tomato variety of intensely sweet flavor.*

¾   lb (375 g) fresh mozzarella cheese, drained

4   tablespoons (2 fl oz/60 ml) extra-virgin olive oil
Salt and freshly ground pepper

12   fresh basil leaves, thinly sliced

2   tablespoons coarsely chopped fresh flat-leaf (Italian) parsley

2   pints (12 oz/375 g) round and/or pear-shaped cherry tomatoes, in a mixture of colors

¼   cup (1½ oz/45 g) Moroccan olives or other oil-cured olives

◈ If using large balls of mozzarella, cut them into ½-inch (12-mm) dice. If using smaller balls, cut them into quarters.

◈ In a bowl, toss the mozzarella with 2 tablespoons of the olive oil and a generous sprinkling of salt and pepper. Add half of the basil and half of the parsley. Toss gently.

◈ If using round cherry tomatoes, cut them in half. If using pear-shaped tomatoes, leave them whole. In another bowl, combine the tomatoes with the remaining 2 tablespoons olive oil, salt and pepper to taste, and the remaining basil and parsley. Toss gently.

◈ Mound the mozzarella in the center of individual plates. Make a ring of the seasoned tomatoes around the edge and garnish with the olives. Serve immediately.

Serves 4–6

Grilled Eggplant and Goat Cheese Spirals

No antipasti selection would be complete without one or two eggplant dishes. Here, the eggplant is grilled, then marinated with herbs and combined with the mellow sharpness of fresh goat cheese.

1   eggplant (aubergine)
    Salt
    Olive oil for brushing
    Freshly ground pepper
⅓   cup (½ oz/15 g) chopped fresh
    chives
3   cloves garlic, minced
    Balsamic vinegar for sprinkling
    Leaves from 12 fresh thyme sprigs,
    finely chopped, or 1 tablespoon
    dried thyme, crumbled
1   log (7 oz/220 g) fresh goat cheese,
    at room temperature

▣ Cut off and discard a thin slice from the stem and blossom ends of the eggplant. Cut the eggplant lengthwise into slices ¼ inch (6 mm) thick. Lay the slices on a double thickness of paper towels and sprinkle generously with salt. Let stand until beads of water appear on the surface, about 20 minutes. Rinse with cold running water to remove the salt and bitter juices, then pat dry with additional paper towels.

▣ Prepare a fire in a charcoal grill, or preheat a ridged stove-top griddle until it is very hot. Brush the eggplant slices lightly on one side with olive oil, then place them on the grill in a single layer, oiled sides down. Brush the tops with additional oil and grill until the eggplant begins to soften and the grill marks are clearly visible, then turn and continue grilling until soft but not too deeply browned, about 4 minutes total. As the eggplant slices are done, use tongs to transfer them to a large platter.

▣ Arrange half of the slices in a single layer on another platter and sprinkle with salt and pepper to taste. Scatter half each of the chives and garlic evenly over the slices and sprinkle with a little balsamic vinegar. Sprinkle all the thyme evenly over the top. Top with the remaining eggplant slices, again in a single layer, and scatter the remaining chives and garlic over the top. Sprinkle with a little more vinegar. Let stand in a cool place for at least 2 hours, or cover and refrigerate for up to 3 days.

▣ When ready to serve, carefully spread each eggplant slice with an equal amount of the goat cheese and roll up into a tight spiral. Secure with a toothpick, if desired. Serve at room temperature.

Serves 4–6

Pizzas and Calzone

Ingenious Neapolitans changed pizzas and calzone forever with the addition of the tomato, a food that Italians once believed to be poisonous. This succulent fruit became the staple topping for most pizzas, a fact immortalized in 1889 with the pizza named for Queen Margherita. This food that has been embraced by so many cultures continues to evolve. As tastes change and ingredients from kitchens around the world become more widely available, contemporary pizzerias try different calzone fillings and pizza toppings, from chicken and spinach in a creamy béchamel sauce to radicchio and shrimp spiced with caramelized garlic.

Special pizza-making equipment can help you achieve authentic results. Intense heat and direct contact of the dough with the heat source are crucial to creating a great pizza, with a well-crisped crust that finishes baking in the same time it takes the topping to cook. Pizza stones or tiles transform a home oven into an environment that resembles a traditional bread oven. Readily adaptable to both gas and electric ovens, are round pizza stones that are placed on an oven rack set at the lowest level. You can also use square stones or unglazed tiles that sit directly on the oven floor. A pizza peel makes sliding a pizza into the oven a safe and simple task, or use an inverted rimless baking sheet.

Pizza with Asparagus and Artichokes

*It is common to see seasonal offerings in pizzerias throughout
Italy. Here, asparagus and artichokes celebrate the arrival of spring.*

Ice water

3 baby artichokes, trimmed *(see glossary, page 340)* and halved lengthwise

Salt

10 asparagus tips, each about 2 inches (5 cm) long

3 thin slices yellow onion, optional

Olive oil, if using onion

4–6 caramelized garlic cloves *(see recipe method on page 44),* optional

½ recipe Neapolitan pizza dough *(recipe on page 116),* completed through the second rising

All-purpose (plain) flour for dusting

5 fresh basil leaves, torn into small pieces

3 oz (90 g) Fontina cheese, sliced

Freshly ground pepper

2 tablespoons freshly grated Italian Parmesan cheese

1 tablespoon coarsely chopped fresh flat-leaf (Italian) parsley

Fill a saucepan three-fourths full with water. Have ready a bowl of ice water. Trim the stems of the artichoke halves even with the bottoms. Add the halves to the saucepan; add salt to taste and bring to a boil. Cook the artichokes until tender when pierced with a knife, about 10 minutes. Remove and immerse in the ice water to halt the cooking. Drain and lay on paper towels to dry.

Ready a second bowl of ice water. Bring a sauté pan three-fourths full of lightly salted water to a boil. Add the asparagus tips and blanch for 6–8 seconds. Remove and immerse in the ice water to halt the cooking. Drain and lay on paper towels to dry.

If using the onion slices, in a small frying pan over medium heat, warm enough olive oil to coat the bottom of the pan lightly. Add the onion and sauté until soft, 8–10 minutes. Remove from the heat and set aside. If using the caramelized garlic cloves, prepare as directed and set aside.

Place a pizza stone or unglazed terra-cotta tiles on the lowest rack of an oven. Preheat to 500°F (260°C).

Place the dough on a lightly floured pizza peel or rimless baking sheet. Sprinkle on a little more flour and press evenly into a disk about 1½ inches (4 cm) thick and 5 inches (13 cm) in diameter. Lift the dough and gently stretch it with your fingers and then over the backs of your fists, using the weight of the dough to allow it to grow in size. Stretch and rotate the dough until it is about ¼ inch (6 mm) thick and 9 inches (23 cm) in diameter and has a rim about ½ inch (12 mm) thick. Try not to let the center of the disk become too thin. Dust the peel or baking sheet with more flour and gently lay the disk in the center.

Arrange the asparagus, artichoke hearts, and onion slices and garlic, if using, evenly atop the dough, then scatter the basil over all. Arrange the Fontina slices evenly over the vegetables, and season to taste with salt and pepper. Gently shake the peel or baking sheet to make sure the pizza has not stuck to it. Using the peel or baking sheet like a large spatula, quickly slide the pizza onto the hot pizza stone or tiles.

Bake until the edges are golden and crisp, 8–9 minutes. Remove the pizza with a large metal spatula and slide it onto a dinner plate. Sprinkle the Parmesan and parsley evenly over the pizza and serve at once.

Makes one 9-inch (23-cm) pizza

Pizza with Tomatoes, Mozzarella and Basil

Legend relates that this delicious and patriotic combination was created for Queen Margherita of Italy in 1889 by Don Raffaele Esposito, owner of the era's most famous pizzeria in Naples. Its ingredients honored the colors of her country's flag—red, white and green.

½ recipe Neapolitan pizza dough *(recipe on page 116)*, completed through the second rising
   All-purpose (plain) flour for dusting

⅓ cup (3 fl oz/80 ml) tomato-basil sauce *(recipe on page 118)*

6 fresh basil leaves

¼ lb (125 g) mozzarella cheese, sliced

▣ Place a pizza stone or unglazed terra-cotta tiles on the lowest rack of an oven. Preheat to 500°F (260°C).

▣ Place the ball of dough on a lightly floured pizza peel or rimless baking sheet. Sprinkle a little more flour on the top of the dough and, using your fingertips, press evenly into a round, flat disk about 1½ inches (4 cm) thick and 5 inches (13 cm) in diameter. Lift the dough and gently stretch it with your fingers and then over the backs of your fists, using the weight of the dough to allow it to grow in size. While you are stretching the dough, gently rotate the disk. Continue stretching and rotating the dough until it is about ¼ inch (6 mm) thick and 9 inches (23 cm) in diameter and has a rim about ½ inch (12 mm) thick. Try not to let the center of the disk become too thin in comparison to the edges. Dust the peel or baking sheet with more flour and gently lay the disk in the center.

▣ Place the tomato-basil sauce in the center of the disk. Using the back of a spoon, gently spread the sauce over the dough, leaving a 1-inch (2.5-cm) border free of sauce. Lay the basil leaves atop the sauce and then arrange the mozzarella slices evenly over all.

▣ Gently shake the peel or baking sheet back and forth to make sure the pizza has not stuck to it. If it has, gently lift off the stuck section and sprinkle a little more flour underneath. Using the peel or baking sheet like a large spatula, quickly slide the pizza onto the hot pizza stone or tiles.

▣ Bake until the edges are golden and crisp, 8–9 minutes. Remove the pizza with a large metal spatula and slide it onto a dinner plate. Serve at once.

Makes one 9-inch (23-cm) pizza

Pizza with Onion, Anchovies and Olives

Cooks on both the Italian and French Rivieras, from Liguria up through Provence, often combine the sweetness of sautéed onions and full-flavored tomatoes with the sharp bite of anchovy and brine-cured olives. Some food historians contend that the famed savory Provençal tart, la pissaladière, *originally comes from the Italian* pizza all'Andrea, *named for the renowned naval officer, Andrea Doria.*

2	tablespoons extra-virgin olive oil, plus olive oil for drizzling
1	small yellow onion, thinly sliced
	Salt and freshly ground pepper
½	recipe Neapolitan pizza dough *(recipe on page 116),* completed through the second rising
	All-purpose (plain) flour for dusting
4–6	plum (Roma) tomatoes, cut into slices ¼ inch (6 mm) thick
5	anchovy fillets, rinsed and patted dry
10	Kalamata or other brine-cured black olives, pitted
½	teaspoon dried oregano, crumbled

◩ Place a pizza stone or unglazed terra-cotta tiles on the lowest rack of an oven. Preheat to 500°F (260°C).

◩ In a large, heavy sauté pan over medium heat, warm the 2 tablespoons olive oil. Add the onion and sauté, stirring occasionally, until completely wilted and golden, about 10 minutes. Season to taste with salt and pepper and remove from the heat.

◩ Place the ball of dough on a lightly floured pizza peel or rimless baking sheet. Sprinkle a little more flour on the top of the dough and, with your fingertips, press evenly into a round, flat disk about 1½ inches (4 cm) thick and 5 inches (13 cm) in diameter. Lift the dough and gently stretch it with your fingers and then over the backs of your fists, using the weight of the dough to allow it to grow in size. While you are stretching the dough, gently rotate the disk. Continue stretching and rotating the dough until it is about ¼ inch (6 mm) thick and 9 inches (23 cm) in diameter and has a rim about ½ inch (12 mm) thick. Try not to let the center of the disk become too thin in comparison to the edges. Dust the peel or baking sheet with more flour and gently lay the disk in the center.

◩ Scatter the onions evenly over the dough. Distribute the sliced tomatoes evenly over the onions. Tear the anchovies into little pieces and scatter them evenly over the tomatoes. Finally, top with the olives and the oregano. Season to taste with salt and pepper and drizzle with a little extra-virgin olive oil.

◩ Gently shake the peel or baking sheet back and forth to make sure the pizza has not stuck to it. If it has, gently lift off the stuck section and sprinkle a little more flour underneath. Using the peel or baking sheet like a large spatula, quickly slide the pizza onto the hot pizza stone or tiles.

◩ Bake until the edges are golden and crisp, 8–9 minutes. Remove the pizza with a large metal spatula and slide it onto a dinner plate. Drizzle with additional olive oil, if desired, and serve at once.

Makes one 9-inch (23-cm) pizza

Pizza with Scallops and Pesto

At seaside pizzerias all over Italy, treasures from the sea find their way atop the familiar disk of dough. In this recipe, the intense heat of the oven sears the marinated sea scallops as they sit on a layer of emerald pesto.

6 large, plump sea scallops, about 5 oz (155 g) total weight, cut in half horizontally if very thick

1 tablespoon extra-virgin olive oil, plus olive oil for drizzling
Juice of ½ lemon

1 tablespoon coarsely chopped fresh flat-leaf (Italian) parsley

2 green (spring) onions, including the pale green tops, thinly sliced
Salt and coarsely ground pepper

½ recipe Neapolitan pizza dough *(recipe on page 116),* completed through the second rising
All-purpose (plain) flour for dusting

1 clove garlic

1 tablespoon Genovese pesto *(recipe on page 119)*

◪ In a small bowl, combine the scallops, 1 tablespoon olive oil, lemon juice, parsley, green onions, and salt and pepper to taste. Stir to mix well, cover and let stand for 20 minutes.

◪ Meanwhile, place a pizza stone or unglazed terra-cotta tiles on the lowest rack of an oven. Preheat to 500°F (260°C).

◪ Place the ball of dough on a lightly floured pizza peel or rimless baking sheet. Sprinkle a little more flour on the top of the dough and, using your fingertips, press evenly into a round, flat disk about 1½ inches (4 cm) thick and 5 inches (13 cm) in diameter. Lift the dough and gently stretch it with your fingers and then over the backs of your fists, using the weight of the dough to allow it to grow in size. While you are stretching the dough, gently rotate the disk. Continue stretching and rotating the dough until it is about ¼ inch (6 mm) thick and 9 inches (23 cm) in diameter and has a rim about ½ inch (12 mm) thick. Try not to let the center of the disk become too thin in comparison to the edges. Dust the peel or baking sheet with more flour and gently lay the disk in the center.

◪ Pass the garlic clove through a press held over the dough, then rub the garlic evenly over the surface. Using the back of a tablespoon, spread the pesto as evenly as possible over the dough. Using a slotted spoon, remove the scallops from their marinade and distribute them over the dough. Sprinkle a little of the marinade over the top.

◪ Gently shake the peel or baking sheet back and forth to make sure the pizza has not stuck to it. If it has, gently lift off the stuck section and sprinkle a little more flour underneath. Using the peel or baking sheet like a large spatula, quickly slide the pizza onto the hot pizza stone or tiles.

◪ Bake until the edges are golden and crisp, 8–9 minutes. Remove the pizza with a large metal spatula and slide it onto a dinner plate. Drizzle with olive oil, if desired, and serve at once.

Makes one 9-inch (23-cm) pizza

Pizza with Smoked Salmon and Mozzarella

This inspired American combination of the sophisticated tastes of smoked salmon and smoked mozzarella found its way back to the high-tech elegance of some urban Italian pizzerias. A squeeze of fresh lemon and a sprinkling of Italian parsley brighten the assertive flavors.

½   recipe Neapolitan pizza dough *(recipe on page 116)*, completed through the second rising
     All-purpose (plain) flour for dusting
2   oz (60 g) thinly sliced smoked salmon
¼   lb (125 g) smoked mozzarella cheese, sliced
1½   teaspoons chopped fresh chives
     Freshly ground pepper
     Extra-virgin olive oil for drizzling
     Juice of ½ lemon
1   tablespoon coarsely chopped fresh flat-leaf (Italian) parsley

Place a pizza stone or unglazed terra-cotta tiles on the lowest rack of an oven. Preheat to 500°F (260°C).

Place the ball of dough on a lightly floured pizza peel or rimless baking sheet. Sprinkle a little more flour on the top of the dough and, using your fingertips, press evenly into a round, flat disk about 1½ inches (4 cm) thick and 5 inches (13 cm) in diameter. Lift the dough and gently stretch it with your fingers and then over the backs of your fists, using the weight of the dough to allow it to grow in size. While you are stretching the dough, gently rotate the disk. Continue stretching and rotating the dough until it is about ¼ inch (6 mm) thick and 9 inches (23 cm) in diameter and has a rim about ½ inch (12 mm) thick. Try not to let the center of the disk become too thin in comparison to the edges. Dust the peel or baking sheet with more flour and gently lay the disk in the center.

Arrange the smoked salmon on the dough. Top evenly with the smoked mozzarella slices and sprinkle with the chives. Season to taste with pepper. Finish with a drizzle of olive oil.

Gently shake the peel or baking sheet back and forth to make sure the pizza has not stuck to it. If it has, gently lift off the stuck section and sprinkle a little more flour underneath. Using the peel or baking sheet like a large spatula, quickly slide the pizza onto the hot pizza stone or tiles.

Bake until the edges are golden and crisp, 8–9 minutes. Remove the pizza with a large metal spatula and slide it onto a dinner plate. Sprinkle the lemon juice and parsley evenly over the top. Drizzle with additional olive oil, if desired, and serve at once.

Makes one 9-inch (23-cm) pizza

Pizza with Yellow Pepper and Capers

This pizza recalls late-night summer meals taken on the large outdoor terraces of country pizzerias in Italy's fabled south. Sweet yellow peppers are combined with mozzarella, capers and tomatoes for an exceptionally pretty pie. An amber beer, icy from the cooler, is the ideal accompaniment.

½ recipe Neapolitan pizza dough *(recipe on page 116)*, completed through the second rising

All-purpose (plain) flour for dusting

¼ lb (125 g) mozzarella cheese, sliced

1 ripe plum (Roma) tomato, cut in half lengthwise and then into slices ¼ inch (6 mm) thick

½ large, meaty yellow bell pepper (capsicum), seeded, deribbed and cut lengthwise into narrow strips

1 teaspoon capers, rinsed and drained

Salt and freshly ground pepper

Extra-virgin olive oil for drizzling

1 tablespoon coarsely chopped fresh flat-leaf (Italian) parsley

◼ Place a pizza stone or unglazed terra-cotta tiles on the lowest rack of an oven. Preheat to 500°F (260°C).

◼ Place the ball of dough on a lightly floured pizza peel or rimless baking sheet. Sprinkle a little more flour on the top of the dough and, using your fingertips, press evenly into a round, flat disk about 1½ inches (4 cm) thick and 5 inches (13 cm) in diameter. Lift the dough and gently stretch it with your fingers and then over the backs of your fists, using the weight of the dough to allow it to grow in size. While you are stretching the dough, gently rotate the disk. Continue stretching and rotating the dough until it is about ¼ inch (6 mm) thick and 9 inches (23 cm) in diameter and has a rim about ½ inch (12 mm) thick. Try not to let the center of the disk become too thin in comparison to the edges. Dust the peel or baking sheet with more flour and gently lay the disk in the center.

◼ Arrange the mozzarella evenly on the pizza dough. Top with the tomato slices, pepper strips and capers. Season to taste with salt and pepper and drizzle with a little olive oil.

◼ Gently shake the peel or baking sheet back and forth to make sure the pizza has not stuck to it. If it has, gently lift off the stuck section and sprinkle a little more flour underneath. Using the peel or baking sheet like a large spatula, quickly slide the pizza onto the hot pizza stone or tiles.

◼ Bake until the edges are golden and crisp, 8–9 minutes. Remove the pizza with a large metal spatula and slide it onto a dinner plate. Sprinkle with the parsley, drizzle with additional olive oil, if desired, and serve at once.

Makes one 9-inch (23-cm) pizza

Pizza with Radicchio and Fontina

A study in muted colors and complex flavors, this pizza from Treviso
in northern Italy combines two popular regional ingredients, radicchio and Fontina
cheese. Tender, pink shrimp are added to enrich the savory dish.

CARAMELIZED GARLIC
6 cloves garlic
  Olive oil, to cover

PIZZA
6 large shrimp (prawns), peeled, deveined and halved lengthwise
1 tablespoon extra-virgin olive oil, plus olive oil for drizzling
  Salt and coarsely ground pepper
½ recipe Neapolitan pizza dough *(recipe on page 116),* completed through the second rising
¼ head radicchio (red chicory), core removed and coarsely chopped
1½ tablespoons finely shredded fresh basil
4–5 oz (125–155 g) Fontina cheese, sliced

◈ To make the caramelized garlic, peel the garlic but leave the cloves whole. In a small, heavy saucepan over medium-low heat, combine the garlic cloves with just enough olive oil to cover. Bring to a gentle simmer and cook the garlic until it is covered with golden dots, about 15 minutes. Watch carefully, as the garlic burns easily. Remove from the heat, let cool and then drain off the oil. Set the garlic aside. Reserve the oil for another use such as drizzling over grilled fish or vegetables.

◈ Place a pizza stone or unglazed terra-cotta tiles on the lowest rack of an oven. Preheat to 500°F (260°C).

◈ In a small bowl, mix together the shrimp, 1 tablespoon extra-virgin olive oil, and salt and pepper to taste.

◈ Place the ball of dough on a lightly floured pizza peel or rimless baking sheet. Sprinkle a little more flour on the top of the dough and, using your fingertips, press evenly into a round, flat disk about 1½ inches (4 cm) thick and 5 inches (13 cm) in diameter. Lift the dough and gently stretch it with your fingers and then over the backs of your fists, using the weight of the dough to allow it to grow in size. While you are stretching the dough, gently rotate the disk.

Continue stretching and rotating the dough until it is about ¼ inch (6 mm) thick and 9 inches (23 cm) in diameter and has a rim about ½ inch (12 mm) thick. Try not to let the center of the disk become too thin in comparison to the edges. Dust the peel or baking sheet with more flour and gently lay the disk in the center.

◈ Scatter the radicchio, garlic and basil over the dough. Top evenly with the cheese and, finally, with the shrimp. Season to taste with salt and pepper and drizzle with a little extra-virgin olive oil.

◈ Gently shake the peel or baking sheet back and forth to make sure the pizza has not stuck to it. If it has, gently lift off the stuck section and sprinkle a little more flour underneath. Using the peel or baking sheet like a large spatula, quickly slide the pizza onto the hot pizza stone or tiles.

◈ Bake until the edges are golden and crisp, 8–9 minutes. Remove the pizza with a large metal spatula and slide it onto a dinner plate. Drizzle with additional extra-virgin olive oil, if desired, and serve at once.

Makes one 9-inch (23-cm) pizza

Pizza with Sausage and Mushrooms

*The simple combination of sausage and mushrooms is often elevated by the use
of chicken or duck sausage and shiitake or portobello mushrooms.*

1 chicken or duck sausage, about ¼ lb (125 g), casing removed and meat crumbled

2 tablespoons extra-virgin olive oil, plus olive oil for drizzling

1 small yellow onion, thinly sliced

1 cup (3 oz/90 g) sliced, stemmed fresh shiitake or portobello mushrooms

1 clove garlic, minced

1 teaspoon minced fresh thyme
    Salt and freshly ground pepper

½ recipe Neapolitan pizza dough *(recipe on page 116),* completed through the second rising
    All-purpose (plain) flour for dusting

¼ lb (125 g) mozzarella or Fontina cheese, sliced

2 tablespoons freshly grated Italian Parmesan cheese

Place the crumbled sausage in a small sauté pan or frying pan over medium heat and sauté, stirring often, until crumbly and cooked through, 10–15 minutes. Remove from the heat and set aside.

In a large, heavy sauté pan over medium heat, warm the 2 tablespoons olive oil. Add the onion and sauté, stirring frequently, until completely wilted, about 10 minutes. Add the mushrooms, garlic and thyme and continue cooking over medium heat until the onions are golden and the mushrooms are tender, about 5 minutes longer. Season to taste with salt and pepper and remove from the heat.

Place a pizza stone or unglazed terra-cotta tiles on the lowest rack of an oven. Preheat to 500°F (260°C).

Place the ball of dough on a lightly floured pizza peel or rimless baking sheet. Sprinkle a little more flour on the top of the dough and, using your fingertips, press evenly into a round, flat disk about 1½ inches (4 cm) thick and 5 inches (13 cm) in diameter. Lift the dough and gently stretch it with your fingers and then over the backs of your fists, using the weight of the dough to allow it to grow in size. While you are stretching the dough, gently rotate the disk.

Continue stretching and rotating the dough until it is about ¼ inch (6 mm) thick and 9 inches (23 cm) in diameter and has a rim about ½ inch (12 mm) thick. Try not to let the center of the disk become too thin in comparison to the edges. Dust the peel or baking sheet with more flour and gently lay the disk in the center.

Spread the onion-shiitake mixture evenly over the dough, then scatter on the sausage. Top evenly with the cheese slices.

Gently shake the peel or baking sheet back and forth to make sure the pizza has not stuck to it. If it has, gently lift off the stuck section and sprinkle a little more flour underneath. Using the peel or baking sheet like a large spatula, quickly slide the pizza onto the hot pizza stone or tiles.

Bake until the edges are golden and crisp, 8–9 minutes. Remove the pizza with a large metal spatula and slide it onto a dinner plate. Sprinkle evenly with the Parmesan and serve at once.

Makes one 9-inch (23-cm) pizza

Pizza with Goat Cheese and Zucchini

Imagine a pastore, or "shepherd," topping a thick piece of bread with his own freshly made goat cheese, a bit of zucchini and a scattering of leeks. This pizza is an homage to such pastoral combinations.

2 tablespoons extra-virgin olive oil, plus olive oil for drizzling

1 small zucchini (courgette), trimmed and cut into thin julienne strips

1 leek, white part only, carefully rinsed and thinly sliced crosswise

1 clove garlic, minced
Salt and coarsely ground pepper

½ recipe Neapolitan pizza dough *(recipe on page 116),* completed through the second rising
All-purpose (plain) flour for dusting

¼ lb (125 g) fresh goat cheese

1 teaspoon dried oregano, crumbled
Juice of ½ lemon

▣ Place a pizza stone or unglazed terra-cotta tiles on the lowest rack of an oven. Preheat to 500°F (260°C).

▣ In a large sauté pan over medium heat, warm the 2 tablespoons olive oil. Add the zucchini, leek and garlic and sauté, stirring occasionally, until the vegetables are barely tender, 3–4 minutes. Season to taste with salt and pepper and remove from the heat. Set aside.

▣ Place the ball of dough on a lightly floured pizza peel or rimless baking sheet. Sprinkle a little more flour on the top of the dough and, using your fingertips, press evenly into a round, flat disk about 1½ inches (4 cm) thick and 5 inches (13 cm) in diameter. Lift the dough and gently stretch it with your fingers and then over the backs of your fists, using the weight of the dough to allow it to grow in size. While you are stretching the dough, gently rotate the disk. Continue stretching and rotating the dough until it is about ¼ inch (6 mm) thick and 9 inches (23 cm) in diameter and has a rim about ½ inch (12 mm) thick. Try not to let the center

of the disk become too thin in comparison to the edges. Dust the peel or baking sheet with more flour and gently lay the disk in the center.

▣ Distribute the zucchini-leek mixture evenly over the dough. Dot the pizza with the goat cheese and sprinkle with the oregano.

▣ Gently shake the peel or baking sheet back and forth to make sure the pizza has not stuck to it. If it has, gently lift off the stuck section and sprinkle a little more flour underneath. Using the peel or baking sheet like a large spatula, quickly slide the pizza onto the hot pizza stone or tiles.

▣ Bake until the edges are golden and crisp, 8–9 minutes. Remove the pizza with a large metal spatula and slide it onto a dinner plate. Sprinkle with the lemon juice and serve at once.

Makes one 9-inch (23-cm) pizza

Pizza with Escarole and Pine Nuts

This traditional pairing of tender escarole with anchovies, pine nuts and bread crumbs is found on the tables of the more rustic pizzerias of Italy and in their more sophisticated Italian counterparts in America and elsewhere.

½ cup (4 fl oz/125 ml) water
2 tablespoons extra-virgin olive oil, plus olive oil for drizzling
½ head escarole (Batavian endive), tough outer leaves and core removed, coarsely chopped
1 clove garlic, minced
½ recipe Neapolitan pizza dough *(recipe on page 116),* completed through the second rising
   All-purpose (plain) flour for dusting
¼ lb (125 g) Fontina cheese, sliced
2 anchovy fillets, rinsed, patted dry and chopped
1 tablespoon pine nuts
   Freshly ground pepper
1 tablespoon toasted fine dried bread crumbs

◻ In a large sauté pan over medium-low heat, combine the water and the 2 tablespoons olive oil. Bring the liquid to a simmer and add the escarole and garlic. Cover and simmer until the escarole is tender, about 7 minutes. Transfer it to a colander to drain. When cool enough to handle, squeeze between the palms of your hands to remove as much liquid as possible.

◻ Place a pizza stone or unglazed terra-cotta tiles on the lowest rack of an oven. Preheat to 500°F (260°C).

◻ Place the ball of dough on a lightly floured pizza peel or rimless baking sheet. Sprinkle a little more flour on the top of the dough and, using your fingertips, press evenly into a round, flat disk about 1½ inches (4 cm) thick and 5 inches (13 cm) in diameter. Lift the dough and gently stretch it with your fingers and then over the backs of your fists, using the weight of the dough to allow it to grow in size. While you are stretching the dough, gently rotate the disk. Continue stretching and rotating the dough until it is about ¼ inch (6 mm) thick and 9 inches (23 cm) in diameter and has a rim about ½ inch (12 mm) thick. Try not to let the center of the disk become too thin in comparison to the edges. Dust the peel or baking sheet with more flour and gently lay the disk in the center.

◻ Arrange the escarole over the dough. Top evenly with the Fontina, then scatter on the anchovies and pine nuts. Season to taste with pepper. Finish with a drizzle of olive oil.

◻ Gently shake the peel or baking sheet back and forth to make sure the pizza has not stuck to it. If it has, gently lift off the stuck section and sprinkle a little more flour underneath. Using the peel or baking sheet like a large spatula, quickly slide the pizza onto the hot pizza stone or tiles.

◻ Bake until the edges are golden and crisp, 8–9 minutes. Remove the pizza with a large metal spatula and slide it onto a dinner plate. Scatter the bread crumbs evenly over the top and serve at once.

Makes one 9-inch (23-cm) pizza

Pizza with Spinach, Sausage, Salami and Red Pepper

This pizza is made in true American style—with more than half a dozen ingredients. Fennel-scented sweet Italian sausages combine well with the other toppings, but choose the type of sausage you prefer.

1   red bell pepper (capsicum)

1   sweet Italian sausage, about ¼ lb (125 g), casing removed and meat crumbled

½   bunch spinach, stems removed
     Salt

½   recipe Neapolitan pizza dough *(recipe on page 116),* completed through the second rising
     All-purpose (plain) flour for dusting

⅓   cup (3 fl oz/80 ml) uncooked tomato sauce *(recipe on page 118)*

2   paper-thin slices yellow onion, each cut in half

4   thin slices salami, torn into pieces

1   thin slice prosciutto, coarsely chopped

¼   lb (125 g) mozzarella cheese, sliced

2   tablespoons freshly grated Italian Parmesan cheese

▦ Preheat a broiler (griller) or preheat an oven to 450°F (230°C). Set the pepper on a baking sheet and place in the broiler or oven. Broil (grill) or bake, turning as necessary, until the skin is charred on all sides. Immediately place in a bowl and cover tightly. Let steam until cool, about 15 minutes. Peel off the charred skin, then pull out and discard the stems and seeds. Cut in half lengthwise and trim away any tough white ribs. Cut into long, narrow strips.

▦ Place a pizza stone or unglazed terra-cotta tiles on the lowest rack of an oven. Preheat to 500°F (260°C).

▦ Place the sausage in a small frying pan over medium heat. Sauté, stirring often, until crumbly and cooked through, 10–15 minutes.

▦ Meanwhile, rinse the spinach but do not dry. Place in a saucepan over medium-low heat, sprinkle with salt, cover and cook, turning occasionally, until wilted, 2–4 minutes. Drain and squeeze to remove the liquid. Chop coarsely.

▦ Place the dough on a lightly floured pizza peel or rimless baking sheet. Sprinkle more flour on top and press evenly into a round disk about 1½ inches (4 cm) thick and 5 inches (13 cm) in diameter. Lift the dough and stretch with your fingers and then over the backs of your fists, while gently rotating the disk. Continue until the dough is ¼ inch (6 mm) thick and 9 inches (23 cm) in diameter and has a rim ½ inch (12 mm) thick. Dust the peel or baking sheet with more flour and lay the disk in the center.

▦ Place the tomato sauce in the center of the disk. Using the back of a spoon, gently spread the sauce over the dough, leaving a 1-inch (2.5-cm) border free of sauce. Scatter the cooked sausage over the sauce, then layer on the spinach, bell pepper, onion, salami and prosciutto. Top evenly with the mozzarella and dust with the Parmesan.

▦ Gently shake the peel or baking sheet back and forth to make sure the pizza has not stuck to it. If it has, lift off the stuck section and sprinkle more flour underneath. Using the peel or baking sheet like a large spatula, quickly slide the pizza onto the hot pizza stone or tiles.

▦ Bake until the edges are golden and crisp, 8–9 minutes. Remove and slide onto a dinner plate. Serve at once.

Makes one 9-inch (23-cm) pizza

Pizza with Sun-Dried Tomatoes

Pumate are the famous sun-dried tomatoes of Apulia, the region tucked into the heel of the Italian boot. Driving along the country roads there, one sees flashes of scarlet on the outsides of many houses. They are plump bunches of Principessa Borghese tomatoes, a variety grown in summer and strung up to dry in the sun throughout the year. Packed in olive oil, they add an intensely sweet tomato flavor to any pizza.

¾ cup (1 oz/30 g) coarsely chopped arugula (rocket)

1 tablespoon extra-virgin olive oil
    Salt and coarsely ground pepper

½ recipe Neapolitan pizza dough *(recipe on page 116)*, completed through the second rising
    All-purpose (plain) flour for dusting

1 clove garlic

2 fresh plum (Roma) tomatoes, cut into small dice

¼ cup (2 oz/60 g) drained oil-packed sun-dried tomatoes, coarsely chopped and oil reserved

¼ lb (125 g) mozzarella cheese, sliced

2 tablespoons freshly grated Italian Parmesan cheese

▨ Place a pizza stone or unglazed terra-cotta tiles on the lowest rack of an oven. Preheat to 500°F (260°C).

▨ In a small bowl, stir together the arugula, olive oil, and salt and pepper to taste.

▨ Place the ball of dough on a lightly floured pizza peel or rimless baking sheet. Sprinkle a little more flour on the top of the dough and, using your fingertips, press evenly into a round, flat disk about 1½ inches (4 cm) thick and 5 inches (13 cm) in diameter. Lift the dough and gently stretch it with your fingers and then over the backs of your fists, using the weight of the dough to allow it to grow in size. While you are stretching the dough, gently rotate the disk. Continue stretching and rotating the dough until it is about ¼ inch (6 mm) thick and 9 inches (23 cm) in diameter and has a rim about ½ inch (12 mm) thick. Try not to let the center of the disk become too thin in comparison to the edges. Dust the peel or baking sheet with more flour and gently lay the disk in the center.

▨ Pass the garlic clove through a press held over the dough, then rub the garlic evenly over the surface. Top with the fresh and sun-dried tomatoes. Spread the seasoned arugula over the tomatoes and distribute the mozzarella over the top.

▨ Gently shake the peel or baking sheet back and forth to make sure the pizza has not stuck to it. If it has, gently lift off the stuck section and sprinkle a little more flour underneath. Using the peel or baking sheet like a large spatula, quickly slide the pizza onto the hot pizza stone or tiles.

▨ Bake until the edges are golden and crisp, 8–9 minutes. Remove the pizza with a large metal spatula and slide it onto a dinner plate. Sprinkle evenly with the Parmesan, drizzle with the oil reserved from the tomatoes and serve at once.

Makes one 9-inch (23-cm) pizza

Calzone with Chicken and Spinach

While not a traditional ingredient in Italian pizzerias, chicken has been embraced by pizza cooks outside of Italy. Here, a creamy filling of tender dark meat, spinach and prosciutto is tucked into a calzone for an especially rich treat.

1 chicken thigh
Salt and freshly ground pepper

BÉCHAMEL SAUCE
½ cup (4 fl oz/125 ml) milk
1 tablespoon unsalted butter
1 tablespoon all-purpose (plain) flour
Salt and freshly ground pepper

1 bunch spinach, stems removed
1 thin slice prosciutto, chopped
2 tablespoons freshly grated Italian Parmesan cheese
½ recipe Neapolitan pizza dough *(recipe on page 116),* completed through the second rising
All-purpose (plain) flour for dusting

◆ Preheat an oven to 400°F (200°C). Place the chicken thigh in a baking pan and season with salt and pepper. Roast until golden brown and the juices run clear when the meat is pricked with a knife, 25–30 minutes. Remove and discard the skin and bone and shred the meat.

◆ To make the béchamel sauce, heat the milk in a small saucepan over medium-low heat until small bubbles appear along the pan edge. In another small saucepan over medium-low heat, melt the butter. Add the flour and whisk to form a smooth paste. Reduce the heat to low and cook, stirring, for about 2 minutes. When the milk is hot, add the butter-flour mixture, whisking constantly until it comes to a simmer. Simmer over medium heat until the sauce thickens enough to coat a spoon, about 20 minutes. Season with salt and pepper. Pour into a cup.

◆ Rinse the spinach but do not dry. Place in a saucepan over medium-low heat, cover and cook, turning occasionally, until wilted, 2–4 minutes. Drain and squeeze to remove the liquid. Chop coarsely.

◆ Place a pizza stone or unglazed terra-cotta tiles on the lowest rack of an oven. Preheat to 500°F (260°C).

◆ In a bowl, combine the shredded chicken, spinach, béchamel, prosciutto and Parmesan. Stir to mix well.

◆ Place the dough on a lightly floured pizza peel or rimless baking sheet. Sprinkle more flour on top and press evenly into a round disk about 1½ inches (4 cm) thick and 5 inches (13 cm) in diameter. Lift the dough and stretch with your fingers and then over the backs of your fists while gently rotating the disk. Continue until the dough is about ¼ inch (6 mm) thick and 8 inches (20 cm) in diameter. Dust the peel or baking sheet with more flour and lay the disk in the center.

◆ Mound the filling in the center of the dough that is nearest to you and fold over the filling, stretching as necessary so the edges meet. Crimp the edges to seal. Tear a steam vent about 1 inch (2.5 cm) long in the center of the top.

◆ Using the peel or baking sheet like a large spatula, quickly slide the calzone onto the hot pizza stone or tiles. Bake until the top is golden brown, 8–9 minutes. Remove from the oven and serve.

Makes 1 calzone

Calzone with Eggplant, Pancetta and Mozzarella

Easily grown by nearly anyone with a bit of sun and a patch of earth, eggplant and tomatoes have long been staples of southern Italian cooking. Pancetta, unsmoked Italian bacon that is simply cured with salt and pepper, and slices of mozzarella add a rich touch to this savory calzone.

¼ cup (2 fl oz/60 ml) extra-virgin olive oil

2 tablespoons coarsely chopped pancetta or thick-cut bacon

2 Asian (slender) eggplants (aubergines), ends trimmed, peeled and diced
Salt and coarsely ground pepper

½ recipe Neapolitan pizza dough *(recipe on page 116),* completed through the second rising
All-purpose (plain) flour for dusting

1½ teaspoons finely shredded fresh basil

3 oz (90 g) mozzarella cheese, sliced

⅓ cup (3 fl oz/80 ml) tomato-basil sauce *(recipe on page 118)*

▣ Place a pizza stone or unglazed terra-cotta tiles on the lowest rack of an oven. Preheat to 500°F (260°C).

▣ In a large sauté pan over medium-low heat, warm the olive oil. Add the pancetta or bacon and sauté, stirring occasionally, until it renders its fat, about 5 minutes. Add the eggplants and increase the heat to medium. Sauté until the eggplants are golden brown and tender, 4–5 minutes. Season to taste with salt and pepper and remove from the heat.

▣ Place the ball of dough on a lightly floured pizza peel or rimless baking sheet. Sprinkle a little more flour on the top of the dough and, using your fingertips, press evenly into a round, flat disk about 1½ inches (4 cm) thick and 5 inches (13 cm) in diameter. Lift the dough and gently stretch it with your fingers and then over the backs of your fists, using the weight of the dough to allow it to grow in size. While you are stretching the dough, gently rotate the disk. Continue stretching and rotating the dough until it is about ¼ inch (6 mm) thick and 8 inches (20 cm) in diameter. Try not to let the center of the disk become too thin in comparison to the edges. Dust the peel or baking sheet with more flour and gently lay the disk in the center.

▣ Mound the eggplant mixture in the center on the half of the dough that is nearest to you. Top with the basil, mozzarella and tomato-basil sauce. Gently fold the top half of the dough over the filling, stretching and adjusting as necessary so the edges meet. Crimp the edges with a fork to seal. Tear a steam vent about 1 inch (2.5 cm) long in the center of the top.

▣ Gently shake the peel or baking sheet back and forth to make sure the calzone has not stuck to it. If it has, gently lift off the stuck section and sprinkle a little more flour underneath. Using the peel or baking sheet like a large spatula, quickly slide the calzone onto the hot pizza stone or tiles.

▣ Bake until the top is golden brown and the bottom is dotted with dark brown spots. Remove the calzone with a large metal spatula and place on a dinner plate. Serve at once.

Makes 1 calzone

Calzone with Assorted Meats and Cheeses

Walk into any salumeria—Italian delicatessen—and the aroma of countless cheeses and cured meats captivates the senses. The pungent flavors of salami, prosciutto and mortadella are mellowed by sweet ricotta and Parmesan cheese in this salute to the tradition of the salumeria.

2 tablespoons extra-virgin olive oil
1 small yellow onion, thinly sliced
   Salt and freshly ground pepper
½ cup (4 oz/125 g) ricotta cheese
2 thin slices salami, coarsely chopped
1 slice prosciutto, coarsely chopped
1 slice mortadella, coarsely chopped
½ recipe Neapolitan pizza dough *(recipe on page 116)*, completed through the second rising
   All-purpose (plain) flour for dusting
¼ cup (2 fl oz/60 ml) tomato-basil sauce *(recipe on page 118)*
1 tablespoon freshly grated Italian Parmesan cheese

◈ Place a pizza stone or unglazed terra-cotta tiles on the lowest rack of an oven. Preheat to 500°F (260°C).

◈ In a large, heavy sauté pan over medium heat, warm the olive oil. Add the onion and sauté until completely wilted and golden, about 10 minutes. Season to taste with salt and pepper and remove from the heat.

◈ In a bowl, combine the onion, ricotta, salami, prosciutto, mortadella and pepper to taste. Stir to mix well.

◈ Place the ball of dough on a lightly floured pizza peel or rimless baking sheet. Sprinkle a little more flour on the top of the dough and, using your fingertips, press evenly into a round, flat disk about 1½ inches (4 cm) thick and 5 inches (13 cm) in diameter. Lift the dough and gently stretch it with your fingers and then over the backs of your fists, using the weight of the dough to allow it to grow in size. While you are stretching the dough, gently rotate the disk. Continue stretching and rotating the dough until it is about ¼ inch (6 mm) thick and 8 inches (20 cm) in diameter. Try not to let the center of the disk become too thin in comparison to the edges. Dust the peel or baking sheet with more flour and gently lay the disk in the center.

◈ Mound the filling in the center on the half of the dough that is nearest to you. Gently fold the top half of the dough over the filling, stretching and adjusting as necessary so the edges meet. Crimp the edges with a fork to seal. Tear a steam vent about 1 inch (2.5 cm) long in the center of the top. Spoon the tomato-basil sauce over the vent and spread it around with the back of a spoon for decoration.

◈ Gently shake the peel or baking sheet back and forth to make sure the calzone has not stuck to it. If it has, gently lift off the stuck section and sprinkle a little more flour underneath. Using the peel or baking sheet like a large spatula, quickly slide the calzone onto the hot pizza stone or tiles. Bake until the top is golden brown and the bottom is dotted with dark brown spots, 8–9 minutes. Remove the calzone with a large metal spatula and place on a dinner plate. Sprinkle the Parmesan cheese over the top and serve at once.

Makes 1 calzone

Focaccia and Panini

Centuries ago in northern Italy, the Etruscans baked *puls,* a thick gruel, under hot ashes, then topped the resultant cakes with oil and herbs, to eat with broth or meat. The Romans dubbed such rustic flat bread *panus focus,* "bread from the hearth," a name that later evolved into *focaccia.*

Focaccia is made from a softer, more yeasty dough than pizza and, unlike pizza, is usually served warm or at room temperature. Seasoned with herbs and sprinkled sparingly with coarse salt, sharp cheese or other piquant condiments, focaccia makes a satisfying accompaniment to a meal. It also becomes the perfect *merenda,* or "snack," on its own or the base for such hearty ingredients as sliced potatoes, pesto sauce and pine nuts.

Focaccia is a natural choice for constructing *panini,* the little sandwiches of Italy. Its rustic charm and appealing texture inspire many contemporary filling combinations, from a vegetarian ensemble of sautéed eggplant, tomatoes, mozzarella and basil to a distinctive combination of halibut, arugula and roasted peppers. However you bake it and top or fill it, focaccia finds a warm welcome on any pizzeria menu.

Focaccia with Red Onion

*This focaccia is found on the menus of pizzerias in Florence, where small,
three-wheel flatbed trucks laden with torpedo-shaped purple onions—their tops
flopping over the edge of the bed—zoom into the city on market days.*

½ recipe herb-flavored focaccia dough *(recipe on page 117)*, completed through the first rising

¼ small red (Spanish) onion, thinly sliced

1½ teaspoons chopped fresh thyme
Extra-virgin olive oil for drizzling

2–3 tablespoons freshly grated Italian Parmesan cheese

Lightly oil an 8-inch (20-cm) cake pan or similar pan. Place the dough in the prepared pan and gently stretch it to the edges, pulling it from the center outward to achieve an even thickness. If the dough springs back toward the center and is difficult to work with, cover and set it aside to relax for 10 minutes, then continue coaxing the dough out to an even thickness. Cover with a kitchen towel and let rise until almost doubled in bulk and very soft and puffy, about 45 minutes.

Preheat an oven to 475°F (245°C).

Using your fingertips, dimple the dough vigorously in several places, leaving indentations about ½ inch (12 mm) deep. Again cover the pan with a towel and let rise for 20 minutes longer.

Arrange the onion and thyme evenly over the risen dough. Drizzle the top with olive oil, then sprinkle on the Parmesan. Bake until golden brown and cooked through, 15–18 minutes. Transfer the pan to a rack and let stand until the focaccia is barely warm, about 10 minutes, then serve.

Makes one 8-inch (20-cm) focaccia round

Focaccia with Pesto and Potatoes

Potatoes and bread have a satisfying affinity for each other. A garlicky pesto sauce adds a luscious spark to this focaccia, perfect for lunch paired with a salad of baby greens. Although covered with potato slices, the pesto bubbles up during baking to contribute its special beauty to the finished round.

½ recipe herb-flavored focaccia dough *(recipe on page 117)*, completed through the first rising

2 tablespoons olive oil

½ small yellow onion, thinly sliced

2–3 tablespoons Genovese pesto *(recipe on page 119)*

1 very small russet or golden-fleshed potato, unpeeled, sliced paper-thin

2 tablespoons pine nuts

2 tablespoons freshly grated Italian Parmesan cheese

▣ Lightly oil an 8-inch (20-cm) cake pan or similar pan. Place the dough in the prepared pan and gently stretch it to the edges, pulling it from the center outward to achieve an even thickness. If the dough springs back toward the center and is difficult to work with, cover and set it aside to relax for 10 minutes, then continue coaxing the dough out to an even thickness. Cover with a kitchen towel and let rise until almost doubled in bulk and very soft and puffy, about 45 minutes.

▣ Preheat an oven to 475°F (245°C).

▣ Using your fingertips, dimple the dough vigorously in several places, leaving indentations about ½ inch (12 mm) deep. Again cover the pan with a towel and let rise for 20 minutes longer.

▣ While the dough is rising, in a small sauté pan over medium-low heat, warm the olive oil. Add the onion and sauté until tender and golden, about 6 minutes. Remove from the heat and let cool.

▣ Using the back of a spoon, spread the pesto evenly over the dough, using the larger amount if you want the finished focaccia to have a fuller pesto flavor. Arrange the potato slices in concentric circles atop the pesto, leaving gaps between the circles. Top evenly with the sautéed onion and the pine nuts. Scatter the Parmesan over the surface, including around the rim. Bake until golden brown and cooked through, 15–18 minutes. Transfer the pan to a rack and let stand until the focaccia is barely warm, about 10 minutes, then serve.

Makes one 8-inch (20-cm) focaccia round

Eggplant, Tomato and Mozzarella Sandwich

Here, the traditional ingredients for eggplant parmigiana are used to make a luscious panino. *For a lighter version, grill rather than sauté the eggplant. The sandwich is delicious made while the eggplant is still warm. You can also marinate the sautéed eggplant with a bit of minced garlic, a few chopped basil leaves and a splash of balsamic vinegar, allowing you to assemble the* panino *another day.*

1	Asian (slender) eggplant (aubergine)
2	tablespoons olive oil
	Focaccia with coarse salt *(recipe on page 72)* or focaccia with red onion *(page 64)*
1	tomato, sliced
2	thin slices Vidalia onion or other sweet onion
3	oz (90 g) fresh mozzarella cheese, sliced
3 or 4	fresh basil leaves
	Salt and freshly ground pepper
	Extra-virgin olive oil for drizzling
2	tablespoons freshly grated Italian Parmesan cheese

▣ Trim the ends from the eggplant and thinly slice crosswise. Discard the end slices that are covered on one side with skin. In a sauté pan over medium heat, warm the olive oil. Add the eggplant and cook, turning once, until tender and golden, 5–7 minutes. Using a slotted spoon, transfer to paper towels to drain.

▣ Slice the focaccia in half horizontally. Lay the bottom half, cut side up, on a cutting board. Arrange the eggplant slices on the bottom half.

Top evenly with the tomato, onion and mozzarella slices and the basil leaves. Season to taste with salt and pepper. Drizzle with olive oil and sprinkle the Parmesan evenly over the top. Place the other half of the focaccia on top, cut side down, and press down firmly with the palm of your hand. Cut the *panino* in half or in quarters for easier eating and serve.

Makes 1 sandwich

Focaccia with Cheese

Taleggio is a soft, creamy Italian cheese with a hint of acidic tang. It melts beautifully atop this savory focaccia. For the Taleggio, you may substitute a good-quality Jack cheese or Fontina.

½ recipe herb-flavored focaccia dough *(recipe on page 117)*, completed through the first rising
2 oz (60 g) Taleggio cheese, coarsely chopped
10 fresh sage leaves
   Salt and freshly ground pepper
   Extra-virgin olive oil for drizzling

▨ Lightly oil an 8-inch (20-cm) cake pan or similar pan. Place the dough in the prepared pan and gently stretch it to the edges, pulling it from the center outward to achieve an even thickness. If the dough springs back toward the center and is difficult to work with, cover and set it aside to relax for 10 minutes, then continue coaxing the dough out to an even thickness. Cover with a kitchen towel and let rise until almost doubled in bulk and very soft and puffy, about 45 minutes.

▨ Preheat an oven to 475°F (245°C).

▨ Using your fingertips, dimple the dough vigorously in several places, leaving indentations about ½ inch (12 mm) deep. Again cover the pan with a towel and let rise for 20 minutes longer.

▨ Top the risen dough evenly with the Taleggio cheese, sage and salt and pepper to taste. Drizzle the top with olive oil, making sure to coat the sage leaves evenly. Bake until golden brown and cooked through, 15–18 minutes. Transfer the pan to a rack and let stand until the focaccia is barely warm, about 10 minutes, then serve.

Makes one 8-inch (20-cm) focaccia round

Focaccia with Coarse Salt

In pizzerias, this simple focaccia is sometimes served with a tumbler of red wine before dinner. It can also be split in half and used to house a variety of fillings for panini.

½ recipe herb-flavored focaccia dough *(recipe on page 117)*, completed through the first rising

1½ teaspoons coarse salt
  Coarsely ground pepper

1½ tablespoons coarsely chopped fresh rosemary
  Extra-virgin olive oil for drizzling

▨ Lightly oil an 8-inch (20-cm) cake pan or similar pan. Place the dough in the prepared pan and gently stretch it to the edges, pulling it from the center outward to achieve an even thickness. If the dough springs back toward the center and is difficult to work with, cover and set it aside to relax for 10 minutes, then continue coaxing the dough out to an even thickness. Cover with a kitchen towel and let rise until almost doubled in bulk and very soft and puffy, about 45 minutes.

▨ Preheat an oven to 475°F (245°C).

▨ Using your fingertips, dimple the dough vigorously in several places, leaving indentations about ½ inch (12 mm) deep. Again cover the pan with a towel and let rise for 20 minutes longer.

▨ Sprinkle the risen dough evenly with the salt and pepper to taste and the rosemary. Drizzle with olive oil. Bake until golden brown and cooked through, 15–18 minutes. Transfer the pan to a rack and let stand until the focaccia is barely warm, about 10 minutes, then serve.

Makes one 8-inch (20-cm) focaccia round

Focaccia with Onion, Walnuts and Gorgonzola

*Cut into thin slices or squares, this focaccia makes a marvelous addition to a simple
antipasto accompanied with a glass of* vino da tavola. *Gorgonzola dolcelatte, which is
sweeter and milder than Gorgonzola piccante, can be found in well-stocked cheese shops.
If Gorgonzola dolcelatte is unavailable, substitute crumbled Cambozola blue cheese.*

½ recipe herb-flavored focaccia dough *(recipe on page 117),* completed through the first rising

2 tablespoons extra-virgin olive oil

½ large yellow onion, thinly sliced

3 oz (90 g) Gorgonzola dolcelatte cheese, coarsely chopped

¼ cup (1 oz/30 g) coarsely chopped walnuts

◙ Lightly oil an 8-inch (20-cm) cake pan or similar pan. Place the dough in the prepared pan and gently stretch it to the edges, pulling it from the center outward to achieve an even thickness. If the dough springs back toward the center and is difficult to work with, cover and set it aside to relax for 10 minutes, then continue coaxing the dough out to an even thickness. Cover with a kitchen towel and let rise until almost doubled in bulk and very soft and puffy, about 45 minutes.

◙ While the dough is rising, in a sauté pan over medium-low heat, warm the olive oil. Add the onion and sauté until golden brown and very soft and sweet, about 20 minutes. Remove from the heat and let cool.

◙ Preheat an oven to 475°F (245°C).

◙ Using your fingertips, dimple the dough vigorously in several places, leaving indentations about ½ inch (12 mm) deep. Again cover the pan with a towel and let rise for 20 minutes longer.

◙ Spread the cooked onion evenly over the risen dough, then scatter the Gorgonzola over the onion. Top with the walnuts. Bake until golden brown and cooked through, 15–18 minutes. Transfer the pan to a rack and let stand until the focaccia is barely warm, about 10 minutes, then serve.

Makes one 8-inch (20-cm) focaccia round

Seared Halibut Sandwich with Roasted Red Pepper and Arugula

The American love of substantial sandwiches meets traditional Italian flavors in this panino.
It is the type of lunch fare found at many of the new and stylish American pizzerias.

½ red bell pepper (capsicum)
¼ lb (125 g) halibut fillet
1 tablespoon olive oil
   Salt and freshly ground pepper
2 tablespoons mayonnaise
1 teaspoon chopped fresh thyme
½ teaspoon Dijon mustard
   Focaccia with red onion *(recipe on page 64)*
½ cup (½ oz/15 g) loosely packed arugula (rocket) leaves
2 thin slices red (Spanish) onion
   Juice of ½ lemon

Preheat a broiler (griller) or preheat an oven to 450°F (230°C). Remove the seeds and ribs from the pepper half and place, cut side down, on a baking sheet. Place in the broiler or oven and broil (grill) or bake until the skin is charred and blistered. Alternatively, using tongs or a fork, hold the pepper half over a gas flame until charred and blistered. Immediately place the pepper half in a bowl and cover tightly with plastic wrap. Let steam until cool, about 15 minutes. Using your fingers, peel off the charred skin. Cut lengthwise into narrow strips. Set aside.

Preheat a gas grill or a ridged stove-top griddle on high, or place a heavy sauté pan (preferably cast iron) over medium-high heat until very hot. Brush the halibut fillet with the olive oil and season to taste with salt and pepper. Add the fish to the hot grill, griddle or sauté pan and cook, turning once, until nicely browned on both sides and opaque at the center, about 3 minutes on each side depending upon thickness.

While the fish is cooking, in a small bowl, whisk together the mayonnaise, thyme and mustard until blended.

Slice the focaccia in half horizontally. Cut the halibut into slices ½ inch (12 mm) thick. Spread the mustard mayonnaise on the cut sides of the focaccia. Distribute the arugula evenly over the bottom of the focaccia. Top evenly with the sliced halibut and then with the pepper strips and onion slices. Sprinkle with the lemon juice and salt and pepper to taste. Place the other half of the focaccia on top, cut side down, and press down firmly with the palm of your hand. Cut the *panino* in half or in quarters for easier eating and serve.

Makes 1 sandwich

Light Meals

The institution of the pizzeria continues to evolve with changing times and the changing tastes of its customers. In no aspect of the menu does this fact show more clearly than in the offerings of light meals.

Smart pizzeria owners know that not every customer will necessarily want to order a pizza. Many people, particularly time-pressed workers who want to grab a quick lunch or moviegoers looking for a bite to eat before a show, are in search of a convenient and satisfying one-dish meal, or *piatto unico*.

The *piatto unico* could be a rich soup brimming with vegetables and the comforting tenderness of rice, or a pasta dish sauced with fresh tomatoes highlighted by a drizzle of balsamic vinegar and piquant accents of capers and shallots. Daily specials on the menu might explore more adventurous territory—herbed, braised artichokes filled with a savory mixture of green lentils and chicken or a new version of the traditional Tuscan bread salad made with grilled slices of a country loaf and freshly cooked shrimp. Of necessity, dishes such as a roasted chicken cooked on a bed of potatoes or a robust lasagna oozing with the richness of four cheeses preserve a direct connection to traditional rustic tastes.

Roasted Chicken Sausages with Red Peppers

In small pizzerias, the forno a legna, *or "wood-fired pizza oven," is often used for
preparing simple main courses such as this hearty dish of roasted sausages and peppers. It can also be
made with traditional Italian sausages—with or without fennel, mild or highly spiced*

8 chicken sausages
10 fresh thyme sprigs
2 tablespoons extra-virgin olive oil
1 large red (Spanish) onion, cut in half through the stem end and thinly sliced
3 cloves garlic, minced
4 red bell peppers (capsicums), seeded, deribbed and cut lengthwise into strips ¼ inch (6 mm) wide
¼ cup (⅓ oz/10 g) coarsely chopped fresh flat-leaf (Italian) parsley
   Salt and freshly ground pepper

❖ Preheat an oven to 450°F (230°C).

❖ Arrange the sausages in a roasting pan just large enough to hold them in a single layer. Tuck the thyme sprigs around them. Pour in water to a depth of ½ inch (12 mm). Roast, turning the sausages once or twice, until the water has completely evaporated and the sausages are nicely browned, 10–15 minutes.

❖ While the sausages are cooking, in a frying pan over medium-low heat, warm the olive oil. Add the onion and sauté, stirring occasionally, until limp, 5–6 minutes. Add the garlic and sauté for 1 minute longer. Stir in the bell peppers and sauté, stirring occasionally, until the peppers just begin to soften, about 10 minutes. Remove from the heat and set aside.

❖ When the sausages have browned, add the bell pepper mixture to the roasting pan along with the parsley and salt and pepper to taste. Return the roasting pan to the oven and continue to roast until the sausages are a deep golden brown and the vegetables are golden, about 15 minutes longer. Transfer to a warmed platter and serve immediately.

Serves 4–6

Summer Linguine

Summertime is made for exploring the abundant offerings at local farmers' markets. Look for small, tender Blue Lake beans or richly flavored flat romanos. Fresh zucchini flowers add their sunny color and subtle squash flavor to this light vegetarian dish.

¼ cup (2 fl oz/60 ml) extra-virgin olive oil, plus olive oil as needed

1 shallot, minced

2 cloves garlic, minced

2 russet or golden-fleshed potatoes, peeled and cut into small dice

1 zucchini (courgette), ends trimmed, cut in half lengthwise and then cut crosswise into half-moons

½ lb (250 g) green beans *(see note)*, ends trimmed and strings removed

¼ lb (250 g) zucchini (courgette) flowers, stamens removed, optional

¼ cup (⅓ oz/10 g) coarsely chopped fresh basil
Salt and freshly ground pepper
Juice of ½ lemon, or to taste

1 lb (500 g) dried Italian linguine

2 tablespoons unsalted butter, at room temperature
Freshly grated Italian Parmesan cheese

▣ In a frying pan over medium-low heat, warm the ¼ cup (2 fl oz/60 ml) olive oil. Add the shallot and garlic and sauté for a few seconds, stirring frequently, just until the flavors are released. Add the potatoes and sauté, gently tossing once or twice, until just tender, about 7 minutes. Add the zucchini, green beans, zucchini flowers (if using) and basil. Continue sautéing, stirring occasionally, until all the vegetables are tender, about 10 minutes longer. Season to taste with salt, pepper and lemon juice.

▣ While the vegetables are cooking, fill a deep pot three-fourths full with lightly salted water and bring to a rolling boil. Add the pasta and stir a few times to prevent it from sticking together or to the pan. Cook until al dente, 7–8 minutes or according to the package directions. Scoop out and reserve ½ cup (4 fl oz/125 ml) of the cooking water. Drain the linguine thoroughly in a colander.

▣ Immediately place the sautéed vegetables with all their juices and the reserved cooking water in a large shallow pasta bowl. Add the linguine and butter, toss to mix well and serve immediately. Pass Parmesan cheese at the table.

Serves 4–6

Artichokes Stuffed with Chicken and Lentils

No one can meander the streets of Rome without coming under the spell of the purple-green spineless artichoke. In season one sees flatbed trucks laden with the long-stemmed beauties. Here, artichokes are cooked Roman style with herbs, stuffed with a savory filling and then briefly baked.

ARTICHOKES

¼ cup (2 fl oz/60 ml) extra-virgin olive oil

½ cup (4 fl oz/125 ml) water

4 cloves garlic, minced

2 tablespoons coarsely chopped fresh flat-leaf (Italian) parsley

2 tablespoons coarsely chopped fresh basil

4 large artichokes, trimmed *(see glossary, page 340)* and halved lengthwise
  Salt and freshly ground pepper

FILLING

½ cup (3½ oz/105 g) small green French lentils

2 tablespoons extra-virgin olive oil

3 cloves garlic, minced

10 oz (315 g) ground (minced) chicken breast meat

¼ cup (⅓ oz/10 g) coarsely chopped fresh flat-leaf (Italian) parsley
  Coarse salt and freshly ground pepper

½ cup (4 fl oz/125 ml) tomato-basil sauce *(recipe on page 118)*

  Lemon wedges, optional

¼ cup (⅓ oz/10 g) coarsely chopped fresh flat-leaf (Italian) parsley, optional

Place the olive oil and water in a frying pan just large enough to hold the 8 artichoke halves. Scatter the garlic and herbs in the pan and arrange the artichoke halves, cut sides down, in a circular pattern with the stems facing toward the center of the pan. Season to taste with salt and pepper. Place over medium-high heat, bring to a simmer, cover and cook until almost tender, about 10 minutes. Remove from the heat and set aside.

To make the filling, in a saucepan, bring a generous amount of lightly salted water to a boil. Add the lentils and reduce the heat so that the water simmers. Cook, uncovered, until the lentils are just tender but still hold their shape, 20–25 minutes. Drain and refresh them under cold running water to halt the cooking. Drain again and set aside.

In a frying pan over low heat, warm the olive oil. Add the garlic and cook gently, stirring frequently, until the garlic turns opaque, 3–4 seconds. Add the ground chicken, raise the heat to medium and sauté, stirring and breaking up the chicken with a wooden spoon so that it cooks evenly, until cooked through and no trace of pink remains, about 10 minutes. Remove from the heat and add the drained lentils, parsley and salt and pepper to taste. Pour in the tomato-basil sauce and toss gently to mix well.

Preheat an oven to 375°F (190°C).

Place the braised artichokes, hollow sides up, in a baking dish in which they fit in a single layer. Divide the filling mixture evenly among the halves, mounding it high for an attractive presentation. Bake until heated through, about 10 minutes.

Remove from the oven and serve the artichokes hot, cold or at room temperature, arranged on a platter or divided among individual plates. Garnish with lemon wedges and parsley, if desired.

Serves 4–6

Bread Salad with Grilled Shrimp

In many cultures where food traditions were formed amid great poverty, there is much ingenuity in the use of stale bread. Panzanella, a Tuscan salad of stale bread soaked in water, squeezed dry and tossed with a varied mix of ingredients, was created in this spirit. This version, which includes shrimp, would be at home on the menu of any contemporary American pizzeria.

4   tomatoes, cut into small dice

1   large cucumber, peeled, seeded and cut into small dice

2   bell peppers (capsicums), any color, seeded, deribbed and cut into small dice

1   shallot, minced

2   tablespoons capers, rinsed, drained and coarsely chopped

1   tablespoon coarsely chopped fresh oregano

¼   cup (⅓ oz/10 g) fresh flat-leaf (Italian) parsley

¼   cup (2 fl oz/60 ml) extra-virgin olive oil, plus olive oil for drizzling on bread

2   tablespoons red wine vinegar

24   large shrimp (prawns), peeled and deveined

     Olive oil for brushing

3   thick slices country-style bread

1   clove garlic

     Salt and freshly ground pepper

     Lemon wedges

◧ In a large serving bowl, combine the tomatoes, cucumber, bell peppers, shallot, capers, oregano and parsley. Add the ¼ cup (2 fl oz/60 ml) extra-virgin olive oil and the vinegar, toss to mix and set aside for at least 1 hour or up to 6 hours.

◧ Prepare a fire in a charcoal grill or preheat a ridged stove-top griddle until it is very hot.

◧ Lightly brush the shrimp with olive oil. Place the shrimp on the grill rack 7–8 inches (18–20 cm) above the fire or on the griddle and cook, turning once, until pink and cooked through, about 6 minutes total. Remove the shrimp from the grill or griddle and toss into the bowl with the prepared vegetables.

◧ Place the bread slices on the grill rack or griddle and grill, turning once, until grill marks are apparent on both sides and the bread is toasted, 3–4 minutes total. Remove the bread from the grill or griddle and quickly rub one side of each slice with the garlic clove. Drizzle a little extra-virgin olive oil over the bread.

◧ Let the bread cool, then tear into 2-inch (5-cm) pieces. Add to the shrimp and vegetables. Season to taste with salt and pepper and toss to mix well.

◧ Divide evenly among individual plates and garnish with lemon wedges. Serve immediately.

Serves 4–6

Chick-pea Soup with Swiss Chard and Tomatoes

Chick-peas and Swiss chard both have an earthy nuttiness that is particularly suited to creating full-flavored vegetarian soups. This soup is brothy; to make a thicker zuppa, *put half the cooked vegetables through a food mill fitted with the coarse disk. To enrich the presentation of the soup, ladle it over a large* crostino *placed in the bottom of each bowl.*

2 tablespoons extra-virgin olive oil
1 yellow onion, coarsely chopped
3 cloves garlic, minced
8 small plum (Roma) tomatoes, coarsely chopped
1 bunch Swiss chard (silverbeet)
1 can (16 oz/500 g) chick-peas (garbanzo beans), drained
6 cups (48 fl oz/1.5 l) water
   Salt and freshly ground pepper

▣ In a heavy soup pot over medium heat, warm the olive oil. Add the onion and sauté, stirring frequently, until wilted but not browned, 3–4 minutes. Add the garlic and stir for a few seconds. Then add the tomatoes, raise the heat to medium-high and cook, stirring occasionally, just until the tomatoes begin to break down and form a sauce, about 10 minutes.

▣ While the tomatoes are cooking, cut off and discard the bottom third of the Swiss chard stems. Cut the remaining stem portions crosswise into pieces ¼ inch (6 mm) wide. Working with several chard leaves at a time, stack them, roll them up lengthwise and then cut crosswise to form ribbons ¼ inch (6 mm) wide.

▣ Add the chard, chick-peas and water to the soup pot and bring to a simmer over medium-high heat. Cook uncovered, adjusting the heat as necessary to maintain a simmer, until the vegetables are tender and the flavors have blended, 30–45 minutes. The soup will be brothy and chunky.

▣ Season to taste with salt and pepper. Ladle the soup into shallow bowls and serve at once.

Serves 4

Orecchiette with Tomato-Shallot Sauce

Roman cooks are famous for hot pasta tossed in a mixture of chopped raw tomatoes, garlic, basil and oil. Variations on this easy, tasty and colorful base are now found all over Italy. Since the ingredients are already on hand for pizza making, this light, refreshing dish is a welcome addition to a pizzeria menu, especially on warm summer nights.

10	ripe yet firm plum (Roma) tomatoes, chopped
2	shallots, minced
2	cloves garlic, minced
1–2	tablespoons capers, rinsed, drained and coarsely chopped
¼	cup (2 fl oz/60 ml) balsamic vinegar
½–1	cup (4–8 fl oz/125–250 ml) extra-virgin olive oil
	Small handful of coarsely chopped fresh flat-leaf (Italian) parsley
10	fresh basil leaves, chopped
	Salt and freshly ground pepper
1	lb (500 g) Italian orecchiette

In a large, shallow pasta bowl, combine the tomatoes, shallots, garlic, capers, vinegar, ½ cup (4 fl oz/ 125 ml) olive oil, parsley, basil, and salt and pepper to taste. For a fuller, richer flavor, add all or part of the remaining ½ cup (4 fl oz/125 ml) olive oil, if desired. Toss well, cover and set aside in a cool place for at least 1 hour or for up to 3 hours.

When ready to serve, fill a deep pot three-fourths full with lightly salted water and bring to a rolling boil. Add the pasta and stir a few times to prevent it from sticking together or to the pan. Cook until al dente, 7–10 minutes or according to the package directions. Drain the pasta thoroughly in a colander and add it to the serving bowl with the sauce mixture. Toss well and serve immediately.

Serves 4–6

Lasagna with Four Cheeses

*Few baked pastas are as rich and satisfying as this dish from northern Italy. The new
"no-boil" lasagna sheets have a marvelous tender texture, although it is wise to dip them briefly
in boiling water for the best result. Regular lasagna noodles can also be used.*

BÉCHAMEL SAUCE

3½ cups (28 fl oz/875 ml) milk
1   fresh rosemary sprig, 2 inches
    (5 cm) long
6   tablespoons (3 oz/90 g) unsalted
    butter
5   tablespoons (1½ oz/45 g) all-
    purpose (plain) flour
    Salt and freshly ground pepper

GARLIC BREAD CRUMBS

1   loaf good-quality country-style
    bread, about ½ lb (250 g), cut
    into 1-inch (2.5-cm) cubes
1   tablespoon minced garlic, or to
    taste
    Salt and freshly ground pepper
    Extra-virgin olive oil, as needed

½   cup (2 oz/60 g) walnuts
1½ cups (12 oz/375 g) ricotta cheese
¾   cup (6 oz/185 g) mascarpone
    cheese
¾   cup (3 oz/90 g) shredded
    Fontina cheese
2   cups (8 oz/250 g) freshly grated
    Italian Parmesan cheese
1   tablespoon minced fresh
    rosemary
3   tablespoons chopped fresh flat-
    leaf (Italian) parsley
    Salt and freshly ground pepper
20 sheets "no-boil" lasagna

◼ To make the béchamel sauce, pour the milk into a saucepan, add the rosemary sprig and place over medium-low heat until small bubbles appear along the pan edge. In a small saucepan over medium-low heat, melt the butter. Add the flour and whisk to form a smooth paste. Reduce the heat to low and cook, stirring, for about 2 minutes. When the milk is hot, add the butter-flour mixture, whisking constantly. Simmer over medium heat until the sauce thickens enough to coat a spoon, about 20 minutes. Remove and discard the rosemary sprig. Season to taste with salt and pepper. Set aside to cool.

◼ To make the bread crumbs, preheat an oven to 350°F (180°C). In a food processor fitted with the metal blade, pulse the bread cubes to produce coarse crumbs. In a large bowl, combine the crumbs, garlic and salt and pepper to taste. Add enough olive oil to moisten the mixture slightly. Spread on a baking sheet and bake until barely golden, 2–4 minutes.

◼ Spread the walnuts on a baking sheet and toast until golden and fragrant, about 10 minutes. Let cool. Raise the oven temperature to 375°F (190°C). In a large bowl, combine the toasted walnuts, ricotta, mascarpone, Fontina, 1 cup (4 oz/125 g) of

the Parmesan, rosemary, parsley, and salt and pepper to taste. Mix well. Add 1 cup (8 fl oz/250 ml) of the béchamel and stir vigorously to mix.

◼ Fill a deep pot three-fourths full with lightly salted water and bring to a rolling boil. Using tongs, dip the "no-boil" lasagna sheets into the boiling water for 10 seconds, then lay them on a kitchen towel to drain.

◼ Spread a thin layer of béchamel over the bottom of a 13-by-9-by-2-inch (33-by-23-by-5-cm) lasagna pan. Top with a layer of pasta, then with a layer of the cheese mixture. Top with a layer ¼ inch (6 mm) thick of the béchamel. Sprinkle with 1 tablespoon of the remaining Parmesan. Top with another layer of pasta sheets. Alternate layers of the cheese mixture and béchamel and Parmesan, until all the ingredients except the Parmesan are used up, ending with béchamel. Scatter the remaining Parmesan and the bread crumbs over the top. Cover and bake until the dish is bubbling, 35–40 minutes. Uncover and bake until the bread crumbs are crunchy, about 10 minutes longer. Let stand for 5–10 minutes before serving.

Serves 6–8

ITALIAN: LIGHT MEALS

Wild Mushroom Soup

In Umbria, a region in the heart of Italy, soups are often made from an extraordinary assortment of mushrooms that have been gathered by families on Sunday outings in the woods. In this recipe, a mixture of cultivated pale brown cremini and white mushrooms are used. Feel free to substitute any full-flavored fresh mushrooms, cultivated or wild, including chanterelles, morels and porcini.

⅓ cup (2 oz/60 g) pine nuts

½ cup (4 fl oz/125 ml) extra-virgin olive oil

1 large yellow onion, finely chopped

3 cloves garlic, minced

10 plum (Roma) tomatoes, chopped

1 lb (500 g) fresh shiitake mushrooms, stems removed, sliced

½ lb (250 g) fresh cremini or white mushrooms, stems removed, sliced

6 cups (48 fl oz/1.5 l) water

1 tablespoon chopped fresh basil

1 tablespoon chopped fresh flat-leaf (Italian) parsley

1 tablespoon chopped fresh rosemary

1 tablespoon chopped fresh thyme

Salt and freshly ground pepper

◈ Preheat an oven to 350°F (180°C). Spread the pine nuts on a baking sheet and toast until golden and fragrant, 5–8 minutes. Remove from the oven and let cool.

◈ In a heavy soup pot over medium heat, warm the olive oil. Add the onion and sauté, stirring frequently, until soft and golden, about 5 minutes. Add the garlic, tomatoes and mushrooms and raise the heat to high. Sauté, stirring often, just until the mushrooms begin to release their liquid, about 7 minutes.

◈ Add the water and herbs and bring to a boil. Reduce the heat to medium-low and simmer uncovered, stirring occasionally, until all the vegetables are tender and the flavors are blended, 25–30 minutes. Season to taste with salt and pepper. Ladle into warmed shallow soup bowls, scatter the pine nuts evenly over the tops and serve immediately.

Serves 4–6

Spinach–Ricotta Dumplings with Red Pepper Sauce

These light dumplings are made from the filling commonly used in stuffing ravioli.
They are called ravioli nudi, *"naked ravioli," because they lack a pasta covering.*

SAUCE

4   large, fleshy red bell peppers
    (capsicums)
2   tablespoons unsalted butter
2   tablespoons extra-virgin olive oil
½   small yellow onion, cut into
    small dice
2   cloves garlic
1   cup (8 fl oz/250 ml) water or
    chicken or vegetable stock
¼   cup (⅓ oz/10 g) coarsely chopped
    fresh flat-leaf (Italian) parsley
5   fresh basil leaves
    Salt and freshly ground pepper
2   tablespoons heavy (double) cream,
    optional

DUMPLINGS

3   bunches spinach, about 1 lb
    (500 g) each, stems removed
3   eggs, lightly beaten
¾   cup (3 oz/90 g) freshly grated
    Italian Parmesan cheese, plus
    cheese for garnishing
¾   cup (3 oz/90 g) freshly grated
    pecorino romano cheese
2   cups (1 lb/500 g) ricotta cheese
3   tablespoons unbleached all-
    purpose (plain) flour, plus flour
    for dredging
1   teaspoon salt
¼   teaspoon freshly ground pepper
2   tablespoons unsalted butter, melted
½   cup (4 oz/125 g) unsalted butter
10 fresh sage leaves

To make the pepper sauce, use a vegetable peeler to remove the thin skin from the peppers. Cut each in half lengthwise and pull out and discard the stem, seeds and ribs. Cut the peppers lengthwise into strips.

In a sauté pan over medium heat, melt the butter with the olive oil. Add the onion and cook, stirring occasionally, until golden, about 7 minutes. Add the garlic and bell peppers and sauté, stirring occasionally, until the peppers soften, about 10 minutes. Add the water or stock, parsley and basil and bring to a simmer. Simmer, uncovered, until the peppers are tender, about 10 minutes longer. Season to taste with salt and pepper. Purée the pepper mixture in a blender or in a food processor fitted with the metal blade and transfer to a bowl. Stir in the cream, if using.

Rinse the spinach but do not dry. Place in a large saucepan over medium-low heat, cover and cook, turning occasionally, until wilted, 2–4 minutes. Drain, squeeze to remove the liquid and chop finely. In a bowl, combine the spinach, eggs, ¾ cup (3 oz/90 g) each of the Parmesan and pecorino romano cheeses, ricotta cheese, 3 tablespoons flour, salt and pepper. Stir well until the mixture resembles a thick, slightly stiff batter. Add flour to a shallow dish to a depth

of ½ inch (12 mm). Form the ricotta mixture into balls about ¾ inch (2 cm) in diameter. Roll them lightly in the flour, coating evenly, and place them on a lightly floured tray.

Preheat an oven to 250°F (120°C). Fill a deep pot three-fourths full with lightly salted water and bring to a gentle simmer. Add the dumplings a few at a time. Nudge them occasionally to ensure that they cook evenly. The dumplings are ready when they rise to the surface and then cook for another minute or so; this will take about 3 minutes in all. Lift out the dumplings and drain thoroughly on an absorbent kitchen towel. Place in an ovenproof dish, drizzle with the 2 tablespoons melted butter and cover to keep warm.

Meanwhile, in a saucepan over medium heat, warm the pepper purée. In a sauté pan over high heat, melt the ½ cup (4 oz/125 g) butter. Add the sage leaves and sauté, stirring frequently, until the sage leaves are crispy, about 5 minutes. Transfer to paper towels to drain.

Pour the purée onto individual plates and place the dumplings on top. Spoon on the sage leaves and some of the butter. Dust with Parmesan cheese.

Serves 4–6

Roasted Chicken with Potatoes

Nearly every casual Italian dining establishment offers roasted chicken. In this version,
a paste of caramelized garlic and herbs is slathered over the chicken to create a savory crust.

20 cloves garlic
    Olive oil, to cover
1 tablespoon chopped fresh oregano, plus oregano sprigs for garnish
1 tablespoon chopped fresh thyme leaves, plus thyme sprigs for garnish
2 tablespoons hot water
2 small chickens, about 2 lb (1 kg) each
    Salt and freshly ground pepper
6 russet or golden-fleshed potatoes, peeled and thinly sliced
2 yellow onions, thinly sliced
    Lemon wedges

◾ Peel the garlic but leave the cloves whole. In a small, heavy saucepan over medium-low heat, combine the garlic cloves with olive oil just to cover. Bring to a gentle simmer and cook the garlic until it is covered with golden dots, about 15 minutes. Watch carefully, as the garlic burns easily. Remove from the heat, let cool and then drain off the oil. Set the oil aside.

◾ In a blender or in a food processor fitted with the metal blade, combine the garlic cloves, chopped oregano and thyme, hot water and a little of the reserved oil, if desired. Purée to form a coarse paste, scraping down the sides of the blender or bowl as necessary. Transfer to a small bowl. Set aside.

◾ Preheat an oven to 400°F (200°C).

◾ Using poultry shears or a heavy knife, cut the chickens in half lengthwise. Cut out and discard the backbone. Season the chickens generously with salt and pepper and let stand at room temperature for 10 minutes.

◾ Rub the garlic paste generously over the chickens, coating all the surfaces. Place the potatoes in an even layer in a roasting pan just large enough to hold the chickens comfortably in a single layer. Top the potatoes with the onions, distributing them evenly, then season with salt and pepper. Drizzle with a bit of the reserved garlic oil; reserve the remaining oil for another use. Lay the chickens, cut sides down, on top of the vegetables and cover the pan with aluminum foil.

◾ Roast until the chickens begin to brown, 20–30 minutes. Raise the oven temperature to 450°F (230°C). Remove the foil and baste the chickens with the accumulated pan juices. Continue to roast, uncovered, until crusty and deep golden brown and the juices run clear when a thigh is pierced, 10–15 minutes longer.

◾ Transfer the chicken and potatoes to a large platter and garnish with lemon wedges and thyme and oregano sprigs.

Serves 4–6

Desserts

Apart from the innate appeal of their food, pizzerias are patronized for their reasonable prices and small, easy-to-comprehend menus. These qualities make it all the more crucial for the pizzeria chef to devise desserts that are simple and economical while also being as delicious as the foods that precede them.

To that end, most pizzerias offer a limited selection of sure-to-please items on the *carta dei dolci,* or "dessert menu." One might be a hand-beaten *granita di cappuccino,* "cappuccino ice," that is easily prepared even by someone with the most rudimentary of cooking skills. A trip to a nearby pastry shop might be in order, so that the pizzeria can offer something a bit more elegant like a *gianduia* tart featuring the popular combination of hazelnuts and chocolate. A special biscotti recipe is often contributed by a relative, the crisp twice-baked cookies served alongside steaming cups of espresso or cappuccino.

Other items prepared on the premises fall into the category of *dolci al cucchiaio,* "spoon desserts," like a creamy pudding made with Arborio rice, or seasonal fruit such as peaches that can be quickly poached on the stove top while the busy cook prepares other dishes in the wood-fired pizza oven.

Sweet Pizza with Fruit and Almonds

A pizzeria sometimes pairs standard dough with sweet toppings to create a rustic dessert. In this example of that tradition, the intense heat of the hot pizza stone helps the ingredients to caramelize quickly and results in a homey dish that is creamy yet not too rich.

Neapolitan pizza dough *(recipe on page 116),* completed through the second rising

All-purpose (plain) flour for dusting

1   cup (8 oz/250 g) mascarpone cheese

2   teaspoons plus 2 tablespoons sugar

2   egg yolks

2   baking apples such as Granny Smith or Gravenstein, halved, cored and thinly sliced

1   pear, halved, cored and thinly sliced

2   tablespoons coarsely chopped almonds

◉ Place a pizza stone or unglazed terra-cotta tiles on the lowest rack of an oven. Preheat to 475°F (245°C).

◉ Cut each ball of dough into 2 equal pieces so that you have 4 balls. One at a time, place the balls on a lightly floured work surface and flatten slightly. Sprinkle a little flour on the top of the dough and, using your fingertips, press evenly until the ball is shaped into a round, flat disk. Gently lift the dough and stretch and rotate it until it is about ¼ inch (6 mm) thick and 6 inches (15 cm) in diameter. Alternatively, using a rolling pin, gently roll out each ball into a round 6 inches (15 cm) in diameter. Try not to let the center of the disks become too thin in comparison to the edges. Gently lay the dough rounds on a lightly floured pizza peel or rimless baking sheet.

◉ In a small bowl, stir together the mascarpone, 2 teaspoons sugar and egg yolks until evenly blended. Spread the mixture over the pizza rounds, dividing it evenly and leaving about 1 inch (2.5 cm) uncovered at the edges. Arrange the apple and pear slices attractively on the rounds, dividing evenly and overlapping the slices slightly. Sprinkle the rounds with the remaining 2 tablespoons sugar and the almonds. Quickly slide the pizzas onto the preheated stone or tiles.

◉ Bake until the edges of the dough are golden brown and the sugar is slightly caramelized, 15–18 minutes. Using a large metal spatula, remove the pizzas from the oven. Slide each pizza onto an individual dessert plate and serve immediately. Alternatively, transfer to a cutting board, cut each pizza in half and serve on individual serving plates.

Makes four 6-inch (15-cm) pizzas; serves 4 or 8

Chocolate Biscotti

Although it would be unlikely to find biscotti served in a traditional pizzeria in the historic center of Naples, they are common in the pizzerias popular today. These delicious cookies are rich with chocolaty flavor and not too sweet and have the perfect consistency for dipping. The almonds add extra crunch.

¼ cup (1½ oz/45 g) whole blanched almonds

3 tablespoons unsalted butter, at room temperature

½ cup (4 oz/125 g) sugar

1 egg

½ teaspoon pure vanilla extract (essence)

¾ cup (4 oz/125 g) all-purpose (plain) flour

¼ cup (¾ oz/20 g) sifted Dutch-process cocoa

½ teaspoon baking powder

⅛ teaspoon baking soda (bicarbonate of soda)

2 oz (60 g) semisweet or bittersweet chocolate, coarsely chopped

◉ Preheat an oven to 400°F (200°C). Spread the almonds in a single layer on a baking sheet. Place in the oven until lightly toasted and fragrant, about 7 minutes. Remove from the oven and let cool. Reduce the oven temperature to 350°F (180°C).

◉ Line the bottom of a large baking sheet with parchment (baking) paper or aluminum foil. Nest the paper-lined sheet in a second baking sheet of the same size; this will prevent the bottoms of the cookies from scorching.

◉ In a large bowl, using a wooden spoon, cream together the butter and sugar until light and fluffy. Add the egg and vanilla and beat well. Set aside.

◉ In a food processor fitted with the metal blade, combine the flour, cocoa, baking powder and baking soda. Pulse briefly to combine, then add the chopped chocolate. Process continuously until the chocolate is finely and evenly chopped. Add the flour mixture to the butter mixture and blend just until combined. The mixture should come together into a soft dough. Add the almonds and mix until evenly distributed.

◉ On a lightly floured work surface, use your hands to shape the dough into a log about 13 inches (33 cm) long and 2½ inches (6 cm) in diameter. Place the log on the prepared baking sheet. Bake until the edges are firm (the center will not seem done yet), 30–35 minutes.

◉ Remove from the oven and let cool until lukewarm, about 30 minutes. Reduce the oven temperature to 300°F (150°C). Slice the log crosswise on a slight diagonal into pieces ¾ inch (2 cm) wide and return to the baking sheet, cut sides down. Bake for 10 minutes. Turn the cookies over and bake until lightly toasted, about 10 minutes longer. Remove from the oven, transfer to a rack and let cool completely. Store in an airtight container for up to 1 month. The biscotti can actually be stored for up to 6 months, if you can keep your hands out of the container. If they have become soft, recrisp them in a 350°F (180°C) oven for 5–6 minutes.

Makes 15–18 cookies

Peaches Poached in Wine

One of the wonders of summer, peaches are showcased in this easy dessert. The amount of sugar added to the poaching liquid will depend upon the wine's relative dryness; the liquid should be just sweet enough to heighten the natural sweetness of the peaches. To dress up the dish, top each serving with a dollop of mascarpone.

6   yellow- or white-fleshed peaches
1   bottle (24 fl oz/750 ml) fruity white or red wine or Champagne
⅓–⅔ cup (3–5 oz/90–155 g) sugar
1   vanilla bean, split lengthwise

◈ Bring a saucepan three-fourths full of water to a boil. One at a time, dip each peach into the boiling water for 5 seconds. Lift out with a slotted spoon and, using a sharp paring knife, peel the peaches. Halve each fruit along the natural line and remove the pits.

◈ In a saucepan large enough to hold all the peaches in a single layer, combine the wine, ⅓ cup (3 oz/90 g) sugar and vanilla bean. Place over low heat and stir until the sugar dissolves. Taste and add more sugar as needed to achieve a pleasant sweetness (see note). Bring to a simmer, add the peaches and simmer until barely tender, 2–5 minutes, depending upon their ripeness.

◈ Transfer the peaches and their cooking liquid to a deep glass bowl (the peaches should be completely covered by the liquid) and let cool to room temperature. Cover tightly with plastic wrap and refrigerate for at least 2 days or for up to 3 days.

◈ To serve, using a slotted spoon, transfer the peach halves to large wineglasses, placing 2 halves in each glass. Half-fill each glass with the poaching liquid and serve.

Serves 6

Hazelnut Tart

*The flavor combination of hazelnuts and chocolate is a longtime Italian favorite and is so
ubiquitous that it has its own name,* gianduia. *The mixture is used in candy, ice cream and biscotti and
in tarts such as this one, which might be found on the pastry cart of an upscale pizzeria.*

PASTRY DOUGH
1   cup (5 oz/155 g) hazelnuts (filberts)
1   cup (5 oz/155 g) unbleached all-purpose (plain) flour
¼   cup (2 oz/60 g) sugar
6   tablespoons (3 oz/90 g) unsalted butter, melted

FILLING
6   tablespoons (3 oz/90 g) cream cheese, at room temperature
½   cup (4 oz/125 g) ricotta cheese
5   tablespoons (2½ oz/75 g) sugar
1½ tablespoons Dutch-process cocoa
2   egg yolks plus 1 whole egg
1½ tablespoons Frangelico (hazelnut liqueur)
½   cup (2½ oz/75 g) coarsely chopped bittersweet chocolate

To make the pastry, preheat an oven to 325°F (165°C). Spread the hazelnuts in a single layer on a baking sheet and place in the oven until they just begin to change color and the skins begin to loosen, 8–10 minutes. Spread the warm nuts on a kitchen towel. Cover with another kitchen towel and rub against the nuts to remove as much of the skins as possible. Let cool, then set aside ¾ cup (4 oz/125 g) of the nuts to use for the filling. Finely chop the remaining nuts and place in a bowl. Raise the oven temperature to 350°F (180°C).

Add the flour and sugar to the chopped hazelnuts and stir to mix. Pour in the melted butter and stir to distribute evenly. The pastry dough should be moist but still crumbly. Transfer the dough into a 9-inch (23-cm) tart pan with a removable bottom and, using your fingertips, press it evenly over the bottom and sides of the pan. Chill for 15 minutes.

Remove the pastry-lined pan from the refrigerator and line with a sheet of aluminum foil or parchment (baking) paper. Fill with pie weights or dried beans. Bake the pastry until the bottom is just set, about 15 minutes. Remove from the oven and remove the weights or beans and the foil or paper. Return the pastry to the oven and continue to bake until the pastry is lightly golden and pulls away from the sides of the pan, about 5 minutes longer. Transfer to a rack to cool completely.

While the tart is cooling, make the filling: In a food processor fitted with the metal blade, combine the cream cheese, ricotta cheese, sugar and cocoa. Process until very smooth, stopping to scrape down the sides of the bowl as needed. Add the egg yolks and whole egg and again process until smooth. Add the Frangelico and pulse again just to blend.

Pour the filling into the tart shell and jiggle the pan to level the filling. Coarsely chop the reserved hazelnuts and scatter them evenly over the surface along with the chocolate. Bake until the center is just set, 25–30 minutes. Transfer to a rack and let cool before serving.

*Makes one 9-inch (23-cm) tart;
serves 8–10*

Vanilla Ice Cream with Strawberries and Balsamic Vinegar

Many small pizzerias lack the facilities for making elaborate desserts. They instead rely on dolci al cucchiaio, *or "spoon desserts," that can be prepared quickly with easily available ingredients. In this popular, rich summertime spoon dessert, piquant balsamic vinegar flavors fresh strawberries and ice cream.*

1   pt (500 ml) vanilla ice cream
2½ cups (10 oz/315 g) strawberries, stems removed, halved lengthwise
¼   cup (2 fl oz/60 ml) balsamic vinegar, or to taste
1   tablespoon sugar
    Coarsely ground pepper

▨ Remove the ice cream from the freezer and let stand at room temperature until it is soft enough to stir into the strawberries, 10–15 minutes, depending upon on how cold the freezer is.

▨ Meanwhile, in a bowl large enough to accommodate the ice cream eventually, stir together the strawberries, ¼ cup (2 fl oz/60 ml) balsamic vinegar, sugar and pepper to taste. The vinegar and sugar will mix with the berries' natural juices to create a sauce-like consistency. Taste and add more vinegar if needed.

▨ When the ice cream is soft enough, add it to the berry mixture. Immediately stir together until the berries and ice cream are evenly distributed. Spoon into tall wineglasses and serve at once.

Serves 4

Caramelized Rice Pudding

Rice pudding is considered a homey treat in Italy, particularly in the north where it is made with the locally grown short-grained Arborio rice. This high-quality rice, generally used for making risotto, results in an especially creamy pudding. The caramelized topping adds a sweet crunch.

3	tablespoons dark rum
1	tablespoon water
⅓	cup (2 oz/60 g) raisins
½	cup (3½ oz/105 g) Arborio rice
2½	cups (20 fl oz/625 ml) half-and-half (half cream), or more if needed
½	vanilla bean, split lengthwise
2	egg yolks
½	cup (4 oz/120 g) sugar
¾	cup (6 fl oz/180 ml) heavy (double) cream
6	figs, cut in half through the stem end

In a small saucepan, combine the rum and water and bring to a boil. Remove from the heat, stir in the raisins and let stand until needed.

In the top pan of a double boiler, combine the rice, 2½ cups (20 fl oz/ 625 ml) half-and-half and vanilla bean. Bring water in the lower pan to a gentle boil; place the top pan over it (the pan should not touch the water). Cover and cook until the liquid is absorbed and the rice is tender, about 1 hour. Check the level of the liquid occasionally to make sure the pan does not go dry. If the rice is still a bit tough and all the liquid has been absorbed, add a little more half-and-half and cook until the rice softens. The rice mixture should be very thick.

Remove the top pan, uncover and set aside to cool for 5 minutes. Combine the yolks and ¼ cup (2 oz/60 g) of the sugar in a small bowl and whisk to blend. Whisk in a small amount of the rice mixture to warm the yolk mixture slightly, then whisk the yolk mixture into the rice mixture. Reposition the top pan over the lower pan of gently simmering water and cook uncovered, stirring occasionally, until thickened, 3–4 minutes. Remove the top pan and transfer the contents to a bowl. Cover with plastic wrap pressed directly onto the surface of the rice to prevent a skin from forming. Refrigerate until completely chilled. (The rice can be prepared to this stage up to 1 day before serving.)

In a bowl, whip the heavy cream until stiff peaks form. Remove and discard the vanilla bean from the rice pudding. Drain the raisins. Using a rubber spatula, fold the cream and the raisins into the rice mixture, distributing the raisins evenly and folding only until no white drifts of cream remain. Pack the pudding firmly into six ½-cup (4-fl oz/ 125-ml) flameproof ramekins. Level the surface, cover and refrigerate until well chilled before serving.

To serve, preheat a broiler (griller). Place the ramekins on a baking sheet. Divide the remaining ¼ cup (2 oz/ 60 g) sugar evenly among the ramekins, sprinkling 2 teaspoons of it evenly over the surface of each pudding. Place the ramekins in the broiler about 2 inches (5 cm) from the heat and broil (grill) until the sugar caramelizes, 2–3 minutes. Rotate the ramekins as needed so they brown evenly. Serve immediately, accompanied with the figs.

Serves 6

Cappuccino Ice

*In this day of complex appliances, it is good to be reminded that delicious desserts
can be made with just a bowl and a whisk. It is just this type of quick-to-assemble granita
that can be tended to easily in between the more demanding culinary tasks in a pizzeria.
For a special treat, accompany the ice with chocolate biscotti (recipe on page 105).*

2½   cups (20 fl oz/625 ml) hot brewed espresso or brewed French- or Italian-roast coffee

5–6 tablespoons (2½–3 oz/75–90 g) sugar

½   cup (4 fl oz/125 ml) half-and-half (half cream) or milk
Unsweetened whipped cream
Chocolate shavings

◨ In a 2½-qt (2.5-l) stainless-steel bowl, combine the hot espresso or coffee and 5 tablespoons (2½ oz/ 75 g) sugar and stir until the sugar is completely dissolved. Add the half-and-half or milk and mix well. Taste and add the remaining 1 tablespoon sugar if desired. Refrigerate until cold, then place, uncovered, in the freezer.

◨ When ice crystals have started to form around the edges, after 30–40 minutes, whisk the mixture vigorously to blend in the crystals. Return the bowl to the freezer and whisk again every 20–30 minutes until the mixture is a mass of coarse ice crystals yet still soft enough to spoon, 2–3 hours total. (If you forget the granita in the freezer and it hardens too much, let stand at room temperature for a few minutes, then whisk it to the correct consistency.)

◨ To serve, divide the ice among small serving bowls. Top each serving with a dollop of whipped cream and some chocolate shavings.

Serves 4–6

BASIC RECIPES

Pizzeria chefs rely on a handful of essential recipes to prepare a wide variety of dishes. A recipe for classic Neapolitan pizza dough is joined by a versatile focaccia. Simple sauces, both an uncooked and a cooked tomato sauce, and a pesto, not only top pizzas but are paired with pasta and other pizza fare.

NEAPOLITAN PIZZA DOUGH

IMPASTO PER PIZZA ALLA NAPOLETANA

A Neapolitan pizza crust must be thin, but not cracker-thin as is traditional in Rome. If you prefer an extra-crisp super-thin crust, roll the dough into a round 11 inches (28 cm) in diameter rather than the 9 inches (23 cm) specified in the pizza recipes. Note that these directions make enough for 2 crusts. The pizza recipes in this book call for only half that amount. You can refrigerate the extra dough for up to 2 days or freeze for up to 1 month, or double the topping ingredients in the recipes and make 2 pizzas.

1½ teaspoons active dry yeast
¼ cup (2 fl oz/60 ml) lukewarm water (105°F/42°C)
1½ tablespoons olive oil
½ cup (4 fl oz/125 ml) cold water
1⅔ cups (8½ oz/265 g) unbleached all-purpose (plain) flour, plus flour for kneading
¾ teaspoon salt

◙ In a large mixing bowl, stir the yeast into the lukewarm water. Let stand until creamy, about 10 minutes. Stir in the olive oil and the cold water, and then whisk in ½ cup (2½ oz/75 g) of the flour and the salt, stirring until smooth. Stir in the remaining flour, ½ cup (2½ oz/75 g) at a time, until the dough comes together in a rough mass.

◙ On a lightly floured work surface, knead the dough until smooth and velvety, 8–10 minutes. It will be soft. Cover loosely with a kitchen towel and let rest for 15 minutes.

◙ Divide into 2 equal portions, knead briefly, then roll each portion into a smooth, tight round ball. To use the dough immediately, sprinkle a little flour on the work surface and set the balls on it. Cover them with a kitchen towel and let rise for 1 hour, then stretch and top the dough as directed in each recipe.

◙ You may also store one or both balls of dough until ready to use. For short-term storage and for a slow rise resulting in more flavor, place the dough balls on a small baking pan lined with a kitchen towel, cover them with a second towel and refrigerate for up to 48 hours; remove from the refrigerator and let stand at room temperature for 10–15 minutes before forming the pizza. For longer storage, slip each flour-dusted ball into a plastic freezer bag, seal tightly and freeze for up to 1 month. Before use, place the frozen dough in a lightly oiled bowl, cover loosely with plastic wrap, and let thaw overnight in the refrigerator or for about 2 hours at room temperature. The thawed dough should be puffy and soft to the touch.

Makes enough for two 9-inch (23-cm) pizza crusts

HERB-FLAVORED FOCACCIA

FOCACCIA ALLE ERBE

Focaccia dough is softer than pizza dough, yielding a nearly cakelike interior once it is baked. Baking the focaccia in cake pans results in rounds 1½ inches (4 cm) thick—perfect for pairing with an unlimited variety of panino fillings or slicing to serve plain as an accompaniment to any meal. If you prefer a crisp crust, drizzle the dough with a generous amount of olive oil before baking. For a soft crust, brush the focaccia with olive oil immediately upon removing it from the oven.

2½   teaspoons (1 package) active dry yeast
1   cup (8 fl oz/240 ml) lukewarm water (105°F/42°C)
2   tablespoons olive oil
2   cups (10 oz/310 g) unbleached all-purpose (plain) flour, plus flour for kneading
1   teaspoon salt
2   tablespoons chopped fresh chives
1   tablespoon chopped fresh thyme
1½   teaspoons finely chopped fresh rosemary
       Extra-virgin olive oil for brushing
       Coarse salt

◙ In a large mixing bowl, stir the yeast into ¼ cup (2 fl oz/60 ml) of the lukewarm water. Let stand until creamy, about 10 minutes. Stir in the remaining ¾ cup (6 fl oz/180 ml) lukewarm water and the olive oil. Add 1 cup (5 oz/155 g) of the flour and the salt and whisk until smooth. Add the chives, thyme and rosemary and mix well, then stir in the remaining 1 cup (5 oz/155 g) flour, ½ cup

(2½ oz/75 g) at a time, until the dough comes together in a rough mass.

◙ On a lightly floured work surface, knead the dough until smooth and velvety, 8–10 minutes. It will be soft. Lightly oil a bowl, place the dough in it and turn the dough to coat with oil. Cover the bowl with plastic wrap and put in a warm place to rise until doubled in bulk, about 1½ hours.

◙ Divide the dough into 2 equal portions and knead briefly. The dough is now ready to be stretched and topped as directed in the recipes or baked plain as directed below. You may also store the dough, as directed for the Neapolitan pizza dough opposite, until ready to use. If you prefer thinner, more resilient focaccia, stretch out the dough into a larger pan.

◙ If plain focaccia is preferred, lightly oil two 8-inch (20-cm) cake pans. Place each portion of dough in a prepared pan and gently stretch it out

to the edges, pulling it from the center outward to achieve an even thickness. If the dough springs back toward the center and is difficult to work with, cover and set it aside for 10 minutes to relax, then continue coaxing the dough out to an even thickness. Cover the pans with kitchen towels and let rise until almost doubled in bulk and very soft and puffy, about 45 minutes.

◙ Preheat an oven to 475°F (245°C). Using your fingertips, dimple the dough in several places, leaving indentations about ½ inch (12 mm) deep. Again cover the pans with towels and let rise for 20 minutes longer.

◙ Bake until golden brown and cooked through, 15–18 minutes. Remove from the oven and immediately brush the tops with a generous amount of extra-virgin olive oil, then sprinkle with coarse salt. Serve hot or at room temperature.

Makes two 8-inch (20-cm) rounds

UNCOOKED TOMATO SAUCE

SALSA DI POMODORO CRUDO

This simple sauce is the traditional topping on a Neapolitan pizza and suits a wide range of pizza preparations. It is light on the palate and fulfills its role as an undernote to pizza, allowing the additional toppings to stand out.
If you are using canned tomatoes, look for the sweetest ones you can find. Taste them out of the can and, if they are a bit too acidic, add a pinch of sugar.

8   ripe plum (Roma) tomatoes or 1 can (16 oz/500 g) plum (Roma) tomatoes with their juices
1   tablespoon extra-virgin olive oil
     Salt and freshly ground pepper

◾ Fit a food mill with the coarse or medium blade and place over a small mixing bowl. Pass the tomatoes through the mill into the bowl. Alternatively, use a food processor: Peel the fresh tomatoes, if using. Place the fresh or canned tomatoes in a food processor fitted with the metal blade and pulse to form a coarse purée. Add the olive oil and season to taste with salt and pepper. Use immediately, or transfer to a tightly covered container and refrigerate for up to 2 days.

Makes about 1½ cups (12 fl oz/375 ml), enough for six 9-inch (23-cm) pizzas

TOMATO-BASIL SAUCE

SALSA DI POMODORO E BASILICO

This flavorful, yet basic, sauce embodies the simple, rustic elegance of classic Italian cooking at its best. It is used in a wide range of Italian dishes, including soups, pastas, baked dishes, risotto and, of course, pizzas, to which it adds a deeper, more fully developed flavor than the uncooked tomato sauce at left.
If you find that your tomatoes lack a good balance of sweetness and acidity, add a few pinches of sugar to bring out their natural sweetness.

¼   cup (2 fl oz/60 ml) extra-virgin olive oil
2   cloves garlic, minced
12 plum (Roma) tomatoes, peeled, seeded and chopped, or 1 can (28 oz/875 g) plum (Roma) tomatoes, chopped, with their juices
8   large fresh basil leaves, coarsely chopped
     Salt and freshly ground pepper

◾ In a large frying pan over medium heat, warm the oil. Add the garlic and sauté for a few seconds just until fragrant. Add the tomatoes and cook, stirring frequently, until they begin to break down and form a sauce, about 10 minutes.

◾ Add the basil, season to taste with salt and pepper and raise the heat to medium-high. Cook, stirring occasionally, until the sauce thickens and is no longer watery, 15–20 minutes.

◾ Use immediately, or transfer to a container with a tight-fitting lid and refrigerate for up to 2 days.

Makes about 2 cups (16 fl oz/500 ml)

ITALIAN: BASIC RECIPES

GENOVESE PESTO

PESTO ALLA GENOVESE

Few sauces represent a season as perfectly as this summer sauce from Liguria. The distinct flavors of basil and garlic, mellowed with Italian Parmesan, give it a versatility matched by few other sauces. It can be used for pasta and pizza, spread on crostini and panini, even used as a marinade for roasted meats. Vary the amount of olive oil according to your own preferences: use less for a light, fluffy texture and more for a denser, heavier and more flavorful sauce.

¼ cup (1 oz/30 g) pine nuts or walnuts

2 cups (2 oz/60 g) firmly packed fresh basil leaves

4–6 cloves garlic

½–1 cup (4–8 fl oz/125–250 ml) extra-virgin olive oil

¼ cup (1 oz/30 g) freshly grated Italian Parmesan cheese

¼ cup (1 oz/30 g) freshly grated Italian pecorino romano cheese
Salt and freshly ground pepper

◻ Preheat an oven to 350°F (180°C). Spread the nuts in a single layer on a baking sheet. Place in the oven until lightly toasted and fragrant, about 8 minutes. Remove from the heat and let cool.

◻ In a food processor fitted with the metal blade or in a blender, combine the basil and garlic and pulse until finely chopped, scraping down the sides of the bowl as necessary. With the motor running, add ½ cup (4 fl oz/125 ml) of the olive oil in a slow, steady stream. Scatter the cheeses over the top, then pulse until the cheeses are absorbed. Again with the motor running, slowly add the remaining oil and process until creamy.

◻ Season to taste with salt and pepper, add the nuts and pulse just until the nuts are coarsely chopped. Use immediately, or pour into a container and top with a thin layer of olive oil. Cover tightly and refrigerate for up to 4 days.

Makes about 2 cups (16 fl oz/500 ml)

ITALIAN: BASIC RECIPES

MEXICAN

While all cuisines are hybrids, developing under diverse social, cultural and historical influences, the roots of Mexican cooking can be traced more easily than most. For centuries, the native populations of the country ate stews and roasts featuring such indigenous ingredients as turkey, quail and seafood, along with three staples that later found their way to the Old World—squashes, beans and corn—and two lively seasonings that gave distinctive personality: chilies and chocolate.

Spanish explorers and settlers, starting with the arrival of Hernán Cortés and his men at the Aztec court in 1519, brought with them a whole new variety of fare that would influence Mexican cooking. Onions, garlic, citrus fruits, sugarcane, wheat, rice, chicken, beef and, most notably, pork, entered the nation's kitchens. Not only did pork become a featured ingredient of the cuisine, but abundant lard introduced an important new cooking method, frying. This edible intermingling of cultures took place throughout the land, and perhaps most dynamically in Spanish convents and missions, which, by offering bed and board to travelers, became early restaurants of a sort. The cantina-style recipes that follow, from Tortilla Soup to Mexican Wedding Cookies, celebrate the best of Mexico's culinary history.

Appetizers

Mexicans might well use the word *antojitos* —"little whimsies"— to describe the recipes on the following pages. The term applies to virtually any dish easily popped into the mouth, whether at the start of a meal or as a snack while strolling through a marketplace.

Like any good starter, these recipes boast impressive versatility. Guacamole, for example, may be scooped up with tortilla chips to accompany beer or sangría; but it also provides a cool, rich garnish for spicy main courses. Ceviche makes an elegant appetizer when presented in a sparkling glass bowl; but you might also see it in a paper cup held in the hand of someone wandering along the seafront in Acapulco or Puerto Vallarta. And empanadas are just as satisfying eaten as a simple lunch as they are a first course.

With that spirit of versatility in mind, you might present a meal composed just of these recipes, perhaps joined by one or two other finger foods, such as beef tacos, grilled beef or chicken drumsticks, that comfortably fit beneath the *antojitos* umbrella. Set them out together on a buffet table, letting guests pick and choose as whimsy dictates.

Roasted Peppers with Melted Cheese

A classic northern Mexican dish, queso fundido—literally, "melted cheese"—makes a delightful starter for a cold-weather meal. Serve with lots of warm tortillas to scoop up the bubbling mixture. For more spice, add crunchy browned chunks of chorizo sausage or drizzle with árbol salsa (recipe on page 227).

1 fresh poblano chili pepper, roasted, peeled and seeded *(see glossary, page 342)*

1 red bell pepper (capsicum), roasted, peeled and seeded *(see glossary, page 340)*

1 yellow bell pepper (capsicum), roasted, peeled and seeded

½ white onion, diced

1½ cups (6 oz/185 g) grated Manchego, mozzarella, Monterey Jack or other good melting cheese

½ cup (2 oz/60 g) grated Cotija, Romano or feta cheese

½ cup (2 oz/60 g) grated panela, dry cottage or dry ricotta cheese
    Freshly ground black pepper

12 small flour or corn tortillas, homemade *(recipes on pages 226–227)* or purchased, heated
    Green salsa *(recipe on page 228)*

❖ Preheat an oven to 375°F (190°C). Cut the poblano pepper and bell peppers lengthwise into strips 3 inches (7.5 cm) long and ¼ inch (6 mm) wide. Place in a bowl, add the onion and toss to mix. Set aside.

❖ In a separate bowl, combine all the cheeses and toss to mix. Set six 1-cup (8–fl oz/250-ml) or one 1½-qt (1.5-l) earthenware or glass baking dish in the oven to heat thoroughly, about 10 minutes.

❖ Distribute the cheeses evenly among the warmed small dishes or spread them evenly in the warmed large dish and return to the oven.

Cook for 5 minutes. Sprinkle the cheeses with the pepper-onion mixture and again return to the oven. Bake until the cheeses are completely melted and beginning to bubble, 5–7 minutes.

❖ Sprinkle with black pepper and serve immediately with warm tortillas and salsa on the side.

Serves 6

Beer-Battered Shrimp with Chipotle-Honey Sauce

Beer adds both flavor and texture to this lovely batter. If you make the batter early, it may thicken, in which case it can be thinned with a little more beer or with water. Too thick a batter will make the shrimp soggy, while a batter that is too thin won't form a complete coating.

BATTER
1   cup (5 oz/155 g) all-purpose (plain) flour
1½ teaspoons cayenne pepper
1   teaspoon salt
1   teaspoon sugar
½   teaspoon baking powder
1   cup (8 fl oz/250 ml) beer

DIPPING SAUCE
2   dried chipotle chili peppers, stemmed and seeded
1   ripe tomato, quartered
½   small yellow onion, sliced
1   clove garlic
½   cup (4 fl oz/125 ml) water
1   teaspoon salt
¼   cup (3 fl oz/90 ml) honey
2   tablespoons red wine vinegar

SHRIMP
Peanut oil for deep-frying
All-purpose (plain) flour for dusting
1¼ lb (625 g) rock shrimp or peeled white shrimp (prawns)

☒ To make the batter, in a bowl, combine the flour, cayenne, salt, sugar and baking powder. Stir to mix. Add the beer all at once and whisk until smooth. Set aside at room temperature for at least 30 minutes or up to 4 hours.

☒ To make the dipping sauce, in a small saucepan, combine the chilies, tomato, onion, garlic, water and salt and bring to a boil. Reduce the heat to low, cover and simmer gently until the ingredients soften and the mixture thickens, about 15 minutes. Remove from the heat and let cool slightly, then transfer to a blender and purée until smooth. Pour the purée into a small bowl and stir in the honey and vinegar. Let cool.

☒ In a large saucepan, pour in peanut oil to a depth of 5 inches (13 cm) and heat to 350°F (180°C) or until a few drops of batter sprinkled into the oil rise immediately to the surface. Spread some flour in a shallow bowl and toss the shrimp in it to coat evenly, tapping off any excess. Drop the shrimp, a few at a time, into the batter. Using tongs or your fingers, remove the shrimp from the batter, draining off the excess, and drop into the hot oil. Deep-fry until light golden and crisp, about 2 minutes. Using a slotted spoon, transfer to paper towels to drain.

☒ Arrange the shrimp on a warmed platter and serve immediately with the dipping sauce.

Serves 6

Melted Cheese-and-Bean Sandwiches with Fresh Salsa

You're likely to find these bubbly, open-faced sandwiches served for breakfast in Mexico City.
An excellent use for leftover beans, they also make a terrific lunch or a snack at any time of day.
Crusty Mexican rolls, called bolillos, *are ideal, but any French or Italian bread will do.*

SALSA FRESCA

2 large ripe tomatoes, seeded and diced

¼ red (Spanish) onion, finely diced

1 fresh jalapeño or serrano chili pepper, stemmed, seeded and finely diced

2 tablespoons coarsely chopped fresh cilantro (fresh coriander)

Juice of ½ lime

½ teaspoon salt

Freshly ground black pepper

SANDWICHES

6 *bolillos* or French or Italian rolls

1½ cups (12 fl oz/375 ml) refried black beans *(recipe on pages 228–229)*

1 cup (4 oz/125 g) grated Manchego, asadero, Monterey Jack or white Cheddar cheese, or a mixture

☒ Preheat a broiler (griller).

☒ To make the salsa, in a small bowl, stir together the tomatoes, onion, chili, cilantro, lime juice, salt and black pepper to taste. Set aside.

☒ Split each roll in half lengthwise and spread each cut side with a layer of beans ¼ inch (6 mm) thick. Sprinkle the cheese(s) evenly over the beans.

☒ Arrange the split rolls on a baking sheet and place in the broiler (griller) 4–6 inches (10–15 cm) below the heat source. Broil (grill) until the bread is crunchy, the cheeses are melted and the beans are bubbly, 6–8 minutes.

☒ Serve hot with the salsa on the side.

Serves 6

Guacamole

Mashed avocado is a common garnish for cantina dishes. Add salt, chili, lime and cilantro, and you have guacamole, a combination that takes its name from ahuacatl (avocado) and molli (mixture), in the language of southern Mexico's Nahuatl Indians. This great dip is best made with dark, bumpy-skinned Hass avocados. Store with the pits resting in the guacamole to help prevent the dip from oxidizing.

3   ripe avocados
1   fresh jalapeño chili pepper, stemmed, seeded and finely chopped
½   white onion, diced
¼   cup (⅓ oz/10 g) coarsely chopped fresh cilantro (fresh coriander)
    Juice of 1 lime
½   teaspoon salt
    Freshly ground black pepper
1   ripe tomato, seeded and diced (optional)
    Lettuce leaf, optional
    Corn tortilla chips

☒ Cut each avocado lengthwise into quarters, removing the pit. Peel off the skin and place the pulp in a bowl. Using a potato masher, spoon or your hand, mash lightly. Add the jalapeño, onion, cilantro, lime juice, salt, pepper to taste and the diced tomato, if using. Mix just until combined; chunks of avocado should remain visible.

☒ To serve, spoon the guacamole into a serving bowl or onto a plate lined with a lettuce leaf. If not serving immediately, poke the avocado pits down into the center of the mixture, cover tightly with plastic wrap and refrigerate for up to 4 hours. Serve chilled, accompanied by tortilla chips.

Serves 4–6

Mussel Ceviche Tostadas

Tostadas take their name from their bases of toasted—that is, crisply fried—tortillas. They are variously topped with beans, lettuce, cheeses and, often, poultry or meat. In coastal towns like Veracruz, however, seafood stars, particularly the "citrus-cooked" seafood known as ceviche, a dish that some food historians believe was introduced to Mexico from Asia by Spanish galleon traders.

3	lb (1.5 kg) mussels in the shell
1	cup (8 fl oz/250 ml) dry white wine
6	bay leaves
2	ripe tomatoes, seeded and diced
1	small red (Spanish) onion, diced
1	cup (5 oz/155 g) small Spanish green olives or other small green olives such as French picholines
3	tablespoons coarsely chopped fresh oregano
⅔	cup (5 fl oz/155 ml) good-quality tomato juice
⅓	cup (3 fl oz/80 ml) fresh orange juice
⅓	cup (3 fl oz/80 ml) fresh lime juice
¼	cup (2 fl oz/60 ml) fruity Spanish olive oil or other fruity olive oil
1	teaspoon salt
½	teaspoon freshly ground pepper
6–8	small corn tortillas, homemade *(recipe on page 226)* or purchased Vegetable oil for frying
1	ripe avocado, pitted, peeled and mashed

◨ Scrub the mussels under cool running water and pull off and discard their beards. Discard any mussels that do not close to the touch.

◨ In a wide sauté pan, combine the wine and bay leaves and bring to a boil. Add enough mussels to the pan to cover the bottom in a single layer; cover, reduce the heat to medium and cook until they open, 3–5 minutes. Using a slotted spoon, lift out the mussels and transfer to a bowl to cool. Cook the remaining mussels in batches in the same liquid, discarding any mussels that do not open. Reserve the cooking liquid for another use.

◨ Remove the mussels from their shells and place them in a nonaluminum bowl. Add the tomatoes, onion, olives, oregano, tomato and citrus juices, olive oil, salt and pepper and stir gently to mix. Cover and refrigerate for 1–2 hours to allow the flavors to blend.

◨ Meanwhile, pour oil to a depth of ½ inch (12 mm) in a small frying pan and heat to 375°F (190°C) on a deep-frying thermometer. Working with 1 tortilla at a time and using tongs, slip the tortilla into the oil and fry, turning once, until crispy but not browned, about 1 minute on each side. Let drain on paper towels while you fry the remaining tortillas.

◨ To serve, place the tortillas on individual plates. Divide the ceviche evenly among the tortillas, spooning it on top. Place a dollop of mashed avocado on each and serve.

Serves 6–8

Sea Bass Ceviche with Lime and Cilantro

You can adapt this wonderful ceviche to many kinds of fish and shellfish, including halibut, snapper, grouper or shrimp. Freshness is so prized in Mexico that it's common for ceviche aficionados to take chopped vegetables and lime juice along on the fishing boat to dress the catch almost the moment it's pulled from the water.

1   lb (500 g) sea bass fillet

¾   cup (6 fl oz/180 ml) fresh lime juice

1   large ripe tomato, seeded and diced

1   small red (Spanish) onion, finely diced

½   cup (¾ oz/20 g) coarsely chopped fresh cilantro (fresh coriander)

2   fresh jalapeño chili peppers, stemmed and sliced crosswise into thin circles

2   cups (16 fl oz/500 ml) bottled clam juice

1   teaspoon salt, or to taste
    Romaine (cos) lettuce leaves if serving in goblets, or leaf lettuce if serving in shallow soup bowls
    Corn tortilla chips

❂ Dice the sea bass into ½-inch (12-mm) cubes and place in a shallow glass or porcelain dish. Add ½ cup (4 fl oz/120 ml) of the lime juice and toss to coat evenly. Let marinate for 30–45 minutes.

❂ Drain the fish and return to the shallow dish. Add the tomato, onion, cilantro, chilies, clam juice, salt and the remaining ¼ cup (2 fl oz/60 ml) lime juice. Stir to mix well, then cover and refrigerate for 1–2 hours to allow the flavors to blend.

❂ Serve the ceviche in tall chilled goblets with spears of romaine and tortilla chips scattered along the edge. Or line shallow soup bowls with leaf lettuce leaves and spoon the ceviche on top. Surround the edges of the bowls with tortilla chips.

Serves 6

Roasted Onions Stuffed with Cheese

An elegant appetizer inspired by country cooking, these fragrant onions also go well as a side dish for spicy skirt steak. The richness and smooth texture of the cheese perfectly complements the sweetness and crunch of the onions. Be sure to roast the onions very slowly to develop their full flavor.

4   medium-large yellow sweet onions, unpeeled

1   tablespoon cumin seeds

½   cup (2 oz/60 g) grated asadero, Manchego, Monterey Jack or other good melting cheese

1   cup (4 oz/125 g) grated Cotija, Romano or other aged cheese

3   tablespoons sour cream

1   tablespoon balsamic vinegar

3   dashes of hot pepper sauce such as Tabasco

½   teaspoon salt

½   teaspoon freshly ground pepper

❧ Preheat a broiler (griller). Place the unpeeled onions in a small baking pan and cover with aluminum foil. Place in the broiler about 5 inches (13 cm) from the heat source and broil (grill), turning every 5–10 minutes, until charred on the outside and soft all the way through, about 1 hour. Remove from the broiler and set aside to cool. Set the oven temperature to 375°F (190°C).

❧ Peel the onions carefully, keeping them intact and discarding the outer charred skin. Cut the onions in half crosswise and, using a finger, remove the centers, forming roasted onion "cups" with walls about ¾ inch (2 cm) thick; reserve the centers. Line the bottom of each onion cup with a piece of the removed roasted onion to prevent the filling from leaking out.

❧ In a small frying pan over medium heat, toast the cumin seeds, shaking the pan frequently, until lightly browned and fragrant, 2–3 minutes. Transfer the seeds to a cutting board and chop coarsely. Chop the remaining removed onion pulp and place in a small bowl. Add both cheeses, sour cream, cumin seeds, vinegar, hot-pepper sauce, salt and pepper and stir to mix well.

❧ Divide the cheese mixture evenly among the onion cups. Place on a baking sheet and bake until browned and bubbling, 15–20 minutes. Serve hot.

Serves 4

Chicken, Chili and Cheese Tamales

Some version of these steamed cornmeal packets are served in every region in Mexico.
Pack each tamale generously and don't worry if they ooze slightly during cooking.

FILLING

4   chicken breast halves

2   cups (16 fl oz/500 ml) chicken stock, or as needed

4   fresh poblano chili peppers, roasted, peeled and seeded *(see glossary, page 342)*, then cut lengthwise into strips 2 inches (5 cm) wide

½   cup (4 fl oz/125 ml) green salsa *(recipe on page 228)*

    Salt and freshly ground black pepper

½   lb (250 g) panela, Manchego or Monterey Jack cheese, cut into thin strips ¼ inch (6 mm) thick and 2 inches (5 cm) long

TAMALE DOUGH

4   fresh poblano chili peppers, roasted, peeled and seeded

½   cup (4 fl oz/125 ml) green salsa

1   cup (8 fl oz/250 ml) chicken stock, reserved from making filling

1   teaspoon baking soda (bicarbonate of soda)

2½ teaspoons salt

1½ lb (750 g) prepared *masa* dough, chilled

½   cup (4 oz/125 g) lard or vegetable shortening, chilled

1   package (8 oz/250 g) dried corn husks, soaked in hot water for at least 2 hours

    Green salsa and *crema* or sour cream

To make the filling, place the chicken breasts in a saucepan and add stock to cover. Bring to a boil, reduce the heat to low and simmer, uncovered, until tender and opaque throughout, about 15 minutes. Using a slotted spoon, transfer the chicken to a plate to cool; reserve the stock for the tamale dough. Remove the meat from the chicken bones, discard the skin and, using your fingers, shred the meat into strips 2 inches (5 cm) long. Place in a bowl and add the chili strips, salsa and salt and black pepper to taste. Toss to mix and set aside with the cheese strips.

To make the dough, in a blender, combine 2 of the chilies, the salsa, reserved chicken stock, baking soda and salt. Blend until smooth. Set aside.

Place the *masa* dough in a bowl and, using an electric mixer set on medium speed, beat until light in texture, about 5 minutes. Slowly add the chicken stock mixture, beating until combined. Increase the speed to high and add the lard or shortening, 1 tablespoon at a time. Continue beating until light and fluffy, about 15 minutes total.

To make the tamales, drain the corn husks and pat dry. Spread 1 large or slightly overlap 2 small softened husks on a work surface, with the narrow end(s) pointing away from you. Leaving about 3 inches (7.5 cm) uncovered at the top and 1½ inches (4 cm) uncovered at the bottom, spread about 2½ tablespoons of the *masa* mixture over the center area of the husk(s). Place a spoonful of the chicken mixture on the *masa* and place 2 or 3 cheese strips on top. Fold one long side of the husk covered with *masa* over the chicken and cheese to enclose the filling completely in *masa* and then fold the opposite long side back over the center. Fold the top down and the bottom up, overlapping the ends. Tie a long shred of a corn husk around the center to secure the ends. Wrap in aluminum foil. Repeat with the remaining ingredients.

Line a large steamer rack with the remaining corn husks and arrange the wrapped tamales on it. Place the rack over (not touching) simmering water in a pan. Cover and steam until the husks pull away from the *masa* without sticking, about 1¼ hours, adding boiling water to the pan as needed to maintain the original level.

To serve, remove the foil and place 2 tamales on each plate. Serve the salsa and the *crema* or sour cream in bowls on the side. Let guests unwrap the husks.

Makes 12–14 tamales; serves 6–7

Swiss Chard Empanadas

The turnovers of Mexico, empanadas are stuffed with all kinds of vegetables, including squashes, mushrooms and the chard used here. Be sure to use plenty of chard and season it well. You'll want to make a large batch of empanadas when you have the time, then store them well wrapped in the freezer for up to several weeks.

EMPANADA DOUGH

2   cups (10 oz/315 g) all-purpose (plain) flour

½   cup (4 oz/125 g) lard or unsalted butter, chilled

2½ tablespoons unsalted butter, chilled

½   teaspoon salt
    About ⅓ cup (3 fl oz/80 ml) ice water

FILLING

2   tablespoons olive oil

1   large white onion, diced

½   teaspoon salt

½   teaspoon freshly ground pepper

2   bunches Swiss chard (silverbeet), about 1 lb (500 g) total weight, trimmed, leaves cut into small pieces and stems cut into ½-inch (12-mm) dice

¾   cup (3 oz/90 g) grated Cotija, Romano or Parmesan cheese

¼   cup (1 oz/30 g) grated asadero, Manchego, Monterey Jack cheese or other good melting cheese
    Squeeze of fresh lime juice

1   egg, beaten, for glaze
    Freshly cracked pepper

☒ To make the dough, in a bowl, combine the flour, lard, butter and salt. Mix lightly with your fingers until the mixture forms pea-sized pieces. Using a fork, stir in the ice water, a little at a time, until a dough forms, and then knead lightly until it comes together in a ball. Wrap in plastic wrap and refrigerate for at least 1 hour or as long as overnight.

☒ To make the filling, in a large frying pan over medium heat, warm the olive oil. Add the onion, salt and pepper and sauté until the onion is soft and begins to turn lightly golden, 7–10 minutes. Add the chard stems and cook for 1–2 minutes. Then add the chard leaves and cook, stirring, until tender, 3–4 minutes. Transfer to a bowl and let cool. Add the cheeses and lime juice and mix well. Taste and adjust the seasonings.

☒ To assemble the empanadas, on a lightly floured board, roll out the dough about ⅛ inch (3 mm) thick. Using a 3-inch (7.5-cm) round cookie cutter, cut out 12 rounds. Place about 2 tablespoons of the filling on one-half of each round, leaving a ½-inch (12-mm) border. Dampen the edges of the dough with a little of the egg glaze, then fold the dough over to enclose the filling. Seal the edges by pressing firmly with the tines of a fork. Arrange the empanadas on a tray, cover with plastic wrap and chill for at least 30 minutes or up to 3 days before baking.

☒ Preheat an oven to 350°F (180°C). Place the empanadas on a baking sheet. Brush the tops with the egg glaze and sprinkle with cracked pepper. Using a sharp knife, cut 2 or 3 small slits in the top of each empanada to allow steam to escape.

☒ Bake until golden, about 30 minutes. Transfer to a rack to cool. Serve warm or at room temperature.

Makes twelve 3-inch (7.5-cm) empanadas; serves 6

Salads

With a climate ranging from the tropics to the subtropics, Mexico is a true cornucopia of fresh produce, and cooks take full advantage of this abundance. Buttery avocados, crisp jicama, tangy watercress, peppers and squashes in a kaleidoscope of colors, and many other riches of the farm and garden enliven the salads you are likely to find in the cantina.

As you might expect from a cuisine that makes the most of seasonal produce—and one that often springs up amidst the same market stalls as well—there is a delightfully impromptu feeling to many cantina salads. Such staples as rice and beans, for example, might be transformed into salads in an instant with the addition of a confetti of squashes or peppers and a simple oil-and-vinegar dressing. Or an array of bright-hued tropical fruits and blood oranges might be combined with crisp, white jicama, and the whole mixture thrown into sharp relief by hot chilies.

As the last example suggests, strong similarities exist between salads and fresh salsas. Indeed, you are likely to find many of the salads that follow offered as accompaniments to grilled meat, pork or chicken, offering their own lively counterpoints to the main course with every bite.

Grilled Vegetable Salad

Perfect for cookouts, this hearty salad can be started as soon as the coals warm up, leaving the vegetables to marinate while the main course cooks. Or you can make the salad a day ahead, as it will improve in flavor overnight. Almost any seasonal vegetable can be substituted for those suggested here.

2   red (Spanish) onions, unpeeled

VINAIGRETTE

¼   cup (2 fl oz/60 ml) red wine vinegar

1   teaspoon salt, or to taste

½   teaspoon freshly ground pepper

3   tablespoons coarsely chopped fresh oregano or marjoram

1   large clove garlic, minced

⅔   cup (5 fl oz/155 ml) olive oil

SALAD

1   medium or 2 small Japanese eggplants (aubergines)

1   zucchini (courgette)

1   yellow crookneck squash

1   bulb fennel

1   large red bell pepper (capsicum), seeded, deribbed and quartered lengthwise
    Lettuce leaves

☒ Preheat a broiler (griller) or prepare a fire in a charcoal grill.

☒ If using a broiler, place the un-peeled onions in a small baking pan and cover with aluminum foil. Place the pan in the broiler or place the onions directly on the grill rack about 5 inches (13 cm) from the heat source. Broil or grill, turning every 5–10 minutes, until charred on the outside and soft throughout, about 1 hour if using a broiler or 20–30 minutes if using a grill. Remove from the broiler or grill rack; set aside to cool slightly.

☒ To make the vinaigrette, in a small bowl, whisk together the vinegar, salt, pepper, oregano or marjoram and garlic. Slowly add the olive oil, whisking constantly.

☒ Trim the ends from the eggplant(s) and squashes and any stalks from the fennel bulb and cut lengthwise into quarters. Place in a bowl with the bell pepper and half of the vinaigrette

and toss to mix. Arrange the vegetables on a broiler pan or directly on the grill rack about 5 inches (13 cm) from the heat source. Broil or grill slowly, turning to cook evenly, until lightly golden and cooked through, 5–10 minutes for the squashes, peppers and eggplants and 15 minutes for the fennel. Remove from the broiler or grill rack and let cool slightly.

☒ Peel the onions and cut into 2-inch (5-cm) pieces. Place in a bowl. Cut all the remaining vegetables into 2-inch (5-cm) pieces as well and add to the bowl. Pour the remaining vinaigrette over the vegetables and toss well to coat.

☒ To serve, line individual plates with lettuce leaves and spoon the vegetables on top.

Serves 4–6

Three Beans and Three Peppers Salad

*Two Mexican pantry staples—beans and peppers—are featured here, with
three different varieties of each playing the central roles. Start testing the beans for
doneness early, as cooking times vary greatly with age and variety.*

½ cup (3½ oz/105 g) dried black beans

½ cup (3½ oz/105 g) dried pinto beans

½ cup (3½ oz/105 g) dried red or kidney beans

1 yellow bell pepper (capsicum)

1 red bell pepper (capsicum)

1 fresh poblano chili pepper

¼ cup (2 fl oz/60 ml) red wine vinegar

1 teaspoon salt

½ teaspoon freshly ground black pepper

1 canned chipotle chili pepper in vinegar or in *adobo* sauce, stemmed, seeded and minced (optional)

⅔ cup (5 fl oz/160 ml) olive oil

1 red (Spanish) onion, finely diced

☙ Sort through all the beans, keeping them separate, and discard any misshapen beans or stones. Rinse well. Place each bean variety in a separate saucepan and add water to cover generously. Bring each to a boil, reduce the heat to medium-low, cover and simmer until the smallest bean is cooked through and creamy inside, about 1½ hours. Drain all the beans in a colander (they can be mixed at this time) and spread them out on a plate to cool slightly.

☙ Meanwhile, remove the stems, seeds and ribs from the bell peppers and poblano chili. Cut the peppers into ¼-inch (6-mm) dice, or a size as similar as possible to that of the cooked beans. In a large bowl, whisk together the vinegar, salt, black pepper and chipotle chili, if using. Slowly add the olive oil, whisking constantly. Toss in the diced peppers, onion and warm beans and mix well.

☙ Cover and refrigerate for at least 2 hours or as long as overnight. Serve the salad chilled.

Serves 4–6

Parsley, Mint and Watercress Salad

One of the most popular greens in Mexico, peppery watercress joins here with the fresh tastes of parsley and mint—an exotic and interesting combination that is also a good way to use up any excess herbs in your garden. Parboiling the garlic for the dressing mellows its sharpness and heightens the earthy flavor and buttery consistency.

DRESSING
Regular table salt
1 head garlic, separated into cloves, peeled and thinly sliced
¾ cup (6 fl oz/180 ml) olive oil
3 tablespoons fresh lemon juice
1 teaspoon sea salt
½ teaspoon freshly ground pepper

SALAD
1 large bunch fresh flat-leaf (Italian) parsley, about ¼ lb (125 g), stemmed
1 large bunch fresh mint, about ¼ lb (125 g), stemmed
2 bunches watercress, about 10 oz (315 g) total weight, stemmed

◩ To make the dressing, bring a small saucepan three-fourths full of water to a boil and add table salt to taste. Add the garlic and parboil for about 3 minutes to soften slightly and mellow the flavor. Drain and let cool.

◩ Place the cooled garlic in a small bowl and add the oil, lemon juice, sea salt and pepper. Whisk to dissolve the sea salt and form a dressing.

◩ In a salad bowl, combine the parsley, mint and watercress. Drizzle the dressing over the greens and toss to coat evenly. Serve immediately.

Serves 4–6

Avocado and Tomatillo Salad

This home-style salad showcases the wonderful contrasts present when rich, creamy avocado, sharp-tasting tomatillos and crunchy croutons come together. The vegetables must be at their peak of ripeness for the best results. The avocado should be only slightly soft, so it holds up during tossing.

CROUTONS

¼ cup (2 fl oz/60 ml) olive oil

⅓ loaf crusty French, Italian or sourdough bread, cut into ¾-inch (2-cm) cubes
    Salt to taste, plus 1 teaspoon
    Freshly ground pepper to taste

SALAD

2 ripe avocados, pitted, peeled and cut into ¾-inch (2-cm) cubes

2 cups (12 oz/375 g) red or yellow cherry tomatoes, or a mixture, halved

2 bunches fresh cilantro (fresh coriander), about 6 oz (185 g) total weight, stemmed
   Lettuce leaves

6 green (spring) onions, thinly sliced

DRESSING

5 tomatillos, husked and quartered

1 tablespoon fresh lime juice

2 tablespoons distilled white or white wine vinegar

¼ cup (2 fl oz/60 ml) olive oil

1 teaspoon salt

½ teaspoon freshly ground pepper

☙ To make the croutons, in a frying pan over medium heat, warm ¼ cup (2 fl oz/60 ml) of the olive oil. Add the bread cubes and shake the pan to coat the cubes lightly on all sides. Sprinkle with salt and pepper to taste, reduce the heat to medium-low and toast, shaking the pan occasionally, until golden brown on all sides, about 15 minutes. Remove from the heat and let cool.

☙ In a bowl, combine the avocados, cherry tomatoes and cilantro; set aside.

☙ To make the dressing, in a blender or a food processor fitted with the metal blade, combine the tomatillos, lime juice, vinegar, olive oil, salt and pepper. Blend well to form a smooth dressing.

☙ Pour the dressing over the avocado mixture and begin to toss lightly to mix. When almost fully mixed, add the croutons and continue to toss until all the ingredients are evenly distributed.

☙ To serve, line a platter or individual salad bowls with lettuce leaves and spoon the avocado mixture on top. Garnish with the green onions and serve immediately.

Serves 4–6

Jicama and Blood Orange Salad

Throughout Mexico, you'll find jicama—a crisp, refreshing, white-fleshed root vegetable—eaten raw as a snack, sprinkled with chili powder. Natives of the Yucatán peninsula also enjoy it paired with exotic fruit in salads such as this one, which features red-fleshed blood oranges. Try this chopped as a salsa for grilled fish, too.

1 jicama, about ¾ lb (375 g)

3 blood oranges

1 papaya (pawpaw) or mango or ¼ pineapple

1 small red (Spanish) onion, thinly sliced

1 teaspoon sea salt

¼ dried habanero chili pepper, seeded and finely chopped or ground to a powder, or cayenne pepper to taste (optional)

3 tablespoons olive oil

Juice of 1 lime

1 bunch fresh cilantro (fresh coriander), about 3 oz (90 g), stemmed

1 bunch fresh mint, about 3 oz (90 g), stemmed

☜ Using a paring knife, peel the jicama, including the fibrous layer just beneath the skin. Thinly slice the flesh and then cut into thin strips 2 inches (5 cm) long and ¼ inch (6 mm) thick. Place in a large bowl.

☜ Working with 1 orange at a time and using a sharp knife, cut a slice off the top and bottom of the oranges to reveal the fruit. Place each orange upright on a cutting board and cut away the peel and any white membrane. Then, holding the orange over the bowl with the jicama, cut along either side of each segment to free it, letting the segments and any juices fall into the bowl. If using a papaya, halve lengthwise, scoop out and discard the seeds and peel the halves. If using a mango, peel it and cut the flesh from the pit. If using pineapple, cut away the peel and the tough core area. Cut the papaya, mango or pineapple into ½-inch (12-mm) dice; you should have about 1½ cups (9 oz/ 280 g). Add to the bowl.

☜ Add the onion, salt, habanero chili or cayenne pepper, olive oil, lime juice, cilantro and mint to the bowl. Toss gently to mix. Cover and refrigerate for 2 hours before serving.

Serves 4–6

Tropical Green Salad

Pumpkin seeds, known in Spanish as pepitas, *have been part of the Mexican pantry since before the arrival of Columbus in the New World, while pomegranate seeds came to the Americas with the Spanish conquistadores. Here these two distinctive ingredients are joined by the musky papaya, a Caribbean native, in a colorful salad that complements simple grilled poultry and meats.*

DRESSING

3 tablespoons red wine vinegar
1 tablespoon fresh orange juice
3 small shallots, minced
1 teaspoon salt
½ teaspoon freshly ground pepper
6 tablespoons (3 fl oz/90 ml)
    extra-virgin olive oil

SALAD

½ cup (2½ oz/75 g) raw hulled
    green pumpkin seeds
1 tablespoon soy sauce
1 pomegranate
1 ripe papaya (pawpaw)
3 small bunches baby arugula
    (rocket), stemmed, carefully
    washed and dried
1 cup (5 oz/155 g) crumbled
    Cabrales or Roquefort cheese

To make the dressing, in a small bowl, whisk together the vinegar, orange juice, shallots, salt and pepper until the salt dissolves. Add the olive oil in a slow stream, whisking constantly until emulsified. Set aside.

In a small, dry frying pan over medium heat, toast the pumpkin seeds until slightly puffed and golden, 3–5 minutes. Add the soy sauce and stir to mix, then immediately remove from the heat. Turn the pumpkin seeds onto a plate to cool.

Cut off the blossom end of the pomegranate, removing some of the membrane but not cutting into the seeds. Score the skin into quarters, then break the fruit apart gently, following the scored lines. Bend back the thin hard skin and pull the seeds free of it. (If this step is done in a basin of water, the membrane and skin will float and the seeds will sink.) Set the seeds aside.

Cut the papaya in half lengthwise and scoop out and discard the seeds. Cut each half into thin slices and place in a large salad bowl.

Add the arugula, cheese and pomegranate seeds to the papaya. Drizzle on just enough of the dressing to coat, then toss gently. Sprinkle the pumpkin seeds over the top and serve. Pass the remaining dressing at the table.

Serves 4

Summer Squash and Rice Salad

A cantina cook might throw together a salad much like this one to use up leftovers. The mixture of rice and vegetables yields a balanced flavor and texture that doesn't become soggy. Success depends upon cooking and seasoning everything separately so the flavors remain pronounced when the ingredients are combined.

8   tablespoons (4 fl oz/125 ml) olive oil

5   assorted small summer squashes such as zucchini (courgettes), yellow crookneck or straightneck, or pattypan, in any combination, trimmed and cut into ¼-inch (6-mm) dice
    Salt and freshly ground pepper

1   yellow onion, diced

2   cloves garlic, crushed

2   teaspoons ground cumin

2   tablespoons distilled white or cider vinegar

2   cups (14 oz/440 g) steamed rice *(recipe on page 229)*, cooled to room temperature

½   cup (¾ oz/20 g) coarsely chopped fresh parsley
    Chopped lettuce leaves

☯ In a frying pan over high heat, warm 2 tablespoons of the olive oil. Add one-third each of the squashes and season to taste with salt and pepper. Sauté, stirring often, until lightly browned and slightly soft, 1–2 minutes. Transfer to a bowl. Cook the remaining squashes, in 2 batches, in the same way, using 2 tablespoons oil with each batch. Let the squashes cool.

☯ In the same frying pan, heat the remaining 2 tablespoons oil over medium heat. Add the onion and sauté until lightly golden, 3–5 minutes. Stir in the garlic and cook briefly. Add the cumin, reduce the heat to low and sauté for about 2 minutes longer. Add to the bowl holding the squashes. Add the vinegar, rice and parsley and toss to mix well. Taste and adjust the seasonings. (At this point, the salad can be covered and refrigerated for up to 3 days. Bring to room temperature before serving.)

☯ To serve, line individual plates with lettuce leaves and spoon the salad on top.

Serves 4–6

Soups and Stews

Cantinas at their most basic—those that serve only one simple dish—will in all likelihood offer a soup or a stew. Nothing could be easier to make: just simmer some vegetables, beans, meat, poultry or seafood in a stock that you've made from flavorful vegetables and bones or trimmings, and the result is a satisfying feast in a bowl.

Many soups and stews typify the thrifty nature of cantina cooking. Tortilla soup and *chilaquiles,* for example, make delicious use of leftover corn tortillas; garlic soup draws complex flavor from a humble seasoning; and chili and the popular meatballs known as albóndigas feature economical ground poultry and meat. Not surprisingly given their central role in the Mexican diet, beans feature in some of the recipes, offering their own earthy satisfaction.

As you look through the recipes on the pages that follow, you will find the stews distinguished from the soups by their heartier, thicker texture and the frequent addition of meat, poultry or seafood. But the border between the two is hazy, and either one, accompanied with tortillas or bread and, perhaps, a salad, can easily become the centerpiece of a meal.

157

Green Gazpacho

*This variation on a traditional Spanish soup is lively and refreshing. You'll
want to serve it ice cold on the hottest of days or before a hearty meal. Simply prepared
cheese quesadillas or lightly salted breadsticks make a lovely accompaniment.*

SOUP

2	slices day-old white bread, crusts removed
1	celery stalk, including leaves, chopped
6	tomatillos, husked and chopped
1	small green bell pepper (capsicum), seeded, deribbed and cut up
2	large or 6 small pickling cucumbers, peeled and cut up
1	fresh jalapeño chili pepper, stemmed, seeded (if desired) and cut up
3	cloves garlic, cut up
1	teaspoon salt
	Juice of 1 lime
¼	cup (⅓ oz/10 g) coarsely chopped fresh cilantro (fresh coriander)
2	cups (16 fl oz/500 ml) vegetable stock or water

MAYONNAISE

2	egg yolks
2	tablespoons tarragon vinegar
1½	teaspoons salt
½	teaspoon freshly ground black pepper
⅔	cup (5 fl oz/155 ml) olive oil
	Chopped fresh chives
½	small avocado, peeled and sliced

☞ Place the slices of bread in a shallow bowl and add water to cover. Let stand for 5 minutes, then squeeze the bread dry. Set aside.

☞ In a food processor fitted with the metal blade, combine the celery, tomatillos, bell pepper, cucumbers, jalapeño chili, the bread, garlic, salt, lime juice and cilantro. Process until finely puréed. Working in batches, transfer to a blender with the vegetable stock or water and purée until smooth. Set aside.

☞ To make the mayonnaise, in a large bowl, whisk together the egg yolks, vinegar, salt and pepper. Gradually add the olive oil, drop by drop, whisking until an emulsion forms. As the mixture thickens, you can begin adding the oil more quickly. (If the mayonnaise becomes overly thick or looks stringy, add 1 tablespoon water and then continue.)

☞ Once all the oil has been added and the mayonnaise is thick, start adding the vegetable purée, ¼ cup (2 fl oz/60 ml) at a time, whisking constantly, until thoroughly blended. Taste and adjust the seasonings. Cover and chill for at least 2 hours or up to 24 hours.

☞ Ladle into chilled bowls. Sprinkle with chopped chives and top each serving with a slice of avocado.

Serves 4–6

Pork and Hominy in a Red Chile Broth

Pozole is a staple of the Mexican table, and each region offers several variations. The stew's name refers to whole-kernel hominy—large kernels of dried corn that have been soaked in unslaked lime to remove their outer skins and puff them up. In this recipe, tougher cuts like pork shoulder or butt give abundant flavor and grow tender with slow, gentle cooking.

1	lb (500 g) boneless stewing pork, cut into 1-inch (2.5-cm) cubes
½	teaspoon salt
4	cups (32 fl oz/1 l) water
4	dried ancho chili peppers, stemmed and seeded
5	cloves garlic
1½	teaspoons dried oregano
2	tablespoons vegetable oil
1	large yellow onion, diced
2	cups (12 oz/375 g) well-drained canned hominy
3	cups (24 fl oz/750 ml) chicken or pork stock, or as needed
	Sliced radishes, shredded lettuce, diced yellow onion, corn tortilla chips, diced avocado and lime wedges for garnish

◪ In a sauté pan, combine the pork cubes and salt with the water. Bring to a boil, reduce the heat to medium and simmer gently, uncovered, until barely tender, about 20 minutes. Remove from the heat and let the pork cool in the liquid. Drain, reserving the liquid in a bowl. Set the meat aside, covering it with a damp towel.

◪ Place the ancho chilies in the reserved warm cooking liquid and let soak for 20 minutes. Transfer the liquid and chilies to a blender. Add the garlic and oregano and purée until smooth. Set aside.

◪ In a heavy saucepan over medium-high heat, warm the vegetable oil. Add the onion and sauté until lightly golden, about 10 minutes. Add the puréed chili mixture, hominy and chicken or pork stock, adding more stock if needed for a more soupy consistency. Stir in the reserved pork. Bring to a boil, reduce the heat to medium-low and simmer gently, uncovered, until the pork is fork-tender, about 30 minutes. Taste and adjust the seasonings.

◪ Ladle the stew into warmed shallow bowls. Arrange the garnishes in small bowls and let guests add to the stew to taste.

Serves 4–6

Cream of Chayote Soup

Related to squashes and cucumbers, mild-flavored chayotes—sometimes called vegetable pears—are believed to be indigenous to Mexico and are grown throughout the country. The most common variety, pale green and about the size and shape of a large pear, are used in this soup. If you can't find them, substitute zucchini (courgettes), which approximate the flavor, or use cauliflower or kohlrabi.

1 large slice bacon or 2 tablespoons unsalted butter

1 yellow onion, diced

1 teaspoon salt

½ teaspoon freshly ground pepper

5 cups (40 fl oz/1.25 l) chicken stock, vegetable stock or water

2 bay leaves

1 small boiling potato, peeled and sliced

4 chayotes, peeled, seeded and sliced

1 cup (8 fl oz/250 ml) heavy (double) cream or half-and-half (half cream)

2 limes, thinly sliced

☒ In a large soup pot over low heat, fry the bacon until almost all the fat is rendered, or melt the butter. Raise the heat to medium, add the onion, salt and pepper and cook, stirring occasionally, until soft, about 5 minutes. Add the stock or water, bay leaves and potato and simmer until the potato slices are soft, about 20 minutes.

☒ When the potato slices are soft, remove and discard the bay leaves and bacon. Add the chayotes and bring to a boil. Return the heat to medium and simmer, uncovered, until the chayotes are soft, about 15 minutes.

☒ Remove from the heat and let cool slightly. Working in batches, purée the soup in a blender until smooth. As each batch is puréed, pour the purée through a sieve placed over a bowl, pressing with the back of a spoon to extract all the juices. Pour the purée back into the pot, add the cream or half-and-half and bring just to a boil. Taste and adjust the seasonings.

☒ Remove from the heat and ladle into warmed bowls. Slip a few lime slices into each bowl and serve hot.

Serves 6

Sea Bass Veracruzana

Seaside restaurants in Veracruz regularly feature fish cooked with onion, garlic, chilies and tomatoes. Sea bass, which takes well to searing and cooks evenly without flaking, makes a good choice. Be sure to get the pan very hot before adding the fish.

1½ lb (750 g) sea bass or other firm-fleshed fish fillets, cut into 4 equal portions
   Salt and freshly ground pepper

3   tablespoons olive oil

1   small yellow onion, thinly sliced

2   cloves garlic, minced

2   fresh jalapeño chili peppers, stemmed and cut into rounds ¼ inch (6 mm) thick

1   lime, cut into 8 wedges

1   ripe tomato, seeded and cut into strips

1½ tablespoons coarsely chopped fresh oregano

½   cup (2½ oz/75 g) small Spanish green olives or other small green olives such as French picholines, pitted

½   cup (4 fl oz/125 ml) dry white wine

¾   cup (6 fl oz/180 ml) fish stock or bottled clam juice

☒ Sprinkle the fish fillets on both sides with salt and pepper. Heat 1 very large or 2 medium-sized sauté pans over medium-high heat for 1 minute. Add the olive oil and when it is hot but not smoking, add the fish fillets, skin side up. Turn the heat to high and sear the fillets on the first side until golden brown, 1–2 minutes. Turn and sear on the second side, 1–2 minutes longer. Remove from the heat.

☒ Using a slotted spatula, transfer the fillets to a rack set over a plate to catch the juices. Return the pan(s) to high heat, add the onion and sauté, stirring often, until lightly golden, 2–3 minutes. Add the garlic, jalapeños, lime wedges, tomato, oregano and olives and sauté, stirring briskly, for 1 minute longer. Add the white wine and boil until reduced by half, 2–3 minutes. Add the fish stock or clam juice and bring to a boil.

Reduce the heat to medium-low and return the fish fillets along with their juices to the pan(s). Cover and simmer gently until opaque throughout, 1–3 minutes depending upon the thickness of the fillets.

☒ Taste the broth and adjust the seasonings. Using the spatula, transfer the fish to warmed shallow soup bowls. Ladle the broth into the bowls, arranging some of the vegetables from the broth on the top of each fillet. Serve immediately.

Serves 4

Poached Eggs in Roasted Tomato Broth

Morning meals in cantinas often feature brothy dishes like this one, which can also double as a light midday repast or dinner in summertime. Mexican cooks sometimes call this simple preparation huevos ahogados, *or "drowned eggs." Be sure to roast the tomatoes until uniformly charred, to develop a smoky flavor.*

4   tomatoes
4   cups (32 fl oz/1 l) chicken stock
2   tablespoons olive oil
1   yellow onion, thinly sliced
1   teaspoon salt
½   teaspoon freshly ground black pepper
3   cloves garlic, minced
2   fresh serrano chili peppers
8   eggs
¼   cup (1 oz/30 g) grated Cotija, Romano or Parmesan cheese
4   large flour tortillas, homemade *(recipe on page 227)* or purchased, heated

◧ Preheat a broiler (griller). Place the tomatoes in a shallow baking pan and place in the broiler 4–6 inches (10–15 cm) from the heat source. Broil (grill), turning occasionally, until charred on all sides, 10–12 minutes.

◧ Remove the tomatoes from the broiler, let cool slightly and cut out the cores. Transfer to a blender, add 1 cup (8 fl oz/250 ml) of the chicken stock and purée until smooth. Set aside.

◧ In a heavy, wide saucepan or deep sauté pan over medium heat, warm the olive oil. When it is nearly smoking, add the onion, salt and pepper and sauté until golden brown, about 15 minutes. Add the garlic and whole serrano chilies and sauté for 1 minute longer. Add the tomato purée and the remaining 3 cups (24 fl oz/ 750 ml) chicken stock and bring to a boil. Reduce the heat to medium and simmer, uncovered, for 10 minutes to blend the flavors.

◧ To poach the eggs, one at a time, crack them into a cup and gently slide them into the simmering broth. Cook the eggs, basting the tops occasionally with spoonfuls of the hot broth, until the whites are set but the yolks are still soft, 4–6 minutes.

◧ Using a slotted spoon, gently lift out the eggs and place 2 in each warmed soup bowl. Ladle the broth over the eggs and garnish with the grated cheese. Serve immediately with the flour tortillas alongside.

Serves 4

Albóndigas Soup with Cilantro Pesto

Taking its name from the word for the meatballs that float in its rich broth, this great one-dish meal is arguably the national soup of Mexico. Make a big pot for a casual party, keeping it warm on the stove top. Adding the cilantro pesto to each serving produces a wonderfully fresh taste.

SOUP

¾ cup (5½ oz/170 g) short-grain white rice

1½ cups (12 fl oz/375 ml) water

4 tablespoons (2 fl oz/60 ml) vegetable oil

2 white onions, diced

½ lb (250 g) ground (minced) pork

½ lb (250 g) ground (minced) beef

1 egg

1 teaspoon ground cumin

1 teaspoon dried oregano

1½ teaspoons salt

1 teaspoon freshly ground pepper

1 clove garlic, minced

1 zucchini (courgette), diced

2 carrots, peeled and diced

2 ripe tomatoes, peeled, seeded and diced

6 cups (48 fl oz/1.5 l) chicken stock

PESTO

½ cup (¾ oz/20 g) coarsely chopped fresh cilantro (fresh coriander)

1 fresh mint sprig, stemmed and chopped

Juice of 2 limes

2 tablespoons olive oil

2 tablespoons water

½ teaspoon salt

☙ Place the rice in a heatproof bowl. Bring the water to a boil and pour it over the rice. Let soak for 40 minutes, then drain; set aside.

☙ Meanwhile, in a sauté pan over medium heat, warm 2 tablespoons of the vegetable oil. Add 1 of the onions and sauté until soft, about 5 minutes. Remove from the heat and let cool.

☙ In a bowl, combine the pork, beef, cooled onion, soaked rice, egg, cumin, oregano, ¾ teaspoon of the salt and ½ teaspoon of the pepper. Using your hands, mix well and form into 1-inch (2.5-cm) balls.

☙ In a large soup pot over medium heat, warm the remaining 2 tablespoons vegetable oil. Add the remaining onion and sauté until soft, about 5 minutes. Add the garlic, zucchini, carrots and tomatoes and cook, stirring, until fragrant, about 5 minutes. Add the chicken stock, stir well and bring to a boil. Carefully slip the meatballs into the pot, reduce the heat to low and simmer uncovered until the meatballs are fully cooked, about 45 minutes. Stir in the remaining ¾ teaspoon salt and ½ teaspoon pepper.

☙ While the soup simmers, make the cilantro pesto: In a mini food processor or a blender, combine the cilantro, mint, lime juice, olive oil, water and salt. Process to a paste.

☙ Ladle the soup into warmed soup bowls and top each serving with a dollop of cilantro pesto. Serve at once.

Serves 6–8

Garlic Soup

Although garlic originally came to Mexico with the Spanish explorers, it is now so ubiquitous that this soup regularly turns up on lunch menus in casual restaurants there. Do not be put off by the amount of garlic; the flavor mellows and sweetens with slow cooking. With its straight-forward flavors and intriguing textures, this makes an ideal first course for a grand feast.

3 tablespoons mild olive oil

9 cloves garlic, halved

½ loaf crusty French bread, cut into 1-inch (2.5-cm) cubes (2 generous cups/5 oz/155 g)

1 teaspoon salt

½ teaspoon freshly ground pepper

8 cups (64 fl oz/2 l) chicken stock

3 eggs, lightly beaten

2 tablespoons fresh epazote *(see glossary, page 343)* or oregano leaves, chopped

1 lime, cut into 6 wedges

☒ Preheat an oven to 325°F (165°C). In a soup pot over low heat, warm the olive oil. Add the garlic and cook slowly, stirring occasionally, until the oil is well flavored and the garlic is soft but has not begun to color, about 5 minutes. Remove from the heat and discard the garlic cloves.

☒ Place the bread cubes in a bowl and pour about half of the garlicky oil over them (leave the remaining oil in the pot). Toss well to coat, sprinkle with the salt and pepper, and spread out on a baking sheet. Bake until golden brown and crisp throughout, 10–15 minutes. Remove from the oven and set aside.

☒ Pour the stock into the soup pot holding the remaining oil. Place over medium heat and bring to a simmer.

Gradually add the eggs to the simmering stock while stirring the stock constantly in a circular motion. Add the epazote or oregano and simmer until the eggs are set, about 3 minutes longer. Remove from the heat.

☒ Divide the croutons among 6 warmed soup bowls and ladle the egg-laced stock into them. Squeeze a wedge of lime over each bowl, then drop the wedge in the bowl. Serve immediately.

Serves 6

Saffron Mussel Stew

You find a lot of Spanish influence in the Yucatán region, where this classic stew originates. The presence of saffron is evidence of Spain's contribution to many of the area's dishes. Serve with a tossed green salad and generous slices of broiled garlic bread.

2	tablespoons olive oil
2	yellow onions, cut into julienne strips
½	teaspoon salt
½	teaspoon freshly ground pepper
4	cloves garlic, sliced
1½	cups (12 fl oz/375 ml) dry white wine
1	fresh thyme sprig
1	teaspoon saffron threads
2½	cups (20 fl oz/625 ml) bottled clam juice or fish stock
1	cup (8 fl oz/250 ml) good-quality tomato juice
3	lb (1.5 kg) small mussels in the shell
½	cup (¾ oz/20 g) coarsely chopped fresh flat-leaf (Italian) parsley

☙ In a large, heavy-bottomed saucepan over medium heat, warm 1 tablespoon of the olive oil. Add half of the onions, salt and pepper and sauté, stirring briskly, until lightly golden, 8–10 minutes. Add the garlic and sauté for 1 minute longer. Then add the white wine and bring to a boil. Boil until reduced by half, 7–8 minutes. Add the thyme, saffron, clam juice or fish stock and tomato juice and bring to a boil. Reduce the heat to low and simmer for 10 minutes to blend the flavors. Strain through a sieve into a bowl and set aside.

☙ Scrub the mussels under cool running water and pull out and discard their beards. Discard any mussels that do not close to the touch.

☙ Place 2 large, wide sauté pans over high heat (or work in batches if only 1 pan is available). Add half of the remaining 1 tablespoon olive oil to each pan. When hot, add half of the remaining onions to each pan and sauté briefly, stirring occasionally, until they just begin to color, about 4 minutes. Add half of the mussels to each pan, spreading them out in a single layer, and sauté, stirring occasionally, for 1–2 minutes. Add half of the strained broth to each pan and bring to a boil. Immediately reduce the heat to medium, cover and cook until all the mussels open, 3–5 minutes. Discard any mussels that do not open.

☙ Add half of the parsley to each pan. Toss to mix and then spoon the mussels into warmed shallow soup bowls. Divide the broth evenly among the bowls and serve immediately.

Serves 4

Turkey Black Bean Chili with Ancho Salsa

Some food scholars say that chili-seasoned stews of meat and beans belong more to Texas and the American Southwest than to Mexico. Certainly, this is a cantina dish of the northern borderlands, and it owes a debt to present-day sensibilities in its health-conscious combination of ground turkey and black beans.

CHILI

2	cups (14 oz/440 g) dried black beans
8	cups (64 fl oz/2 l) water
2	fresh árbol chili peppers
3	bay leaves
2	tablespoons vegetable oil
1	lb (500 g) coarsely ground (minced) turkey
1	large yellow onion, diced
1	teaspoon salt, or to taste
½	teaspoon freshly ground black pepper
½	teaspoon cayenne pepper
3	cloves garlic, minced
2	fresh poblano chili peppers, stemmed, seeded and diced
1½	tablespoons chili powder
1½	tablespoons ground cumin
2	cups (16 fl oz/500 ml) chicken stock, or as needed

SALSA

4	dried ancho chili peppers, stemmed and seeded
½	cup (4 fl oz/125 ml) fresh orange juice
¼	cup (2 fl oz/60 ml) fresh lime juice
1	teaspoon salt
2	tablespoons extra-virgin olive oil

☒ Sort through the black beans and discard any misshapen beans or stones. Rinse well. In a large saucepan, combine the beans, water, árbol chilies and bay leaves and bring to a boil. Reduce the heat to medium, cover and simmer until tender, about 1 hour. Remove the chilies and bay leaves and discard. Set aside.

☒ Meanwhile, make the salsa: In a cast-iron frying pan over medium heat, toast the ancho chilies, turning frequently to avoid scorching, until soft and brown, 1–2 minutes. Remove from the heat, chop and place in a bowl. Add the orange and lime juices, salt and olive oil. Mix well and let stand at room temperature for at least 30 minutes or up to 2 hours before serving. (The salsa can be covered and refrigerated for up to 2 days.)

☒ In a large pot over medium heat, warm the 2 tablespoons vegetable oil. Add the turkey and cook, stirring often, until browned, about 10 minutes. Add the onion, salt, black pepper and cayenne pepper and sauté over medium heat, stirring occasionally, until lightly golden, about 10 minutes. Add the garlic, poblano chilies, chili powder and cumin and cook, stirring, until fragrant, 2–3 minutes. Add the black beans and their liquid and the 2 cups (16 fl oz/500 ml) chicken stock and cook, uncovered, until the flavors have blended and the mixture has thickened, 30–40 minutes. Taste and adjust the seasonings, adding more chicken stock if needed for the desired consistency.

☒ Ladle the chili into warmed bowls and top each serving with a dollop of the salsa.

Serves 6

Red Chicken and Tortilla Soup

The most common use for leftover tortillas throughout Mexico, chilaquiles *are essentially pieces of stale tortilla cooked or softened in chili sauce. Depending upon the cantina, this can translate into cheesy casseroles, thick porridges or brothy soups. This version relies on red salsa, but green can be substituted.*

SOUP

6   cups (48 fl oz/1.5 l) chicken stock
1   lb (500 g) skinless, boneless chicken breasts
    Salt to taste, plus 1 teaspoon
    Freshly ground pepper to taste, plus ½ teaspoon
2   tablespoons vegetable oil
1   yellow onion, diced
3   cloves garlic, minced
2   cups (16 fl oz/500 ml) red salsa *(recipe on page 228)*
1   cup (8 fl oz/250 ml) water
2   handfuls corn tortilla chips

GARNISHES

¼   cup (⅓ oz/10 g) coarsely chopped fresh cilantro (fresh coriander)
¼   yellow onion, diced
¼   cup (1 oz/30 g) grated Cotija, Romano or Parmesan cheese
¼   cup (2 fl oz/60 ml) *crema (see glossary, page 342)* or sour cream

☒ In a deep frying pan, bring the chicken stock to a boil. Sprinkle the chicken breasts with salt and pepper to taste and add to the stock. Reduce the heat to medium, cover and cook until tender and opaque throughout, 8–10 minutes. Using a slotted spoon, remove the chicken breasts, wrap in a damp towel and set aside to cool. Reserve the stock.

☒ In a large saucepan over medium heat, warm the vegetable oil. Add the onion, 1 teaspoon salt and ½ teaspoon pepper and sauté until soft, about 5 minutes. Add the garlic and sauté until soft but not browned, 2–3 minutes longer. Add the salsa, reserved chicken stock and water. Bring to a boil over high heat, reduce the heat to medium and simmer, uncovered, for 10 minutes to blend the flavors.

☒ Using your fingers, shred the cooled chicken meat into long, thin strips. Add to the pan along with the tortilla chips. Stir well, taste and adjust the seasonings. Continue to simmer over medium heat for 3–4 minutes to soften the chips slightly. The chips should still be half crispy.

☒ Ladle the soup into warmed soup bowls. Garnish each serving with cilantro, onion, cheese and a spoonful of *crema* or sour cream. Serve immediately.

Serves 4–6

Pinto Bean Soup with Fresh Salsa

Despite its creamy taste, this simply prepared soup is surprisingly low in fat. A cantina cook might well make up a batch from the previous day's leftover beans. It is the perfect antidote to a blustery day, and the fresh, sharp garnish contrasts nicely with the natural richness of the beans.

SOUP

1½	cups (10½ oz/330 g) dried pinto beans
7	cups (56 fl oz/1.75 l) water
¼	cup (2 fl oz/60 ml) vegetable oil
2	yellow onions, diced
1	teaspoon salt
½	teaspoon freshly ground pepper
4	cloves garlic, minced
6	cups (48 fl oz/1.5 l) chicken stock, vegetable stock or water

SALSA

3	ripe plum (Roma) tomatoes, diced
½	small red (Spanish) onion, finely diced
¼	cup (⅓ oz/10 g) coarsely chopped fresh cilantro (fresh coriander)
	Juice of 1 lime
	Salt and freshly ground pepper

Crema (see glossary, page 342) or sour cream

☒ Sort through the beans and discard any misshapen beans or stones. Rinse well. Place the beans in a saucepan and add the water. Bring to a boil, reduce the heat to medium-low, cover and simmer until the smallest bean is cooked through and creamy inside, about 1½ hours. Remove from the heat and set aside.

☒ In a large saucepan over medium heat, warm the vegetable oil. Add the onions, salt and pepper and sauté until the onions are lightly browned, about 10 minutes. Add the garlic and sauté for 1–2 minutes longer. Add the beans and their liquid and the stock or water. Bring to a boil, reduce the heat to medium and simmer uncovered, stirring occasionally, until the beans start to break apart, 20–30 minutes. Remove the beans from the heat and let cool slightly.

☒ Meanwhile, make the salsa: In a bowl, stir together the tomatoes, onion, cilantro, lime juice and salt and pepper to taste. Cover and refrigerate until you are ready to serve.

☒ Working in batches, transfer the bean mixture to a blender and purée until smooth. Transfer the purée to a clean saucepan and reheat over low heat, stirring frequently, until hot. (If not serving immediately, keep warm over very low heat, stirring often.)

☒ Ladle the soup into warmed shallow bowls and top each serving with a spoonful of salsa and a dollop of *crema* or sour cream.

Serves 6

Tortilla Soup

This hearty soup, a favorite in central Mexico but served throughout the country, results from cooking leftover tortillas with other cantina staples: onion, garlic, chilies and salsa. When left for a few hours, the soup will thicken, and can be thinned with more liquid or served as a starchy side dish.

SOUP
2	tablespoons vegetable oil
1	yellow onion, diced
1	teaspoon salt
2	cloves garlic, minced
1	dried chipotle chili pepper, stemmed and seeded (optional)
1½	cups (12 fl oz/375 ml) red salsa *(recipe on page 228)*
5	cups (40 fl oz/1.25 l) chicken stock, vegetable stock or water
½	lb (250 g) corn tortilla chips

GARNISHES
¼	cup (⅓ oz/10 g) coarsely chopped fresh cilantro (fresh coriander)
½	small yellow onion, diced
1	lime, cut into 6 wedges

☒ In a saucepan over medium heat, warm the vegetable oil. Add the onion and salt and cook, stirring occasionally, until golden brown, about 15 minutes. Add the garlic and the chipotle chili, if using, and cook for 1–2 minutes longer. Then add the salsa and stock or water and bring to a boil. Reduce the heat to medium-low and simmer, uncovered, for about 20 minutes to blend the flavors. Stir in the tortilla chips and simmer until the chips soften and begin to break apart, 10–15 minutes longer.

☒ Remove and discard the chipotle chili, if used. Ladle the soup into warmed bowls and garnish each serving with cilantro and onion. Squeeze a wedge of lime over each bowl, then drop the wedge into the bowl. Serve immediately.

Serves 6

Pork Stew with Green Chilies

One of the most widespread ways to cook and serve pork in Mexico, and a staple of lunch counters, this hearty dish highlights the rich, slowly cooked meat with the sharpness of tomatillos and the heat of chilies.

1½ lb (750 g) tomatillos, husked

4 lb (2 kg) pork butt or shoulder, trimmed of fat and cut into 2-inch (5-cm) cubes

2 teaspoons salt

1 teaspoon freshly ground black pepper
   All-purpose (plain) flour for dusting

¼ cup (2 fl oz/60 ml) vegetable oil

3 yellow onions, cut into 1-inch (2.5-cm) squares

2 fresh Anaheim or poblano chili peppers, stemmed, seeded and cut into 1-inch (2.5-cm) squares

2 fresh jalapeño chili peppers, stemmed, seeded and finely chopped

2 green bell peppers (capsicums), seeded, deribbed and cut into 1-inch (2.5-cm) squares

3 cloves garlic, finely minced

1 tablespoon dried oregano, crumbled

2 teaspoons ground cumin

2 tablespoons coriander seeds, crushed and soaked in water to cover for 15 minutes, then drained

2 bay leaves

¼ cup (⅓ oz/10 g) coarsely chopped fresh cilantro (fresh coriander)

4 cups (32 fl oz/1 l) chicken stock

◨ Preheat a broiler (griller). Place the tomatillos in a shallow pan and place in the broiler about 2 inches (5 cm) from the heat source. Roast, turning occasionally, until charred on all sides, 5–8 minutes. Remove from the broiler and, when cool enough to handle, core and chop the tomatillos. Set aside.

◨ Sprinkle the pork on all sides with the salt and black pepper. Spread some flour on a plate and dust the pork with the flour to coat evenly, tapping off any excess. In a heavy-bottomed frying pan over medium-high heat, warm the vegetable oil. Working in small batches, add the pork cubes and brown well on all sides, 3–5 minutes. Using a slotted spoon, transfer the pork to a large soup pot.

◨ Discard any fat remaining in the frying pan and place the pan over medium heat. Add the onions and sauté, stirring occasionally, until soft, about 5 minutes. Add all of the chilies and bell peppers and sauté until fragrant, 3–4 minutes. Add the garlic and sauté for 1–2 minutes longer.

◨ Transfer the sautéed onions and peppers to the soup pot. Add the chopped tomatillos, oregano, cumin, coriander seeds, bay leaves, cilantro and chicken stock and bring to a boil. Reduce the heat to low and simmer gently, uncovered, until the pork is tender when pierced with a fork, 2–3 hours.

◨ Taste and adjust the seasonings, then spoon the stew into warmed bowls and serve hot.

Serves 6–8

Main Courses

One of the most appealing features of cantina cooking is the scent of savory juices as they drip onto glowing coals and vaporize, transforming into aromatic wisps of smoke that lure customers from blocks away.

Grilled main courses are a hallmark of Mexico's casual cuisine, taking full advantage of the ease with which food may be cooked over an open fire. The keeper of a tiny market stall will build that fire in a small metal drum, while a big taco stand on the plaza keeps its coals ablaze beneath a grill as big as a bed. At home, the recipes on the following pages work just as well on a backyard barbecue, or, if weather or space does not permit, on a stove-top grill or under a broiler.

Of course, other cooking methods are found in cantinas, too, including the gentle simmering used to enhance traditional Mexican moles; the baking essential to enchiladas; and the high-heat frying that forms the golden crust of chiles rellenos. What these dishes have in common with grilled foods is the relative economy and ease with which they are prepared—and the fact that their taste is every bit as delicious as the wonderful aromas that fill the air while they cook.

183

Grilled Beef Tacos

In the beef-eating north, taco stands everywhere feature some form of charcoal-grilled
skirt steak. Offer an array of condiments, letting guests fill warm, handmade tortillas to taste.
Try the tacos with flour tortillas, too, just as they are often served in northern Mexico.

QUICK SALSA

4	ripe plum (Roma) tomatoes, seeded and coarsely chopped
2	fresh serrano chili peppers, stemmed and coarsely chopped
3	tablespoons fresh lime juice
1	teaspoon salt
½	teaspoon freshly ground black pepper

GARNISHES

¼	cup (⅓ oz/10 g) coarsely chopped fresh cilantro (fresh coriander)
2	avocados, pitted, peeled and diced
2	tomatoes, seeded and diced
6	green (spring) onions, including the tender green tops, sliced on the diagonal
¼	head white cabbage, shredded

TACOS

1½	lb (750 g) trimmed skirt, flank or tri-tip steaks
	Salt and freshly ground black pepper
2	cloves garlic, minced
2	tablespoons olive oil
	Juice of 1 lime
18	small or 12 large corn tortillas, homemade *(recipe on page 226)* or purchased

☞ Prepare a fire in a charcoal grill.

☞ To make the salsa, in a food processor fitted with the metal blade, combine the tomatoes, chilies, lime juice, salt and black pepper and purée until very smooth. Pour into a bowl and set aside. You should have about 1¼ cups (10 fl oz/310 ml). Prepare all the garnishes and place in separate bowls.

☞ Ten minutes before the grill is ready, season the steaks evenly with salt and black pepper, rub with the garlic and olive oil and then drizzle evenly with the lime juice.

☞ Just before grilling the steaks, warm the tortillas on the grill: Fill a shallow pan with water and, one at a time, briefly dip each tortilla in the water and immediately place on the grill rack. Grill for 30 seconds, then turn and grill for 30 seconds longer. Stack the tortillas as they come off the grill and wrap them in a damp towel and then in aluminum foil until serving. (They will keep warm for up to 30 minutes.)

☞ When the fire is very hot, place the steaks on the grill rack about 3 inches (7.5 cm) from the coals and grill, turning once, until evenly caramelized on the outside but still pink in the center, 1–2 minutes per side.

☞ Transfer the steaks to a cutting board and let rest for 3–5 minutes before slicing. Using a sharp knife, cut across the grain into slices ¼ inch (6 mm) thick. Serve immediately with the warmed tortillas, salsa and garnishes. Let diners assemble their own tacos at the table.

Serves 6

Chicken Mole Drumsticks

Although the extravagantly spiced, sometimes chocolate-enriched sauces known as moles can be quite complicated, everyone raves about their depth of flavor. This simplified recipe takes only an hour or so to make, but you may still want to cook up a double batch and freeze half. Serve with plenty of white rice.

12	large chicken drumsticks
	Salt
	Freshly ground black pepper
5	dried mulato chili peppers
3	dried pasilla chili peppers
2	dried ancho chili peppers
5	cups (40 fl oz/1.25 l) boiling water
¼	cup (2 fl oz/60 ml) vegetable oil
1	yellow onion, diced
2	cloves garlic, minced
2	tablespoons skinless peanuts
2	tablespoons golden raisins (sultanas)
4	tomatillos, husked, peeled and chopped
1	corn tortilla, homemade *(recipe on page 226)* or purchased, lightly toasted over an open flame and broken into small pieces
¼	teaspoon aniseeds
6	coriander seeds
1	whole clove
10	whole peppercorns
½	cup (1½ oz/45 g) sesame seeds
1½	cups (12 fl oz/375 ml) chicken stock
1	oz (30 g) bittersweet chocolate, coarsely chopped
4	limes, cut into wedges

☙ Rinse the chicken drumsticks and pat dry. Sprinkle with salt and pepper and set aside.

☙ Stem, core, seed and derib all the chilies. In a large, heavy-bottomed pot over medium heat, toast the chilies, turning once, until fragrant and the skins begin to blister, 3–5 minutes. Transfer the chilies to a heatproof bowl, add the boiling water and let stand until cool. Working in batches, transfer the cooled chilies and their soaking water to a blender and purée until smooth. Transfer to a bowl. Set the purée and the blender aside. Wipe the pot clean.

☙ Place the pot over medium heat and add the vegetable oil. When the oil is hot, add the drumsticks and brown well on all sides, about 10 minutes. Using tongs, transfer the drumsticks to a serving dish and keep warm. Add the onion to the same pot and sauté over medium heat until golden, about 10 minutes. Add the garlic and sauté for 1 minute, then add the peanuts and raisins and continue to sauté for 1 minute longer. Stir in the tomatillos and tortilla and cook, stirring occasionally, until soft, about 5 minutes. Remove from the heat and set aside.

☙ In a small, dry frying pan over medium heat, toast the aniseeds and coriander seeds until fragrant, 2–3 minutes. Transfer to a spice grinder or a mortar, add the clove and peppercorns and grind or pulverize until coarsely crushed.

☙ In the same small, dry pan over medium heat, toast the sesame seeds, stirring often, until golden, about 3 minutes. Add half of the seeds to the blender and reserve half for garnish. Add the reserved sautéed vegetables (do not wash the pot), ground spices and chicken stock to the blender. Purée until smooth.

☙ Add the puréed chilies to the same large pot used to sauté the vegetables. Cook over low heat, stirring often in the fat remaining in the pot, until thickened, 8–10 minutes. Add the puréed vegetables and chocolate and season to taste with salt. Stir well. Add the chicken pieces, cover and simmer gently over low heat until the chicken is tender and opaque throughout when pierced with a knife, about 45 minutes.

☙ Serve the drumsticks generously topped with the sauce. Sprinkle with the reserved sesame seeds and garnish with lime wedges.

Serves 6

Chiles Rellenos

From season to season, region to region and even field to field, poblano chilies can vary in hotness: the only way to test their heat is to taste one. These stuffed chilies can be made and refrigerated up to a day ahead. If the cheese filling is too rich for you, add more vegetables such as corn kernels or peas.

⅓ lb (155 g) Manchego or Monterey Jack cheese, grated

¼ lb (125 g) panela or farmer cheese, grated

2 oz (60 g) añejo or Romano cheese, grated

8 fresh poblano chili peppers, roasted and peeled *(see glossary, page 342)* but kept whole

½ cup (2½ oz/75 g) all-purpose (plain) flour

4 eggs, beaten

½ teaspoon salt

½ teaspoon freshly ground black pepper

Vegetable oil for frying

1 cup (8 fl oz/250 ml) red salsa *(recipe on page 228)*

1 cup (8 fl oz/250 ml) green salsa *(recipe on page 228)*

6 tablespoons (3 fl oz/90 ml) *crema* or sour cream, optional

◧ In a bowl, combine the cheeses and toss to mix. Make a lengthwise slit in each chili and remove the stem, seeds and ribs. Mold ½ cup (2 oz/60 g) of the cheese mixture into a torpedo shape and place it inside a chili. Fold the chili around the cheese to enclose it completely and set aside while filling the remaining 7 chilies in the same way.

◧ Preheat an oven to 350°F (180°C). Spread the flour on a plate. In a wide bowl, using a whisk, beat the eggs until foamy, 3–5 minutes. Then whisk in the salt and pepper and set aside.

◧ In a wide cast-iron frying pan over medium heat, pour in the vegetable oil to a depth of 1 inch (2.5 cm) and heat until almost smoking (about 375°F/190°C). Working with 1 chili at a time, dip it in flour and turn to coat, patting off any excess. Dip 2 chilies at a time into the beaten eggs, then slip them into the hot oil. Fry until lightly browned, 2–4 minutes. Flip and brown the other side, 2–4 minutes longer. Using a slotted spoon, transfer to a paper towel–lined baking sheet to drain. Repeat with the other chilies.

◧ When all the chilies have been browned, remove the paper towel and place the baking sheet in the oven until the cheese at the center of each chili has melted, 4–6 minutes.

◧ To serve, coat one half of each of 4 individual plates with red salsa and the other half with green salsa. Place 2 chilies on each plate and spoon a dollop of *crema* or sour cream on top, if desired. Serve immediately.

Serves 4

Grilled Citrus–Marinated Chicken Breast

Mexican cooks often marinate chicken in citrus juices before grilling. Don't marinate the meat longer than overnight, however, or it will become too soft. When grilling, sear the skinless side first to seal in the juices, then finish cooking more slowly off to one side of the grill. Serve with green rice and refried black beans (recipes on pages 229 and 228).

MARINADE

1 cup (8 fl oz/250 ml) fresh orange juice
2 tablespoons fresh lime juice
1 dried chipotle chili pepper, stemmed and seeded
1 cup (8 fl oz/250 ml) red salsa *(recipe on page 228)*
¼ cup (2 fl oz/60 ml) olive oil
1 teaspoon salt

4 boneless chicken breast halves
   Fresh orange slices, optional
   Fresh cilantro (fresh coriander) sprigs, optional

In a small saucepan, combine the orange juice, lime juice and chili pepper and bring to a boil. Reduce the heat to medium and simmer, uncovered, until the chili is plump, about 5 minutes. Remove from the heat and let cool.

Transfer the cooled citrus mixture to a blender and add the salsa, olive oil and salt. Purée until smooth.

Rinse the chicken breasts and pat dry. Place the chicken breasts in a shallow nonaluminum dish. Pour the purée evenly over the top, cover and let marinate in the refrigerator for 2–4 hours.

Prepare a fire in a charcoal grill or preheat a broiler (griller).

When the fire is hot or the broiler is ready, remove the chicken breasts from the marinade. Place them skin side down on the grill rack about 5 inches (13 cm) from the coals, or arrange them skin side up on a broiler pan and place in the broiler about 4 inches (10 cm) from the heat source. Grill or broil for 2–3 minutes. Turn and cook on the second side for 2–3 minutes. Continue to cook the chicken, turning every 2–3 minutes to avoid burning, until tender and opaque throughout. The total cooking time should be 12–20 minutes, depending upon the size of the breasts.

Transfer the chicken to a warmed platter. Garnish with orange slices and cilantro sprigs, if desired, and serve immediately.

Serves 4

Grilled Skirt Steak with Onion–Cilantro Relish

Spicy marinades are well suited to hearty cuts of meat like skirt steak. Take care not to marinate the steak too long, though, or the meat will be tough and stringy. The marinade is excellent with pork, lamb or chicken, too. Serve with fresh tortillas and refried beans (recipes on pages 226–228).

MARINADE

4	dried Anaheim chili peppers
4	dried árbol chili peppers
2	teaspoons cumin seeds
1	clove garlic, minced
1	fresh jalapeño chili pepper, stemmed, seeded and coarsely chopped
½	cup (4 fl oz/125 ml) red wine vinegar
½	cup (4 fl oz/125 ml) olive oil
1½	teaspoons salt
1	lb (500 g) trimmed skirt steak

RELISH

1	small white onion, minced
1	fresh serrano chili pepper, stemmed, seeded and minced
½	cup (¾ oz/20 g) coarsely chopped fresh cilantro (fresh coriander)
1	teaspoon salt
	Juice of 1 lime
1	tablespoon olive oil

☙ To make the marinade, remove the stems from all the dried chilies, then shake out and discard the seeds. Place the chilies in a small saucepan with water just to cover. Bring to a boil, remove from the heat and let stand for 20 minutes to soften. Drain.

☙ In a small, dry frying pan over medium heat, toast the cumin seeds until lightly browned and fragrant, 2–3 minutes. In a blender, combine the softened chilies, cumin seeds, garlic, jalapeño chili and red wine vinegar. Purée until thick and smooth, 1–2 minutes. Add the olive oil and salt and blend again until well mixed.

☙ Place the skirt steak in a shallow nonaluminum dish and pour the marinade over it. Let marinate at room temperature for 1 hour.

☙ Prepare a fire in a charcoal grill or preheat a broiler (griller).

☙ Just before placing the steak on the grill or in the broiler, make the relish: In a small bowl, stir together the onion, serrano chili, cilantro, salt, lime juice and olive oil. Set aside until you are ready to serve.

☙ When the fire is hot or the broiler is ready, place the steak on the grill rack about 3 inches (7.5 cm) from the coals, or place in a broiler pan at the same distance from the heat source. Grill or broil, turning once, until seared on the outside but still pink in the center, 1–2 minutes per side.

☙ To serve, slice the steak across the grain and on the diagonal. Arrange the slices on a platter and serve with the relish on the side.

Serves 4

Chorizo and Roasted Pepper Ragout over Quinoa

Shop around for the finest chorizo available, and take care not to overcook it. Quinoa, an ancient grain native to the South American Andes and prized for both its flavor and nutrients has been rediscovered in recent years. Here, the tiny, round grains make a splendid bed for juicy sausages and a vegetable topping.

QUINOA

3   tablespoons unsalted butter
1   cup (3 oz/90 g) broken vermicelli
½   yellow onion, diced
6   cups (48 fl oz/1.5 l) chicken stock or water
3   cups (14 oz/440 g) quinoa (organic, if possible)

RAGOUT

2   tablespoons olive oil
1   yellow onion, cut into julienne strips
4   cloves garlic, minced
2   teaspoons paprika
1   teaspoon ground cumin
2   red bell peppers (capsicums), roasted, peeled and seeded *(see glossary, page 340),* then cut into julienne strips
2   green bell peppers (capsicums), roasted, peeled and seeded, then cut into julienne strips
2   fresh poblano chili peppers, roasted, peeled and seeded *(see glossary, page 342),* then cut into julienne strips
1   cup (8 fl oz/250 ml) chicken stock
    Salt and freshly ground black pepper
6   large chorizo sausages

☒ Prepare a fire in a charcoal grill or preheat a broiler (griller).

☒ To prepare the quinoa, in a saucepan over medium heat, melt the butter. Add the vermicelli and cook, stirring often, until the noodles turn golden brown, 4–6 minutes. Add the onion and sauté until the onion is soft and begins to turn golden, 3–5 minutes. Add the stock or water and bring to a boil. Add the quinoa and return to a boil. Reduce the heat to medium, cover and cook until the centers of the grains are soft, 20–30 minutes.

☒ Meanwhile, make the ragout: In a large saucepan over medium heat, warm the olive oil. Add the onion and sauté until it begins to turn golden, 3–4 minutes. Add the garlic and continue to sauté for 1–2 minutes longer. Stir in the paprika and cumin and cook for 1 minute. Add all the bell peppers, the chilies and the chicken stock and cook uncovered, stirring occasionally, until the mixture thickens, 10–15 minutes. Season to taste with salt and pepper.

☒ While the peppers are cooking, place the sausages on the grill rack about 3 inches (7.5 cm) above medium-hot coals, or arrange them on a broiler pan and place in the broiler at about the same distance from the heat source. Grill or broil, turning often, until cooked throughout, 8–10 minutes.

☒ To serve, spoon the quinoa onto a warmed platter or individual plates and arrange the sausages on the quinoa. Top with the pepper mixture and serve.

Serves 4–6

Vegetable Enchiladas

*At its most basic, an enchilada is a tortilla dipped in chili sauce. This unusual variation
pleases even avid meat eaters with a vegetarian filling inspired by rustic potato dishes and enriched
by popular Mexican cheeses. Add rice and beans or a tossed salad for a memorable feast.*

FILLING

¾   lb (375 g) red potatoes, unpeeled

3   fresh poblano chili peppers, roasted, peeled and seeded *(see glossary, page 342),* then cut into julienne strips

2   red bell peppers (capsicums), roasted, peeled and seeded *(see glossary, page 340),* then cut into julienne strips

½   yellow onion, diced

1   cup (4 oz/125 g) shredded panela or Monterey Jack cheese

½   cup (2 oz/60 g) grated Cotija, Romano or Parmesan cheese

ANCHO SAUCE

1   tomato

4   dried ancho chili peppers, stemmed and seeded

2   cups (16 fl oz/500 ml) hot tap water

1   teaspoon salt

½   teaspoon freshly ground pepper

¼   yellow onion, coarsely chopped

2   cloves garlic, chopped

1   teaspoon ground cumin

1   teaspoon distilled white vinegar

2   teaspoons dried oregano, crumbled

2   tablespoons olive oil

    Vegetable oil for frying

12   corn tortillas, homemade *(recipe on page 226)* or purchased

To make the filling, in a saucepan, combine the potatoes with water to cover. Bring to a boil over medium-high heat. Boil gently until the potatoes are tender when pierced with a fork, about 15 minutes. Drain and let cool, then cut the unpeeled potatoes into ½-inch (12-mm) dice. Place in a bowl. Add the poblano chilies, bell peppers, onion and both cheeses and stir to mix well. Set aside.

To make the sauce, preheat a broiler (griller). Place the tomato in a small shallow baking pan. Place in the broiler 4–6 inches (10–15 cm) from the heat source. Broil (grill), turning occasionally, until charred on all sides, 10–12 minutes. Remove from the broiler, let cool slightly and cut out the core. Set aside.

In a small, dry frying pan over medium heat, toast the chilies, turning once, until fragrant and the skins begin to blister, 3–5 minutes. Remove from the heat and let cool, then place the chilies in a bowl, add the hot water and let soak for 15 minutes to soften.

Transfer the chilies and their soaking liquid to a blender and add the salt, pepper, onion, garlic, cumin, vinegar, oregano and roasted tomato. Purée until smooth, then strain through a sieve into a shallow bowl.

In a heavy-bottomed pot over medium heat, warm the olive oil. Add the purée and cook, stirring constantly, until the sauce thickens slightly, 5–10 minutes.

Meanwhile, preheat an oven to 350°F (180°C). Spread a 12-inch (30-cm) square of plastic wrap on a work surface.

In a shallow frying pan over medium heat, pour in the vegetable oil to a depth of ¼ inch (6 mm). When the oil is hot, fry the tortillas one at a time, turning once, until limp but not crisp, about 30 seconds per side. Using tongs, transfer the tortillas to paper towels to drain. One at a time, dip each limp tortilla in the sauce and then lay it on the plastic wrap. Place about one-twelfth of the filling on the tortilla in a line not quite to the edge of the round and roll up the tortilla. As the tortillas are filled, place them seam side down and side by side in a warmed glass or ceramic baking dish. When all the enchiladas are made, top each one with a few spoonfuls of the remaining sauce.

Place the enchiladas in the oven until warmed throughout, 10–15 minutes. Serve hot.

Serves 4–6

Grilled Shrimp with Mango Salsa

Perfect for a hot summer night, this tropical dish partners grilled seafood with the exotic sweetness of mangoes and the punch of cilantro. Although mangoes are native to India, they came to the New World via Brazil in the 1700s, and are now widely available all over Mexico. The salsa complements fish or chicken as well.

2 cups (16 fl oz/500 ml) olive oil

8 cloves garlic, thinly sliced
  Juice of 2 limes

1 teaspoon salt

½ teaspoon freshly ground black pepper

2 lb (1 kg) large shrimp (prawns), peeled and deveined (20–24 shrimp)

SALSA

2 ripe mangoes

6 green (spring) onions, including tender green tops, thinly sliced

2 fresh jalapeño chili peppers, stemmed, seeded (if desired) and finely diced

¼ cup (⅓ oz/10 g) coarsely chopped fresh cilantro (fresh coriander)
  Juice of 2 limes

1 teaspoon salt

  Lime wedges, optional

☙ In a frying pan over medium heat, warm the olive oil. Add the garlic and cook, stirring occasionally, until soft, 3–5 minutes. Remove from the heat, pour into a shallow non-aluminum dish and let cool. Add the lime juice, salt and pepper. Mix well.

☙ Using bamboo skewers, thread 4 or 5 shrimp onto each skewer, passing the skewer through points near both the head and tail sections of each shrimp. Place the skewers in the olive oil mixture, turning to coat evenly. Cover and let marinate in the refrigerator for at least 2 hours or up to 12 hours.

☙ To make the salsa, peel each mango and cut the flesh from the pit. Cut into ¼-inch (6-mm) dice and place in a bowl. Add the green onions, chilies, cilantro, lime juice and salt. Stir to mix, cover and refrigerate for at least 30 minutes before serving.

☙ Prepare a fire in a charcoal grill.

☙ When the fire is hot, place the skewers on the grill rack about 3 inches (7.5 cm) from the coals and grill, turning once, until the shrimp turn pink and are opaque throughout, about 3 minutes per side.

☙ To serve, arrange a bed of salsa on each plate and top with a skewer of shrimp, or remove the shrimp from each skewer and arrange atop the salsa. Garnish with lime wedges, if desired, and serve.

Serves 4–6

Fish Fillets in a Bath of Garlic

Garlic sauce, known as mojo de ajo, *is a favorite topping for Mexican seafood. This version adds a touch of ancho chili. Make the sauce quickly while the fish finishes cooking, and take care not to brown the garlic or chilies. Serve with red or white rice (recipes on page 229).*

6   halibut or sea bass fillets, 6 oz (185 g) each
     Salt to taste, plus 1 teaspoon
     Freshly ground black pepper to taste, plus ½ teaspoon

8   tablespoons olive oil

20   cloves garlic, thinly sliced

1   dried ancho chili pepper, stemmed, seeded and chopped

⅔   cup (5 fl oz/150 ml) fish stock or bottled clam juice
     Juice of 3 limes

½   cup (¾ oz/20 g) coarsely chopped fresh flat-leaf (Italian) parsley

☒ Preheat an oven to 350°F (180°C).

☒ Sprinkle the fish fillets with salt and pepper. Place a large cast-iron or other heavy-bottomed frying pan over medium-high heat. When hot, add 3 tablespoons of the olive oil. When the oil is hot, add the fish fillets and sear, turning once, until lightly golden on both sides, 1–2 minutes per side. Transfer the fillets to an ovenproof platter or shallow baking dish and place in the oven to finish cooking until opaque throughout, 3–5 minutes depending upon thickness of fillets.

☒ Meanwhile, add the remaining 5 tablespoons olive oil to the same pan and place over medium-low heat. Add the garlic, the 1 teaspoon salt and the ½ teaspoon black pepper.

Sauté for 1–2 minutes. Add the ancho chili and continue to sauté until fragrant, 1–2 minutes longer. Add the fish stock or clam juice and any juices that have collected in the platter or dish holding the fish fillets and raise the heat to medium-high. Boil until reduced by half, 1–2 minutes. Add the lime juice and parsley and bring to a boil, then remove from the heat.

☒ Pour the sauce over the fish fillets on the platter. Or, if using a baking dish, transfer the fillets to a warmed platter and pour the sauce over the top. Serve immediately.

Serves 6

Grilled Lobster Rosarita

A renowned specialty of seaside cantinas in the Baja California enclave of Rosarita Beach, grilled lobster is served all along the Mexican coast. Maine lobsters and spiny lobsters from tropical waters both work fine. Serve with refried pinto beans, steamed white rice and warm corn tortillas (recipes on pages 226–229).

4	live lobsters, 1½ lbs (750 g) each
	Sea salt to taste, plus 1–2 teaspoons
	Freshly ground black pepper to taste, plus 1 teaspoon
3	tablespoons olive oil
6	shallots, chopped
2	cloves garlic, minced
3	fresh red jalapeño chili peppers, stemmed, seeded and chopped
3	fresh green jalapeño chili peppers, stemmed, seeded and chopped
2	teaspoons ground cumin
2	teaspoons paprika
½	teaspoon cayenne pepper
	Juice of 2 limes
2–4	tablespoons unsalted butter
	Lime wedges

☒ Prepare a fire in a charcoal grill or preheat a broiler (griller).

☒ Using a sharp knife, pierce the lobsters between their eyes to kill them. Working with 1 lobster at a time, place back side up and, starting where the tail and head sections meet, cut in half lengthwise, first cutting the tail portion and then the head. Pull out and discard the intestinal vein and any organs. Season the meat to taste with salt and black pepper. Repeat with the remaining lobsters.

☒ Just before you are ready to cook the lobsters, in a wide sauté pan over medium heat, warm the olive oil. When it is hot, add the shallots and sauté until lightly golden, 3–5 minutes. Add the garlic and the jalapeños and continue to sauté for 1–2 minutes longer. Add the cumin, paprika and cayenne pepper and cook, stirring, until the aromas are released but the spices are not burned, 1–2 minutes. Remove from the heat and stir in the lime juice, butter, 1–2 teaspoons salt and 1 teaspoon black pepper.

☒ Place the lobsters on the grill rack shell side down 3–5 inches (7.5–13 cm) from the coals, or arrange them shell side up on a broiler pan and place in the broiler at the same distance from the heat source. Grill or broil, rotating the lobster halves onto their sides and moving them away from the hottest part of the fire as necessary to prevent burning, until the meat is opaque, about 8 minutes. (Do not turn the meat directly toward the fire at any point.)

☒ Spoon the butter mixture over the lobsters during the last few minutes of grilling. Serve hot with plenty of lime wedges.

Serves 4

Desserts

*C*omida hecha, compañía deshecha, goes an old Mexican saying that censures fair-weather friends: "The meal finished, the company departs." As cantina cooks know from experience, however, there is no better way to hold the attention of a diner than to serve an enticing dessert.

Cantina-style desserts understandably tend toward recipes that can be made ahead of time and keep well, such as moist cakes, rich puddings and iced concoctions. As in the savory courses that come before them, they feature locally grown ingredients, from the citrus fruits of the subtropics to the coconuts and bananas of the tropical regions to the chocolate of the Aztec court. Not surprisingly, good Mexican-grown coffee offers the perfect complement to the naturally assertive flavors.

All of these ingredients, along with those that feature in the other desserts on the following pages, serve another important function, that of soothing the palate after a meal that was more likely than not spiced with chili peppers. Frozen desserts like ice cream or sorbet literally lower the heat, while creamy sweets such as rice pudding or Mexico's national dessert, flan, offer a calming conclusion to such a vibrant repast.

Creamy Lime Pie

The perfect end to a chili-spiced meal, this easy pie cools and soothes the taste buds even as its sharp, citrusy flavor continues to excite them. When choosing limes for the recipe, look for ones that are yellowish and soft when squeezed; they'll provide more juice and more flavor.

1 recipe empanada dough *(recipe on page 140)*, chilled

¾ cup (6 fl oz/180 ml) fresh lime juice

1 lb (500 g) cream cheese, at room temperature

1 can (14 fl oz/440 ml) sweetened condensed milk

Finely grated zest of 1 lime

1 cup (8 fl oz/250 ml) *crema* or crème fraîche

¼ cup (1 oz/30 g) confectioners' (icing) sugar

1 lime, for garnish

☞ On a lightly floured work surface, roll out the dough into a round about 12 inches (30 cm) in diameter and ¼ inch (6 mm) thick. Drape the round over the rolling pin and transfer to a 9- or 10-inch (23- or 25-cm) glass or ceramic pie plate. Ease the pastry into the pie plate, pressing it gently against the bottom and sides. Trim the edges, leaving a generous ½-inch (12-mm) overhang. Fold the overhang under, then crimp the edges decoratively. Cover and chill for 30–60 minutes.

☞ Preheat an oven to 350°F (180°C). Prick the bottom and sides of the pastry with a fork. Line the pastry with parchment (baking) paper or waxed paper, allowing the edges to hang over the sides and fill with pie weights or dried beans. Bake until only very lightly browned, 20–25 minutes. Remove from the oven and immediately remove the weights and paper. Transfer the pie shell to a rack and let cool completely.

☞ In a food processor fitted with the metal blade, combine the lime juice, cream cheese and condensed milk. Process until smooth, scraping down the sides of the work bowl often. Add the lime zest and process to mix thoroughly. Pour into the pie shell and place in the refrigerator.

☞ In a bowl, using a whisk, beat the *crema* or crème fraîche and confectioners' sugar until soft peaks form. Using a rubber spatula, spread the mixture over the top of the pie, creating peaks evenly over the surface. Slice 8 thin rounds from the center of the lime and cut each round once from the center to the edge. Form a twist from each round and place these twists, evenly spaced, on the pie.

☞ Cover and chill for 4–6 hours or as long as overnight before serving.

Makes one 9- or 10-inch (23- or 25-cm) pie; serves 8

Mexican Wedding Cookies

Different regional variations of light, crumbly cookies like these are served on special occasions—be it weddings, christenings or Christmas—throughout Mexico. The fact that you're just as likely to find such recipes in German cookbooks as in Mexican ones is evidence of the cuisine's rich blending of cultures.

1 lb (500 g) unsalted butter, at room temperature

1 cup (4 oz/125 g) confectioners' (icing) sugar, plus extra for dusting

2 tablespoons vanilla extract (essence)

1 teaspoon salt

2 cups (8 oz/250 g) finely chopped pecans

5 cups (15 oz/470 g) sifted cake (soft-wheat) flour

◧ Preheat an oven to 350°F (180°C). Butter 2 baking sheets.

◧ In a bowl, using an electric mixer set on medium speed, beat together the butter and the 1 cup (4 oz/125 g) confectioners' sugar until light and fluffy, 10–15 minutes. Add the vanilla, salt and pecans and beat just until combined. Using a wooden spoon, stir in the flour, being careful not to overmix.

◧ Form the dough into torpedo shapes about the size of small walnuts and place on the prepared baking sheets. Bake just until very lightly browned on the bottoms, 10–12 minutes, switching pan positions halfway through baking.

◧ Remove from the oven and set the baking sheets on wire racks to cool. Place confectioners' sugar in a large bowl. When the cookies are cool enough to handle, place a few at a time in the bowl and toss gently to coat them on all sides. As the cookies continue to cool, occasionally toss them again with sugar, trying to coat with as much sugar as possible. When fully cooled, serve the cookies or place in an airtight container and store at room temperature for up to 1 week.

Makes about 50 cookies

Vanilla Caramel Flan

*The universal dessert of the Mexican cantina, flan offers a true test of baking skill, so keep
your eye on the oven for the perfect moment to remove the custard. This version is extra caramelly;
be sure to cook the sugar very slowly to coax it to just the right degree of darkness.*

CARAMEL
1½ cups (12 oz/375 g) sugar
1   cup (8 fl oz/250 ml) water

FLAN
2   cups (16 fl oz/500 ml) milk
2   cups (16 fl oz/500 ml) half-
     and-half (half cream)
¾   cup (6 oz/185 g) sugar
8   whole eggs, plus 4 egg yolks
1   tablespoon vanilla extract
     (essence)
     Boiling water, as needed

❧ Preheat an oven to 325°F (165°C).

❧ To make the caramel, in a saucepan over medium heat, combine the sugar and water. Cook, swirling the pan occasionally, until the mixture begins to turn golden, 12–15 minutes. Reduce the heat to low and continue cooking and swirling occasionally until the mixture is dark brown and smells of caramel, about 5 minutes.

❧ Remove the caramel from the heat and pour into a 9-inch (23-cm) round cake pan or eight ¾-cup (6-fl oz/180-ml) custard cups. Using a kitchen towel or hot pad, tilt the pan or cups, swirling the caramel to coat the bottom and sides evenly. Let stand for a few minutes; the caramel will cool down and form a layer about ¼ inch (6 mm) thick on the bottom and sides. Then pour the excess caramel back into the saucepan it was cooked in.

❧ To make the flan, pour the milk into the saucepan holding the excess caramel and place over low heat. Cook, stirring frequently, until the caramel has dissolved in the milk, 3–5 minutes. Strain the warm milk mixture through a fine-mesh sieve set over a bowl. Add the half-and-half and stir to mix well. Add the sugar, whole eggs and egg yolks, and vanilla. Whisk until blended, then strain through the fine-mesh sieve into the prepared pan or cups. Set the pan or cups in a roasting pan and place the roasting pan in the oven. Pour boiling water into the roasting pan to reach halfway up the sides of the cake pan or custard cups.

❧ Bake until the center of the custard(s) feel just firm when pressed gently with the fingertips, 45–55 minutes for the large pan or 30–40 minutes for the individual cups. Remove from the oven and let cool for about 1½ hours. Then cover with plastic wrap and refrigerate overnight or for up to 4 days.

❧ To serve, run a knife along the inside edge of the pan or cups to loosen. Invert a serving dish over the pan or a saucer over each cup. Quickly invert and carefully lift off the pan or cup. Carefully pour excess caramel into a small sauce pitcher.

❧ Serve chilled. Offer the extra caramel alongside.

Serves 8

Spiced Apple Cake with Guava Cream Cheese

This fragrant spice cake, laden with fresh apples, goes together quickly. If you can't find guava jam in your area, feel free to substitute plum, cherry or any other preserves you have on hand. The cake is also terrific at brunch, where it pairs well with a cup of great coffee.

CAKE

2 eggs
1 cup (8 fl oz/250 ml) vegetable oil
¼ cup (2 fl oz/60 ml) fresh orange juice
2 cups (1 lb/500 g) sugar
2 cups (10 oz/315 g) all-purpose (plain) flour
4 teaspoons ground cinnamon
1 teaspoon salt
2 teaspoons baking soda (bicarbonate of soda)
4 cups (1 lb/500 g) peeled, cored and finely chopped Granny Smith or other tart green apples (about 4 apples)
1 cup (4 oz/125 g) walnuts, coarsely chopped

GUAVA CREAM CHEESE

¼ cup (3 oz/90 g) guava jam
1 tablespoon fresh lime juice
⅔ cup (5 oz/155 g) cream cheese, at room temperature

☙ Preheat an oven to 325°F (165°C). Butter and flour a 10-inch (25-cm) round cake pan.

☙ To make the cake, in a bowl and using an electric mixer set on medium speed, beat the eggs until frothy, 3–4 minutes. Add the vegetable oil and orange juice and mix thoroughly. In a separate bowl, stir together the sugar, flour, cinnamon, salt and baking soda. Add the flour mixture to the egg mixture and beat on low speed until thoroughly combined. Fold in the apples and walnuts.

☙ Pour the batter into the prepared pan. Bake until firm to the touch and a toothpick inserted into the center comes out clean, about 1 hour; cover the top with aluminum foil if it begins to overbrown. Remove from the oven and let cool in the pan on a rack for 5 minutes, then invert onto the rack. Let cool completely.

☙ Meanwhile, make the guava cream cheese: In a bowl, combine the jam, lime juice and cream cheese. Using a fork, mash and stir briskly until light and fluffy.

☙ To serve, place the cake on a serving plate. Using an icing spatula or knife, spread the guava cream cheese evenly over the top.

Makes one 10-inch (25-cm) cake; serves 8

Tangerine Sorbet in Chocolate Shells

*After a feast, when you think you couldn't eat even one more bite, this superb sorbet
makes a perfect dessert. Fruit ices are popular in Mexico, and this version heralds the abundant
tangerine season. The lacy chocolate cups dress up the dessert for a special dinner party.*

SORBET
2   tablespoons grated tangerine zest
3½ cups (28 fl oz/875 ml) fresh tangerine juice (18–20 tangerines)
½   cup (4 fl oz/125 ml) fresh lemon juice (3 or 4 lemons)
1¼ cups (10 oz/315 g) sugar
¼   cup (2½ fl oz/75 ml) light corn syrup

SHELLS
½   cup (2 oz/60 g) ground blanched almonds
½   cup (2½ oz/75 g) all-purpose (plain) flour
¼   cup (2½ fl oz/75 ml) light corn syrup
¼   cup (2 oz/60 g) sugar
¼   cup (2 oz/60 g) unsalted butter
1   oz (30 g) unsweetened chocolate
½   teaspoon vanilla extract (essence)

Shredded tangerine zest for garnish, optional

☒ To make the sorbet, in a bowl, combine the tangerine zest and juice, lemon juice, sugar and corn syrup. Stir until the sugar dissolves. Transfer to an ice cream maker and freeze according to the manufacturer's instructions. Pack into a freezer container and place in the freezer until set, 2–4 hours.

☒ Preheat an oven to 350°F (180°C). Butter a baking sheet.

☒ To make the shells, in a bowl, stir together the almonds and flour until thoroughly mixed. In a small, heavy-bottomed saucepan over low heat, combine the corn syrup, sugar, butter and chocolate. Heat, stirring constantly, until the mixture just comes to a boil. Remove from the heat and stir in the vanilla. Add the flour mixture and stir until fully blended.

☒ Drop the dough by tablespoonfuls onto the prepared baking sheet, leaving at least 3 inches (7.5 cm) on all sides to allow room for spreading and forming no more than 4 shells on the sheet. Bake until they spread out and are lacy, 8–10 minutes. Remove from the oven and let cool for 1–1½ minutes. Using a thin metal spatula, lift the baked rounds from the baking sheet and drape each round over an inverted coffee cup. Let cool completely, then carefully lift off the shells and set aside. Repeat with the remaining dough, to form 8 shells in all. (The shells can be stored in an airtight container for up to 3 days.)

☒ To serve, place the shells on small dessert plates. Fill each shell with an equal amount of the sorbet and garnish with tangerine zest, if desired. Serve immediately.

Serves 8

Date Ice Cream with Almond Crunch Topping

Ultrasweet dates, a favorite Mexican sweet, always seem to prompt a craving for ice-cold milk, so it makes perfect sense to feature them in this milky concoction. The crunchy topping will keep for weeks in an airtight container in the refrigerator, ready for any sundae you make.

TOPPING
½   cup (1½ oz/45 g) old-fashioned rolled oats
½   cup (2½ oz/75 g) hulled pumpkin seeds
½   cup (2½ oz/75 g) chopped almonds
1½ tablespoons vegetable oil
1½ tablespoons honey
1½ tablespoons apple juice
⅛   teaspoon salt

ICE CREAM
2   cups (16 fl oz/500 ml) nonfat milk
1   lb (500 g) fresh dates, preferably medjool
6   egg yolks
¾   cup (6 oz/185 g) firmly packed brown sugar
3   cups (24 fl oz/750 ml) half-and-half (half cream)
2   teaspoons vanilla extract (essence)

✎ To make the topping, preheat an oven to 300°F (150°C). Lightly oil a baking sheet or line it with parchment (baking) paper.

✎ In a bowl, combine the oats, pumpkin seeds and almonds and stir to mix. In a small saucepan over low heat, combine the vegetable oil, honey, apple juice and salt and stir until combined, the salt has dissolved and the mixture is warm. Pour the warm honey mixture over the oat mixture and toss to coat evenly. Spread out the mixture on the prepared baking sheet and bake, stirring occasionally, until golden, about 20 minutes. Transfer to a rack and let cool, then pack in a small airtight container and place in a freezer until needed.

✎ To make the ice cream, pour the milk into a saucepan and place over low heat. Heat, stirring often with a wooden spoon, until only 1 cup (8 fl oz/250 ml) remains, about 20 minutes. Remove from the heat and let cool completely.

✎ Remove the pits from the dates and chop into pea-sized pieces. Place half of the pieces on a plate and place in the freezer until needed. Place the remaining date pieces in a blender, add the cooled milk and purée until smooth.

✎ In a bowl, combine the egg yolks and brown sugar and whisk vigorously until lemon colored. In a saucepan, bring the half-and-half to a rolling boil and immediately pour over the yolk mixture while whisking constantly. Add the date-milk mixture and the vanilla, mix well and set aside to cool completely.

✎ Transfer to an ice cream maker and freeze according to the manufacturer's instructions. Stir the reserved date pieces into the ice cream and pack into a freezer container. Place in the freezer until set, 2–4 hours.

✎ To serve, scoop into chilled ice cream dishes, top with the almond crunch topping and serve at once.

Makes 1½ qt (1.5 l); serves 6

Banana Coconut Cake

Sweet bananas are grown predominantly along the Gulf Coast, where they are frequently cooked with butter and sugar and then flambéed. This extra-moist cake combines them with coconut, a favorite ingredient in Mexican candies. Look for wide shards of flaked coconut in health food stores.

CAKE
¾ cup (6 oz/185 g) plus 2 tablespoons unsalted butter, at room
   temperature
1½ cups (12 oz/375 g) sugar
3 eggs
½ cup (4 fl oz/125 ml) buttermilk
1⅓ cups (11 oz/345 g) mashed ripe
   banana
2½ cups (7½ oz/235 g) sifted cake
   (soft-wheat) flour
1 teaspoon baking powder
¾ teaspoon salt
¾ teaspoon baking soda (bicarbonate
   of soda)
½ cup (2 oz/60 g) finely chopped
   pecans

CUSTARD
¾ cup (6 fl oz/180 ml) plus 1
   tablespoon unsweetened
   coconut milk
1 cup (8 fl oz/250 ml) whole milk
½ cup (4 oz/125 g) sugar
¼ cup (1 oz/30 g) cornstarch
   (cornflour)
4 egg yolks

TO ASSEMBLE CAKE
3 bananas, peeled and sliced
¼ cup (2 fl oz/60 ml) lemon juice
2 tablespoons sugar
1 cup (4 oz/125 g) unsweetened
   flaked or shredded dried coconut,
   toasted *(see glossary, page 342)*

◨ Preheat an oven to 350°F (180°C). Butter and flour two 9-inch (23-cm) round cake pans. To make the cake, in a large bowl and using an electric mixer set on medium speed, beat together the butter and sugar until light and fluffy, about 10 minutes. Beat in the eggs, one at a time. Continue beating until very light and fluffy, about 10 minutes longer. Mix in the buttermilk and mashed banana.

◨ In a separate bowl, sift together the flour, baking powder, salt and baking soda. Add the flour mixture to the butter mixture and beat on low speed just until moistened. Increase the speed to medium and beat for 1 minute. Then, using a wooden spoon, fold in the pecans.

◨ Pour the batter into the prepared pans, dividing it evenly. Bake until a toothpick inserted into the center comes out clean, 25–35 minutes. Transfer to racks and let cool in pans for 5 minutes, then invert the cakes onto the racks to cool completely.

◨ Meanwhile, make the custard: Line a rimmed baking sheet with parchment (baking) paper or plastic wrap and set aside. In a heavy sauce-pan, combine the coconut milk and whole milk and bring to a boil. Remove from the heat and set aside.

In a bowl, stir together the sugar and cornstarch. Add the eggs yolks and stir briskly until blended. Whisk half of the hot milk into the sugar-yolk mixture to temper it, then whisk the sugar-yolk mixture into the remaining hot milk in the saucepan. Place over medium heat and cook, stirring constantly, until smooth and thick, 3–4 minutes. Spread the custard on the prepared baking sheet; cover with a sheet of parchment paper or plastic wrap to prevent a skin from forming. Refrigerate until cool.

◨ Preheat an oven to 350°F (180°C).

◨ To assemble the cake, in a bowl, toss the banana slices with the lemon juice and sugar. Trim the top of a cake layer so that it is level and place on a serving plate. Spread with a thin layer of the custard, arrange the banana slices on top, and then spread a thin layer of custard over the bananas. Place the second cake layer on top, bottom down, and spread the top with the remaining custard. Garnish with the coconut, mounding it on top. Serve at once or cover and refrig-erate for up to 24 hours.

Makes one 9-inch (23-cm) cake; serves 8

Kahlúa Chocolate Bread Pudding

Everybody in Mexico loves chocolate, which is often partnered with the taste of cinnamon and coffee. Here, those three flavors combine in a bread pudding that, although rustic in origin, makes an elegant presentation when served warm with a drizzle of Kahlúa sauce and whipped cream.

STREUSEL

1	cup (4 oz/125 g) pecans
¼	cup (2 oz/60 g) firmly packed brown sugar
¼	cup (1½ oz/45 g) all-purpose (plain) flour
1	teaspoon ground cinnamon
¼	teaspoon salt
3	tablespoons chilled unsalted butter

PUDDING

4	oz (125 g) unsweetened chocolate
¾	cup (6 oz/185 g) firmly packed brown sugar
1½	cups (12 fl oz/375 ml) heavy (double) cream

CUSTARD

6	whole eggs, plus 2 egg yolks
¾	cup (6 oz/185 g) granulated sugar
1	teaspoon vanilla extract (essence)
¾	loaf day-old French bread, about ¾ lb (375 g), cut into ½-inch (12-mm) cubes

SAUCE

6	tablespoons (3 oz/90 g) unsalted butter
1	cup (8 fl oz/250 ml) Kahlúa or other coffee liqueur
½	cup (4 oz/125 g) granulated sugar
1	egg

Unsweetened whipped cream

☜ To make the streusel, preheat an oven to 325°F (165°C). Spread the pecans on a baking sheet and toast until lightly browned and fragrant, about 10 minutes. Remove from the oven, let cool and chop coarsely. Leave the oven set at 325°F (165°C). In a bowl, combine the nuts, brown sugar, flour, cinnamon, salt and butter. Using your fingertips, mix until crumbly. Set aside in a cool place.

☜ To make the pudding, butter an 8½-by-4½-inch (21.5-by-11.5-cm) glass loaf pan and dust with granulated sugar. Place the chocolate in a heatproof bowl and set over (not touching) simmering water in a pan. Heat, stirring constantly, until the chocolate melts. Add the brown sugar and cream and whisk until smooth. Remove from the heat and set aside.

☜ To make the custard, in a large bowl, combine the whole eggs and egg yolks, sugar and vanilla. Whisk until well mixed. Add about ½ cup (4 fl oz/125 ml) of the custard to the chocolate mixture to temper it, whisking vigorously. Then add the chocolate mixture to the remaining custard and whisk until blended. Add the bread cubes, stir to coat evenly and let stand until the bread has absorbed the liquid, about 15 minutes.

☜ Pour the pudding-custard mixture into the prepared loaf pan. Top evenly with the pecan streusel and set in a roasting pan. Place in the oven and add boiling water to reach halfway up the sides of the loaf pan. Bake until the center feels slightly firm to the touch, about 2 hours.

☜ While the pudding is baking, make the sauce: Place the butter in a heatproof bowl over (not touching) simmering water in a pan. When the butter has melted, add the Kahlúa and sugar and whisk until the sugar has dissolved. Whisk in the egg and cook over simmering water until slightly thickened, about 10 minutes. Strain through a fine-mesh sieve into a serving pitcher.

☜ Remove the pudding from the oven and let cool slightly. Cut into 6–8 equal pieces and place on dessert plates. Pour a pool of the Kahlúa sauce along one side of each piece of pudding and place a spoonful of whipped cream on the other side. Serve at once.

Serves 6–8

221

Rum Raisin Rice Pudding

Rice pudding runs a close second to flan (recipe on page 210) as Mexico's favorite dessert. While some special-occasion versions might add a splash of brandy to the recipe, this variation nods to the Caribbean by including raisins that have been plumped in rum.

1   cup (7 oz/220 g) short-grain white rice
4   cups (32 fl oz/1 l) nonfat milk
4   cinnamon sticks
1   can (14 fl oz/440 ml) sweetened condensed milk
1   vanilla bean, split lengthwise
    Ice water, as needed
¾   cup (6 fl oz/180 ml) dark rum
1   cup (6 oz/185 g) golden raisins (sultanas)
    Ground cinnamon

☒ Rinse the rice in several changes of water until the water runs clear. Drain well.

☒ In a saucepan, combine the nonfat milk and cinnamon sticks and bring to a boil over medium-high heat. Add the rice and return to a boil. Reduce the heat to medium-low and cook uncovered, stirring occasionally, until the centers of the grains are just barely soft, 12–15 minutes.

☒ Add the sweetened condensed milk to the rice mixture and then scrape the seeds from the vanilla bean halves into the pan. Add the vanilla pods as well, stir to combine, cover and continue to simmer over low heat until the rice is plump and tender and the sauce is the consistency of heavy (double) cream, 10–15 minutes longer. Remove from the heat and place over a bowl of ice water to stop the cooking. Stir the mixture occasionally as it cools. When cool, discard the vanilla pods and cinnamon sticks, transfer to a bowl, cover and refrigerate until well chilled, about 2 hours.

☒ Meanwhile, in a heavy-bottomed saucepan over low heat, combine the rum and raisins. Simmer until the raisins have plumped and the rum is almost gone, about 5 minutes. Remove from the heat and let cool.

☒ Fold the raisins into the chilled rice pudding. Serve icy cold with a dusting of ground cinnamon on top.

Serves 4–6

Chocolate Nut Tart

Really a pecan pie with a Mexican twist, this luscious tart is perfect for holiday entertaining. Although elegant, it is also heartwarmingly homey, which explains why you might also see something like it on the countertop of a Mexico City cafetería, ready to be served to the lunchtime crowd.

PASTRY DOUGH

½ cup (4 oz/125 g) unsalted butter, at room temperature

1⅓ cups (5½ oz/170 g) confectioners' (icing) sugar

1 egg

1 teaspoon salt

1¾ cups (9 oz/280 g) all-purpose (plain) flour

FILLING

3 eggs

¾ cup (5½ oz/170 g) firmly packed brown sugar

½ cup (5 fl oz/155 ml) dark corn syrup

2 tablespoons dark molasses

6 tablespoons (3 oz/90 g) unsalted butter, melted

2 teaspoons vanilla extract (essence)

2 teaspoons ground cinnamon

1 teaspoon salt

2 cups (9 oz/280 g) slivered blanched almonds

¾ cup (4 oz/125 g) chopped semisweet chocolate

Unsweetened whipped cream

☒ To make the pastry dough, in a bowl, combine the butter and confectioners' sugar. Using a wooden spoon, cream together until very light and fluffy. Add the egg and salt and beat until combined. Add the flour and stir until the mixture comes together to form a dough. Divide the dough in half and pat each half into a ball. Wrap in plastic wrap and refrigerate 1 ball for 2–3 hours or as long as overnight. Reserve the other half to make another tart; it can be frozen for up to 2 months.

☒ Preheat an oven to 325°F (165°C).

☒ On a lightly floured work surface, roll out the ball of dough into a round about 12 inches (30 cm) in diameter and ⅛–¼ inch (3–6 mm) thick. Drape the round over the rolling pin and transfer to a 10-inch (25-cm) tart pan with a removable bottom. Ease the pastry into the tart pan, pressing it gently against the bottom and sides. Trim the edges even with the pan rim. Place in the refrigerator to chill for 15 minutes.

☒ Prick the bottom and sides of the pastry with a fork. Bake until golden, 10–12 minutes. Transfer to a rack to cool. Leave the oven set at 325°F (165°C).

☒ To make the filling, in a large bowl, whisk together the eggs, brown sugar, corn syrup, molasses, melted butter, vanilla and cinnamon until well blended. Add the salt, almonds and chocolate and mix to coat evenly.

☒ Pour the filling into the tart shell and bake until the center is set, 35–40 minutes. To test, press gently on top with your fingertips. Transfer to a rack and let cool.

☒ To serve, remove the pan sides and, using a spatula, slide off the pan bottom onto a serving plate. Cut into wedges and serve with whipped cream.

Makes one 10-inch (25-cm) tart; serves 6–8

BASIC RECIPES

Four basic foods serve as the cornerstones of virtually any cantina meal. Tortillas made from cornmeal or wheat flour are the bread of Mexico. Chili-laced salsas season almost every savory dish, whether during cooking or at the dining table. Beans and rice are such staples that, accompanied with tortillas and salsa, they can form a humble but nutritious meal on their own.

CORN TORTILLAS
TORTILLAS DE MAIZ

The basic bread of Mexico, freshly made corn tortillas have a rich, earthy aroma and a wonderful flavor to which store-bought varieties simply can't compare. Masa harina, *a Mexican-style cornmeal, provides authentic flavor and texture. A* comal, *an old-fashioned Mexican stove-top griddle, is the ideal cooking surface, although any griddle or pan will do just fine.*

2 cups (10 oz/315 g) *masa harina*
   Pinch of salt
1 cup (8 fl oz/250 ml) lukewarm
   water, or as needed

☒ In a large bowl, combine the *masa harina* and salt. Gradually stir in the 1 cup (8 fl oz/250 ml) lukewarm water until smooth. The dough should be slightly sticky and form a ball when pressed together. To test, flatten a small ball of dough between your palms or 2 sheets of plastic wrap. If the edges crack, add more lukewarm water, a little at a time, until the edges are smooth.

☒ Divide the dough into 12 or 18 pieces, depending upon the size tortillas you need. Roll each piece into a ball. Place the balls on a plate and cover with a damp kitchen towel. Heat a dry griddle, cast-iron frying pan, heavy nonstick pan or *comal* (see note above) over medium heat.

☒ *To form tortillas with a tortilla press,* slit open a heavy-duty plastic bag and use the plastic to line the lower surface of an opened tortilla press, allowing it to extend slightly beyond the edges. Place a ball of dough in the center of the press, top with a second piece of plastic and close the press to flatten the dough. Open the press and carefully peel off the plastic.

☒ *To form tortillas with a rolling pin,* flatten the ball of dough between 2 sheets of plastic wrap on a work surface and roll out to a thickness of about 1/16 inch (2 mm).

☒ Lay the tortillas, one at a time, on the preheated griddle or pan and cook, pressing the top gently with your fingertips to make it puff and turning once, until it appears cooked but not browned, 30–45 seconds on each side.

☒ As the tortillas are cooked, transfer them to a kitchen towel and let cool briefly, then stack and wrap in the towel to keep moist and warm.

When all the tortillas are cooked, serve immediately. Or let cool, wrap in plastic wrap and store in the refrigerator for up to 1 week. To reheat for serving, sprinkle each tortilla with a few drops of water and heat on a preheated nonstick pan for 10–15 seconds on each side. Stack on a kitchen towel and wrap to keep warm until serving.

Makes twelve 6-inch (15-cm) tortillas or eighteen 4-inch (10-cm) tortillas

FLOUR TORTILLAS
TORTILLAS DE HARINA

Only slightly more difficult to make than corn tortillas, because of the increased elasticity of the dough, these thin wheat-flour disks of northern Mexico are wonderful served with grilled meats. If you like, you can shape them a day or two in advance and store them in the refrigerator, to be cooked just before serving.

2½ cups (12½ oz/390 g) all-purpose (plain) flour
⅓   cup (3 oz/90 g) plus 2 tablespoons vegetable shortening
1   teaspoon salt
1   cup (8 fl oz/250 ml) warm water

In a bowl, combine the flour, shortening and salt. Using your fingers, rub the ingredients together until completely combined and the mixture looks crumbly. Mix in the warm water until the ingredients come together in a ball. Knead the dough in the bowl until smooth, about 3 minutes.

Divide the dough into 12 equal pieces and roll each piece into a ball. Place the balls on a plate and cover with a kitchen towel or plastic wrap. Let rest in the refrigerator for at least 30 minutes or as long as overnight.

On a lightly floured board, roll out each ball into a thin 6-inch (15-cm) round, frequently turning the rounds over to prevent sticking. Lay the rounds in a single layer on the lightly floured board, cover with kitchen towels and let rest for 30 minutes. Or stack between pieces of parchment (baking) paper or waxed paper, wrap well in plastic wrap and refrigerate for up to 2 days.

To cook, heat a dry griddle or heavy nonstick frying pan over medium heat. One at a time, cook the tortillas, turning once, until puffy and slightly golden, 30–45 seconds on each side. Transfer to a platter lined with a kit-chen towel and let cool briefly, then stack and wrap in a damp towel to keep warm.

When all the tortillas are cooked, serve immediately. Or let cool, wrap in plastic wrap and store in the refrigerator for up to 5 days. To reheat, wrap the tortillas in aluminum foil and place in a preheated 350°F (180°C) oven for about 15 minutes.

Makes twelve 6-inch (15-cm) tortillas

ÁRBOL SALSA
SALSA DE CHILE DE ÁRBOL

This salsa pairs the rich complexity of roasted tomatoes and tomatillos with peppery árbol chilies. Serve with any dish in need of spice.

1   lb (500 g) plum (Roma) tomatoes, cored
½   lb (250 g) tomatillos, husked
½   cup (1 oz/30 g) dried árbol chili peppers, seeded
1   bunch fresh cilantro (fresh coriander), stemmed
½   small yellow onion, sliced
3   cloves garlic, sliced
1   cup (8 fl oz/250 ml) water
2   teaspoons salt

Preheat a broiler (griller). Place the tomatoes and tomatillos in a shallow baking pan. Broil (grill), turning occasionally, until charred on all sides, 10–12 minutes.

In a small, dry frying pan over medium heat, toast the chilies, turning once, until the skins begin to blister, 3–5 minutes. Transfer the chilies to a saucepan and add the tomatoes, cilantro, onion, garlic, water and salt. Bring to a boil, reduce the heat to medium and simmer until the chilies are soft, 10–12 minutes.

Let cool, then transfer to a blender. Purée until smooth, then strain through a sieve placed over a bowl. Serve warm or at room temperature. To store, cover and refrigerate for up to 5 days or freeze for up to 1 month.

Makes about 2½ cups (20 fl oz/625 ml)

RED SALSA

SALSA ROJA

This all-purpose cooked salsa forms a simple dip for chips, a topping for tacos or enchiladas, a pool of sauce for chiles rellenos or a key flavoring in soups, rices and stews. Variations couldn't be easier: substitute smoky chipotle chilies for the jalapeños, for example, or add chopped cilantro just before serving to give it a fresher flavor.

2 tablespoons vegetable oil
1 yellow onion, thinly sliced
2 cloves garlic, sliced
1 fresh jalapeño chili pepper, stemmed, seeded and thinly sliced
1 teaspoon salt, or to taste
2 cups (12 oz/375 g) canned plum (Roma) tomatoes with their juices

☙ In a saucepan over medium heat, warm the vegetable oil. Add the onion and sauté until soft, about 10 minutes. Add the garlic, chili pepper and salt and cook for 2 minutes longer. Add the tomatoes and their juices and reduce the heat to low. Cook the tomatoes, stirring occasionally to break them up, until soft and the juices have reduced by half, 10–15 minutes.

☙ Let cool slightly, then transfer to a blender. Purée until smooth, then strain through a sieve placed over a bowl. Set aside to cool completely for use as a table salsa. Or reheat gently over low heat to use hot. To store, cover tightly and keep in the refrigerator for up to 4 days or in the freezer for up to 1 month.

Makes about 2 cups (16 fl oz/500 ml)

GREEN SALSA

SALSA VERDE

Bottled green salsa can't compare to freshly made. Whether you use it as a dip, on empanadas or tacos, or cooked in soups or stews, its piquant character perfectly perks up rich flavors.

¾ lb (375 g) tomatillos, husked and quartered
2 fresh serrano chili peppers, coarsely chopped
¼ small yellow onion, sliced
⅓ cup (3 fl oz/80 ml) water
1 teaspoon salt, or as needed
⅓ cup (⅓ oz/10 g) coarsely chopped fresh cilantro (fresh coriander)

☙ In a blender or food processor fitted with the metal blade, combine the tomatillos, chilies, onion and water; process briefly until chunky. Add the 1 teaspoon salt and the cilantro and purée until no large chunks remain, about 2 minutes longer.

☙ Taste and add more salt, if needed. Pour into a bowl and serve, or cover and refrigerate for up to 3 days.

Makes about 2 cups (16 fl oz/500 ml)

REFRIED BEANS

FRIJOLES REFRITOS

No Mexican meal is complete without this creamy staple. Although pinto beans fried in lard are the more traditional choice, black beans fried in vegetable oil meet the more health-conscious demands of today. The beans go best with rice.

2 cups (14 oz/440 g) dried black or pinto beans
8 cups (64 fl oz/2 l) water
⅔ cup (5 oz/155 g) lard or (5 fl oz/160 ml) vegetable oil
1 large yellow onion, diced
1–2 teaspoons salt
½ teaspoon freshly ground pepper
   Fresh cilantro (fresh coriander) leaves, optional

☙ Sort through the beans and discard any misshapen beans or stones. Rinse well. Place the beans in a saucepan and add the water. Bring to a boil, reduce the heat to medium-low, cover and simmer until the smallest beans are cooked through and creamy inside, about 1½ hours.

☙ Remove the beans from the heat. Using a potato masher, mash the beans with their cooking liquid until evenly mashed.

☙ In a sauté pan over medium heat, warm the lard or oil. Add all but about ¼ cup (1¼ oz/38 g) of the

diced onion, salt to taste and pepper and sauté briskly until the onion is translucent and just begins to brown, about 10 minutes. Add the mashed beans and cook, stirring, until the excess liquid evaporates and the beans begin to pull away from the pan sides, about 10 minutes. Cook without stirring until a thin layer of the mashed beans begins to stick to the pan bottom. Scrape up the layer and reincorporate it into the beans. Repeat this step 2 or 3 times, allowing the beans to begin to stick and then scraping them up, until the beans are thick and creamy.

☒ To serve, spoon the beans onto a warmed platter or individual plates and top with the reserved diced onion. Garnish with cilantro, if desired, and serve hot. Store leftover beans, covered, in the refrigerator for up to 4 days. To reheat, return the beans to a wide sauté pan, add a little water and place over medium heat, stirring constantly to heat evenly.

Makes 3–4 cups (24–32 fl oz/ 750 ml–1 l); serves 4–6

STEAMED RICE

ARROZ BLANCO AL VAPOR

Rice was first carried to Mexico on the sixteenth-century Spanish trade galleons that plied the waters between Manila and Acapulco. It has been an integral part of the diet ever since, often paired with the country's ubiquitous beans.

2 cups (14 oz/440 g) long-grain white rice
3 cups (24 fl oz/750 ml) water
2 tablespoons unsalted butter
1 teaspoon salt

☒ Place the rice in a large bowl (not a colander) and rinse under cold running water for 5 minutes. Drain.

☒ In a saucepan, bring the water to a boil. Add the butter, rice and salt and return to a boil. Reduce the heat to low, cover and cook until the water is absorbed, about 20 minutes.

☒ Remove from the heat and let stand, covered, for a few minutes. Fluff with a fork and serve.

Makes about 5 cups (25 oz/780 g); serves 4–6

RED OR GREEN RICE

ARROZ ROJO O VERDE

These two rice dishes make colorful, tasty accompaniments to simple grilled meats and fish.

2 cups (14 oz/440 g) long-grain white rice
¼ cup (2 fl oz/60 ml) vegetable oil
1 yellow onion, diced
2 cloves garlic, minced
1½ cups (12 fl oz/375 ml) chicken stock
1½ cups (12 fl oz/375 ml) red salsa plus 2 or 3 fresh whole red serrano chili peppers, for red rice
1 cup (8 fl oz/250 ml) green salsa puréed with 3 fresh poblano chili peppers, roasted and peeled *(see glossary, page 342),* for green rice

☒ Place the rice in a large bowl (not a colander) and rinse under cold running water for 5 minutes. Drain.

☒ In a saucepan over high heat, warm the oil. Add the onion and garlic and sauté until golden, about 5 minutes. Add the rice and sauté for 5 minutes longer. Pour in the chicken stock.

☒ For red rice, add the red salsa and serrano chilies; for green rice, add the green salsa and poblano chilies. Bring to a boil. Reduce the heat to low, cover and cook until the stock is absorbed, about 20 minutes.

☒ Remove from the heat and let stand, covered, for a few minutes. Fluff with a fork and serve.

Makes about 5 cups (25 oz/780 g); serves 4–6

ASIAN

Wherever there exists an empty spot in the midst of busy street traffic, the intrepid Asian street vendor sets up a "sidewalk cafe," complete with tottering table, folding stools and mismatched dishes. Within minutes, the grill is fired up, and tempting aromas entice hungry customers to grab an empty seat and indulge in delicious street fare.

In the beginning, Asian street foods were primarily snack foods—a crisp onion pancake in Taiwan, a curried vegetable samosa in Singapore, a corn and shrimp fritter in Indonesia, a pork bun in China. Today, the definition has expanded to encompass more substantial offerings as well. These might include such complete meals as Cantonese *won ton mein* (noodle and dumpling soup), Thai *mee grob* (crispy noodles), Indonesian *rendang daging* (dry beef curry), Malaysian *laksa* (curry noodles) and Singaporean chili crab.

Since street food recipes originated in the home, they easily make the return journey. The recipes in this section are versatile—from a collection of appetizers that can be offered with cocktails or served together as a light meal, to cafe salads and soups that can be mixed and matched for lunch or dinner. However you compose your menu, these Asian favorites celebrate the spirit of casual dining.

Snacks and Appetizers

Asians are inveterate noshers. From early morning until late at night, they are easily lured into a bit of culinary pleasure by the slightest appetizing aroma that wafts in their direction. They eat like birds—little meals, several times a day. Vendors selling irresistible offerings of these little finger foods are found along the sidewalks of most Asian cities. One might detour for a banana fritter, maybe some satay, a piece of onion bread or a crisp samosa to take off the edge of hunger just before dinner, in the mid-afternoon, or after the cinema. These goodies are among the small yet immeasurable pleasures of life—treats eaten on the run that deliver immediate gratification.

When Asians think of a snack or appetizer, they consider some rather substantial preparations as well. A stir-fried noodle dish, a hearty chicken soup crowned with potato patties, a fruit and vegetable salad, a mound of fried rice or a lotus leaf parcel plump with rice and chicken are all deemed snacks by Asian standards, and they can be found elsewhere in this book. These robust offerings are eaten at all hours of the day and may easily constitute a light meal.

Whether you whip up a fritter from Indonesia or an omelet from Vietnam in your kitchen, you will be savoring a fascinating delicacy of the Far East.

Steamed Pork Baskets

These tasty dumplings are among the most popular and quickest selling of all Chinese appetizers, a fact that has earned them the name siu mai, *or "cook-and-sell" dumplings. Except for their round shape, the thin dough sheets used for making them are identical to square wonton wrappers, which may be substituted.*

FILLING

4   dried Chinese black mushrooms, soaked in warm water to cover for 30 minutes
1   lb (500 g) coarsely chopped pork butt
¾   lb (375 g) shrimp (prawns), peeled, deveined, patted dry and coarsely chopped
¼   cup (1¼ oz/37 g) finely chopped bamboo shoots
1½   tablespoons light soy sauce
¼   cup (2 fl oz/60 ml) chicken stock
1   tablespoon cornstarch (cornflour)
1   teaspoon salt
1½   teaspoons sugar
      Pinch of ground white pepper
1½   teaspoons Asian sesame oil

½   lb (250 g) *siu mai* wrappers or wonton wrappers (about 48 wrappers)
      Vegetable oil

◙ To make the filling, remove the mushrooms from the water and squeeze dry. Cut off the stems and discard. Finely chop the caps and place in a bowl. Add the pork, shrimp, bamboo shoots, soy sauce, chicken stock, cornstarch, salt, sugar, white pepper and sesame oil. Stir to mix well. Cover and refrigerate for at least 3 hours or as long as overnight.

◙ Place 1 tablespoon of the filling in the middle of a wrapper. (If using wonton wrappers, trim the corners with scissors to make rounds.) Bring the edges of the wrapper up and around the filling. With your index finger and thumb, pinch tiny pleats around the sides to form a straight-sided fluted basket. Tap down the filling to firm it up and leave the top open-faced. Wrap your index finger around the midsection to give the basket a waist, then tap the bottom of the dumpling against the counter-top so that it flattens slightly and can stand on its own. Set on a baking sheet, cover with a sheet of waxed paper and continue making the dumplings with the remaining wrappers and filling.

◙ Bring a wok half full of water to a boil. Grease the bottom of a bamboo steaming basket or a heatproof plate with vegetable oil. Arrange the dumplings in the basket or on the plate, keeping them separate. Set the steaming basket in the wok or the plate on a rack in the wok; cover and steam over (not touching) the boiling water for 15 minutes.

◙ Remove the basket or plate from the steamer and serve the dumplings hot or at room temperature. Store any leftovers in the refrigerator for up to 5 days. Reheat by steaming for 5 minutes or place in a microwave for 1 minute on high power.

Makes about 48 dumplings

Fish Cakes with Pickled Cucumber Relish

Asian fish cakes tend to have a spongy texture that appeals to the Asian palate. They are traditionally made with a mild whitefish, although salmon makes a delicious substitute. Fresh fish paste, ground daily, can be found at better Asian fish markets; or make your own by grinding fish fillets in a food processor at home.

RELISH

⅓ cup (3 fl oz/80 ml) distilled white vinegar
¼ cup (2 oz/60 g) sugar
1 teaspoon salt
¼ cup (2 fl oz/60 ml) water
1 English (hothouse) cucumber
1 large shallot, thinly sliced
1 fresh small red chili pepper, seeded and chopped
1 teaspoon dried shrimp powder, optional
1 tablespoon coarsely chopped fresh cilantro (fresh coriander)
1 tablespoon coarsely chopped dry-roasted peanuts

FISH CAKES

1 lb (500 g) salmon fillets or whitefish paste *(see note above)*
1 tablespoon Thai fish sauce
2 teaspoons Thai roasted chili paste *(nam prik pao)* or 1½ teaspoons red curry paste *(recipe on page 337)*
1 egg, lightly beaten
¼ teaspoon salt
1 tablespoon cornstarch (cornflour)
¼ lb (125 g) green beans, trimmed and cut crosswise into slices ⅛ inch (3 mm) thick
2 tablespoons coarsely chopped fresh cilantro (fresh coriander)
Peanut or vegetable oil for frying

◙ To make the cucumber relish, in a saucepan over medium heat, combine the vinegar, sugar, salt and water. Bring to a simmer, stirring to dissolve the sugar and salt. Remove from the heat and let cool.

◙ Peel the cucumber and cut in half lengthwise. Cut crosswise into very thin slices and place in a bowl. Add the shallot, chili, dried shrimp powder (if using) and cilantro and stir to mix well. Pour the vinegar dressing over the cucumber mixture and set aside. Just before serving, sprinkle the peanuts on top.

◙ To make the fish cakes, if using fillets, cut the fish into 1-inch (2.5-cm) cubes and place in a food processor fitted with the metal blade. Process until a fairly smooth paste forms. Transfer to a large bowl. If using whitefish paste, simply place in the bowl. Add the fish sauce, chili paste or curry paste, egg, salt, cornstarch, green beans and cilantro. Stir to mix well.

◙ Moisten your hands with water and form the mixture into about 24 cakes each about 2 inches (5 cm) in diameter and ½ inch (12 mm) thick. As the cakes are formed, set them on an oiled baking sheet.

◙ In a frying pan over medium-high heat, pour in oil to a depth of 1 inch (2.5 cm) and heat to 375°F (190°C) on a deep-frying thermometer. Using an oiled slotted spatula, lower a few fish cakes into the oil and fry, turning once, until golden brown and crisp, about 2 minutes per side. Transfer to paper towels to drain. Place on a platter and keep warm while frying the remaining fish cakes.

◙ To serve, divide the cucumber relish among individual dipping saucers. Arrange 3 or 4 cakes on each serving plate and place a saucer of the cucumber relish alongside. Serve warm.

Makes about 24 fish cakes; serves 8–12

Fried Spring Rolls

The Vietnamese traditionally wrap these fried rolls in soft lettuce leaves,
tucking shredded carrot, cucumber, mint and cilantro between the leaf and roll.
The "roll-in-a-lettuce-roll" is then dipped into a sauce and eaten out of hand.

Fish sauce and lime dipping
sauce *(recipe on page 337)*

TABLE SALAD PLATTER

1   head butter (Boston) lettuce,
    leaves separated, carefully washed
    and dried
1   bunch fresh mint, stemmed
1   bunch fresh cilantro (fresh
    coriander), stemmed
1   large carrot, peeled and finely
    julienned
1   English (hothouse) cucumber,
    peeled and finely julienned

SPRING ROLLS

1   bundle (2 oz/60 g) dried bean
    thread noodles
2   tablespoons dried small tree ear
    mushrooms
1   cup (4 oz/125 g) finely
    julienned, peeled carrots
1   teaspoon salt
1   yellow onion, finely minced
4   shallots, finely minced
4   cloves garlic, finely minced
1   cup (2 oz/60 g) bean sprouts
1   tablespoon Vietnamese fish sauce
½   teaspoon freshly ground pepper
1   lb (500 g) ground (minced) dark
    chicken meat or pork
36 dried rice paper rounds, each
    6½ inches (16.5 cm) in diameter
1   tablespoon sugar
    Peanut or corn oil for frying

◙ Prepare the dipping sauce and the table salad platter and set aside.

◙ To make the spring rolls, place the noodles and tree ear mushrooms in separate bowls. Add warm water to cover to each bowl and let stand until soft, about 30 minutes.

◙ Meanwhile, place the julienned carrots in a colander and sprinkle with the salt. Let stand for 10 minutes to drain. Squeeze gently to remove excess liquid. Drain the bean thread noodles and cut into 2-inch (5-cm) lengths. Drain and rinse the mushrooms; chop coarsely.

◙ In a large bowl, combine the carrots, noodles, mushrooms, onion, shallots, garlic, bean sprouts, fish sauce, pepper, and chicken or pork. Using your hands, mix together well.

◙ To form the rolls, first soften the rice papers: Dampen several clean kitchen towels with water. Fill a pie plate with cold water. Add the sugar and stir to dissolve it. Spread a damp towel on a flat work surface. Dip 1 rice paper round at a time into the water and spread it flat on the towel. Continue dipping and laying the rice papers in a single layer. When you run out of room, lay a damp towel on top of the rounds and continue, always alternating a layer of rice papers

with a damp towel. Let the rice papers stand until pliable, about 1 minute or longer. For each roll, shape 2 tablespoons filling into a compact cylinder about 1 inch (2.5 cm) in diameter and 3 inches (7.5 cm) long and place along the lower edge of a wrapper. Fold the curved bottom edge up and over the filling in one tight turn. Fold the outside edges in, then roll up into a snug cylinder. Set on a baking sheet, seam side down, and cover with plastic wrap. Repeat with the remaining filling and wrappers.

◙ To fry the rolls, pour oil to a depth of 1½ inches (4 cm) in a large frying pan. Place over medium-high heat and heat to 350°F (180°C) on a deep-frying thermometer. Using long chopsticks or tongs, lower a few rolls into the pan, leaving plenty of space between them. Fry, turning often, until golden brown and crisp, about 5 minutes. Transfer to paper towels to drain. Place on a platter and keep warm while frying the remaining rolls.

◙ Serve the rolls hot or at room temperature with the salad platter and dipping sauce (see note above).

Makes 36 spring rolls

239

Chicken Potstickers

Traditionally made with pork, Chinese potstickers work equally well with chicken. In a pinch, wonton skins may be used for the homemade wrappers; reduce the cooking time to 3 minutes.

WRAPPERS
2   cups (10 oz/315 g) all-purpose (plain) flour, plus extra as needed
¼   teaspoon salt
¾   cup (6 fl oz/180 ml) boiling water

FILLING
2   cups (6 oz/185 g) finely chopped napa cabbage
¼   cup (1½ oz/45 g) blanched spinach, chopped
1   lb (500 g) ground (minced) dark chicken meat
½   teaspoon peeled and grated fresh ginger
2   tablespoons finely chopped garlic chives or green (spring) onion
1   teaspoon salt
½   teaspoon sugar
¼   teaspoon ground white pepper
1   tablespoon light soy sauce
1   tablespoon Chinese rice wine or dry sherry
1   teaspoon Asian sesame oil
1½ teaspoons cornstarch (cornflour)

DIPPING SAUCE
6   tablespoons (3 fl oz/90 ml) distilled white vinegar
3   tablespoons light soy sauce
    Chili oil

    Vegetable oil for frying

◙ To make the wrappers, in a food processor fitted with the metal blade, combine the 2 cups (10 oz/315 g) flour and salt and pulse once to mix. With the motor running, slowly pour in the boiling water. Continue to process until a rough ball forms and the dough pulls away from the sides of the work bowl, 15–20 seconds. Transfer to a lightly floured work surface. Knead until smooth and no longer sticky, about 2 minutes. Cover with a kitchen towel and let rest for 30 minutes.

◙ Meanwhile, make the filling: Place the cabbage and spinach in a kitchen towel, wring out the excess liquid and place in a bowl. Add all the remaining filling ingredients and stir until combined. Cover and refrigerate until ready to use.

◙ Uncover the dough and knead briefly. Cut in half. Roll out one half about ⅛ inch (3 mm) thick. Using a round cookie cutter 3½ inches (9 cm) in diameter, cut out rounds. Set the rounds aside, lightly covered with the kitchen towel. Repeat with the remaining dough and all scraps.

◙ To make the sauce, stir together the vinegar and soy sauce. Add chili oil to taste. Set aside.

◙ To make the potstickers, put 1 tablespoon of the filling in the middle of a dough round. Fold the round in half and pinch the edges together at one end of the arc. Starting from that point, make 6 pleats or tucks along the curved edge to enclose the filling. As each potsticker is made, place seam-side up on a baking sheet, pressing down gently so it will sit flat. Cover with the kitchen towel and continue forming and placing the potstickers on the baking sheet until all are made.

◙ Heat a 9-inch (23-cm) nonstick frying pan over medium-high heat. When hot, add about 2 teaspoons vegetable oil. Arrange 8–10 potstickers, seam side up and just touching, in a spiral in the pan. Fry until the bottoms are browned, about 1 minute. Add water to come halfway up the sides of the potstickers and bring to a boil. Immediately cover, reduce the heat to low and steam-cook for 8 minutes, adding more water if necessary to keep the pan wet. Uncover, increase the heat to high and cook until the liquid is absorbed and the bottoms are crispy, about 30 seconds longer. Transfer to a serving plate and keep warm; fry the remaining potstickers.

◙ Divide the dipping sauce among individual saucers. Serve the potstickers hot with the sauce.

Makes about 24 dumplings; serves 4–6

Pork Satay

*Although the concept of satay—cooking meats on skewers—originated in
Indonesia, it has been enthusiastically adopted by nearly every Southeast Asian cuisine
and fashioned to suit the local taste and palate. This satay is a favorite Thai recipe.*

2 tablespoons brown sugar

1½ teaspoons ground coriander

1 teaspoon ground cumin

½ teaspoon ground turmeric

1 tablespoon fresh lime juice

1½ teaspoons Thai fish sauce

2 tablespoons coconut cream *(see glossary, page 342)*

1½ lb (750 g) pork butt or tenderloin, cut into ¾-inch (2-cm) cubes

SATAY SAUCE

1 oz (30 g) tamarind pulp, coarsely chopped *(see glossary, page 348)*

½ cup (4 fl oz/125 ml) boiling water

1 tablespoon peanut or corn oil

2 tablespoons red curry paste *(recipe on page 337)*

1 tablespoon sweet paprika

1 cup (8 fl oz/250 ml) coconut milk

⅓ cup (1½ oz/45 g) ground dry-roasted peanuts or 6 tablespoons (3 oz/90 g) chunky peanut butter

2 tablespoons palm sugar or brown sugar

1 tablespoon fish sauce

½ teaspoon salt

◙ In a bowl, stir together the brown sugar, coriander, cumin, turmeric, lime juice, fish sauce and coconut cream to form a marinade. Add the pork and mix thoroughly to coat. Cover and let marinate for 2 hours at room temperature. Place 18 bamboo skewers, each 8 inches (20 cm) long, in enough water to cover for at least 30 minutes.

◙ To prepare the sauce, in a small bowl, soak the tamarind pulp in the boiling water for 15 minutes. Mash with the back of a fork to help dissolve the pulp. Pour through a fine-mesh sieve into another small bowl, pressing against the pulp to extract as much liquid as possible. Discard the pulp; set the liquid aside.

◙ Place a wok or saucepan over medium heat. When it is hot, add the oil, curry paste and paprika. Reduce the heat to low and cook, stirring, for 1 minute. Add the coconut milk and stir continuously over low heat until the red-stained oil peeks through the paste, about 3 minutes. Add the ground peanuts or peanut butter and palm sugar or brown sugar and simmer, stirring occasionally, for about 5 minutes.

Stir in the tamarind liquid, fish sauce and salt and cook for 1 minute longer. If the sauce is too thick, thin it with a little water. Remove from the heat and keep warm.

◙ Prepare a fire in a charcoal grill or preheat a gas grill to medium-high heat. Thread 4 or 5 pieces of pork onto each skewer. The pieces should touch but do not press them together. Place the skewers on the grill rack and grill until grill marks are apparent on the underside, about 2 minutes. Turn the skewers over and continue grilling until the pork is browned on all sides and firm to the touch, about 1 minute longer.

◙ To serve, transfer the skewers to a platter. Pour the sauce into a shallow serving bowl and serve alongside.

Makes 18 satay skewers; serves 6

Spicy Potato Samosas

A favorite Singaporean snack is the samosa, a traditional Indian savory pastry stuffed with spicy vegetables. This recipe comes from Singaporean Chinese cooks who make samosas with crispy spring roll wrappers rather than the traditional handmade flaky pastry dough.

FILLING

3   baking potatoes, about 1 lb (500 g), peeled
2   tablespoons ghee or vegetable oil
1   yellow onion, finely chopped
3   cloves garlic, finely chopped
1   teaspoon peeled and finely chopped fresh ginger
½   cup (2½ oz/75 g) frozen petite peas, thawed
½   cup (2½ oz/75 g) finely diced carrots, blanched for 3 minutes and drained
2   fresh small green chilies, seeded and chopped
2   teaspoons curry powder
½   teaspoon ground turmeric
1   teaspoon salt
2   teaspoons sugar
2   tablespoons chopped fresh cilantro (fresh coriander)
1   tablespoon fresh lemon juice

WRAPPERS

1   package (1 lb/500 g) frozen spring roll wrappers, thawed
2   tablespoons all-purpose (plain) flour
2   tablespoons water
    Peanut oil for frying

    Chinese plum sauce for dipping

◙ To make the filling, place the potatoes in a saucepan, add water to cover generously and bring to a boil over medium-high heat. Boil until tender when pierced with a fork, about 20 minutes. Drain and let cool, then peel and cut into ¼-inch (6-mm) dice.

◙ In a nonstick wok or large frying pan over medium-high heat, warm the ghee or oil. Add the onion, garlic and ginger and sauté until softened, about 3 minutes. Add the potatoes, peas, carrots and chilies; gently mix with the onion mixture. Increase the heat to high and fry until the potatoes have a dry consistency, about 3 minutes longer. Season with the curry powder, turmeric, salt, sugar, cilantro and lemon juice. Stir together gently and remove from the heat. Set aside to cool.

◙ Remove 16 spring roll wrappers from the package; freeze the remaining wrappers in an airtight plastic bag for another use. In a small bowl, mix the flour with the water to form a paste; set aside. Cut the spring roll wrappers into 3 equal strips. Cover the unused strips with a damp cloth. Lay 1 strip vertically to you on a work surface. Place a well-packed heaping tablespoon of the filling at the end nearest you. Pull the left-hand corner over the filling on the diagonal to the opposite (right) edge to create a 45-degree angle and corner. Fold up to enclose the top edge, then continue folding the bottom triangle toward the top edge, enclosing the filling completely. Brush the last flap of the triangle with the flour-water paste to seal the triangle. Set on a baking sheet and cover with a kitchen towel. Repeat with the remaining strips and filling.

◙ In a wok or deep frying pan over medium-high heat, pour in oil to a depth of at least 2 inches (5 cm) and heat to 375°F (190°C) on a deep-frying thermometer. Using a slotted spoon, gently lower several triangles into the oil, making sure they can float freely. Fry, turning as needed, until golden brown and crisp, 1–2 minutes. Transfer to paper towels to drain.

◙ Serve the samosas hot with plum sauce for dipping.

Makes about 48 triangles

Fresh Spring Rolls

This variation on the traditional Vietnamese spring roll is refreshing, healthful and herbaceous. Vegetables, herbs and meats are wrapped in rice paper and eaten dipped in a blend of fish sauce and lime juice.

Fish sauce and lime dipping sauce *(recipe on page 337)*

3–4 oz (90–125 g) dried thin rice stick noodles

Boiling water, as needed

¾ lb (375 g) boneless pork loin, in one piece

Salt

12 large shrimp (prawns), peeled and deveined

12 dried large rice paper rounds, each 8½ inches (21.5 cm) in diameter

12 large red-leaf lettuce leaves or other soft, pliable lettuce, stiff stems discarded

1 large carrot, peeled and finely julienned, then tossed with 1 teaspoon sugar until softened, about 10 minutes

1 small English (hothouse) cucumber, peeled and finely julienned

12 fresh mint sprigs

12 fresh cilantro (fresh coriander) sprigs, plus extra leaves for filling

1 tablespoon coarsely chopped dry-roasted peanuts

◎ Prepare the dipping sauce; set aside.

◎ Place the noodles in a bowl, and add boiling water to cover. Let stand for 1 minute. Drain, rinse with cold water, drain again and set aside.

◎ Place the pork in a saucepan, add water to cover and salt to taste. Bring to a boil. Cover, reduce the heat to medium-low and simmer until opaque throughout, about 20 minutes. Drain and let cool. Cut across the grain into very thin slices about 2 inches (5 cm) long and ½ inch (12 mm) wide. Set aside.

◎ Bring a saucepan three-fourths full of water to a boil. Add salt to taste and the shrimp. Boil until they curl slightly and are opaque throughout, 1–2 minutes. Drain and rinse with cold water. Cut each shrimp in half lengthwise, pat dry and set aside.

◎ To prepare the rice papers, dampen several clean kitchen towels with water. Fill a pie plate with cold water. Spread a damp towel on a flat work surface. Dip 1 rice paper round at a time into the water and spread it flat on the towel. Continue dipping and laying the rice papers in a single layer. When you run out of room, lay a damp towel on top of the rounds and continue, always alternating a layer of rice papers with a damp towel. Let the rice papers stand until pliable, about 1 minute or longer.

◎ To assemble, place 1 pliable rice paper round on the work surface and position a lettuce leaf on the lower third of it, tearing the leaf as needed to make it fit and leaving uncovered a 1-inch (2.5-cm) border on the right and left edges. Take a small amount (about one-twelfth) of the rice stick noodles and spread in a line across the width of the leaf. Arrange one-twelfth each of the pork slices, carrot and cucumber, and 1 sprig of mint on the noodles. Fold the bottom edge of the rice paper over to cover the ingredients, then roll up tightly one complete turn. Fold in the left and right edges to enclose the filling. Across the top length of the roll, place 1 sprig of cilantro and 2 pieces of shrimp, end to end and cut side down. Finish rolling up the rice paper to contain the shrimp and form a taut spring roll. Set seam-side down on a baking sheet. Cover with a damp towel. Make the remaining rolls in the same way. The rolls may be made several hours in advance; cover with a damp towel and plastic wrap and refrigerate. Bring to room temperature before serving.

◎ Divide the sauce among individual dipping saucers and then divide the peanuts evenly among the saucers. Serve the rolls with the sauce.

Makes 12 rolls

Shrimp Toasts

*Most likely of Chinese origin, shrimp toasts have found their way into other
Asian kitchens. The Vietnamese use French baguettes and often serve the crispy toasts
alongside their favorite table condiment—fish sauce and lime dipping sauce.*

Fish sauce and lime dipping sauce
(recipe on page 337)

1	loaf day-old French baguette
2	cloves garlic
4	shallots
½	teaspoon peeled and grated fresh ginger
1	lb (500 g) shrimp (prawns), peeled and deveined
½	teaspoon sugar
1	teaspoon salt
¼	teaspoon freshly ground pepper
1	tablespoon cornstarch (cornflour)
¼	cup (1 oz/30 g) sesame seeds
	Peanut or vegetable oil for frying

◙ Prepare the dipping sauce; set aside.

◙ Cut the bread on the diagonal into slices ½ inch (12 mm) wide. Set aside.

◙ In a food processor fitted with the metal blade, combine the garlic, shallots and ginger; process until finely minced. Add the shrimp, sugar, salt, pepper and cornstarch; process until finely chopped but not puréed.

◙ Spread about 1 tablespoon of the shrimp mixture evenly over each slice of bread; smooth the tops. Sprinkle the tops evenly with the sesame seeds, pressing them lightly into the paste. Place the slices, shrimp side up, on a baking sheet and cover with plastic wrap until ready to fry.

◙ In a wok or deep frying pan, pour in oil to a depth of 1½ inches (4 cm) and heat to 350°F (180°C) on a deep-frying thermometer. Carefully add the slices, shrimp side down, and fry until golden brown on the underside, about 2 minutes. Turn over and continue to fry until golden brown on the second side, about 1 minute longer.

◙ Using a slotted spoon, transfer the toasts to paper towels to drain. Arrange on a serving dish and serve warm with the dipping sauce.

Makes about 24 toasts

248

Crispy Vegetable–Stuffed Crêpe

This Vietnamese yellow-tinged crêpe is crispy and eggless and encases a cache of crunchy fresh vegetables. The table salad platter (dia raù) and dipping sauce are traditional accompaniments.

Fish sauce and lime dipping sauce *(recipe on page 337)*

TABLE SALAD PLATTER
2 heads lettuce, washed and leaves separated
2 cups (4 oz/125 g) finely julienned, peeled carrots
2 small English (hothouse) cucumbers, peeled and julienned
2 cups (1 oz/30 g) loosely packed fresh mint leaves
12 pickled shallots, sliced (optional)

CRÊPE BATTER
1 cup (4 oz/125 g) rice flour
½ teaspoon *each* salt, sugar and ground turmeric
¾ cup (6 fl oz/180 ml) coconut milk
1¼ cups (10 fl oz/310 ml) water, or as needed
2 green (spring) onions, thinly sliced

FILLING
6 oz (185 g) boneless and skinless chicken breast or thigh meat
6 oz (185 g) shrimp (prawns), peeled and deveined
3 tablespoons peanut oil
3 large cloves garlic, minced
6 large fresh mushrooms, thinly sliced
1 red bell pepper (capsicum), seeded, deribbed and thinly sliced
1 lb (500 g) bean sprouts, blanched for 5 seconds and drained

◙ Prepare the dipping sauce and the table salad platter and set aside.

◙ To make the crêpe batter, in a bowl, mix together the flour, salt, sugar and turmeric. Stir in the coconut milk and 1¼ cups (10 fl oz/ 310 ml) water. Add more water if needed to form the consistency of a thin pancake batter. Stir in the green onions and set aside.

◙ To make the filling, cut the chicken into ⅓-inch (9-mm) dice and cut the shrimp in half lengthwise. Set aside.

◙ Heat a 9-inch (23-cm) nonstick flat-bottomed wok or frying pan over medium-high heat. When hot, add about 2 teaspoons of the oil and tilt the pan to spread the oil evenly over the bottom and sides. Pour off the excess oil into a bowl and reserve. Add one-sixth each of the garlic, chicken and shrimp and stir-fry for 30 seconds, then spread the mixture evenly over the pan bottom.

◙ Stir the batter briefly and pour ½ cup (4 fl oz/125 ml) of the batter into the pan, tilting the pan to spread a thin film across the bottom and up the sides. Scatter one-sixth each of the mushrooms, bell pepper and bean sprouts over one-half of the batter. Cover the pan, reduce the heat to medium and cook until steam seeps out from under the lid, about 3 minutes. Remove the cover and increase the heat to medium-high. Continue cooking until the crêpe shrinks away from the pan sides, appears dry and has a crisp bottom, about 1 minute longer. Using a spatula, fold the crêpe in half like an omelet, slide it onto a plate and serve at once. Repeat with the remaining oil, filling and batter.

◙ To serve, cut each crêpe crosswise into 4 or 5 sections. Take 1 lettuce leaf and place some carrot, cucumber, mint leaves, and pickled shallots, if using, into the center of the leaf. Top with a section of the crêpe and roll up the leaf to enclose it. Dip into the dipping sauce and eat out of hand.

Makes 6 crêpes; serves 12

Corn, Shrimp and Pepper Fritters

Corn was introduced to Indonesia by Spanish colonists in the seventeenth century. It proved as agriculturally viable as rice in some parts of the archipelago. A favorite Indonesian street-food snack, corn fritters have an addicting aroma that lingers long after they are cooked.

2   cups (12 oz/375 g) corn kernels (from about 3 large ears)
½   lb (250 g) shrimp (prawns), peeled, deveined and coarsely chopped
2   shallots, finely chopped
1   small green or red bell pepper (capsicum), or ½ of each, seeded, deribbed and finely chopped
1   fresh small red chili pepper, seeded and finely minced
2   cloves garlic, finely chopped
1   egg
¼   cup (1½ oz/45 g) all-purpose (plain) flour
¼   teaspoon baking soda (bicarbonate of soda)
1   teaspoon ground coriander
½   teaspoon ground cumin
1   teaspoon salt
2   tablespoons water
    Peanut or corn oil for frying
    Sriracha sauce *(see glossary, page 347)* for dipping, or a squeeze of lime or lemon juice

◙ In a food processor fitted with the metal blade, process the corn into a coarse paste. (Do not purée.) Scrape the corn into a large bowl. Add the shrimp, shallots, bell pepper, chili, garlic and egg; mix well. In a small bowl, stir together the flour, baking soda, coriander, cumin, salt and water. Add to the corn mixture and mix well.

◙ In a large, heavy frying pan over medium-high heat, pour in oil to a depth of at least 1 inch (2.5 cm) and heat to about 375°F (190°C) on a deep-frying thermometer. Drop a few generous tablespoonfuls of the corn mixture into the oil, leaving enough space for each fritter to spread. Fry until golden brown and crisp on the underside, about 1 minute. Turn over and continue to fry until brown and crisp on the second side, about 1 minute longer. Using a slotted spoon, transfer the fritters to paper towels to drain. Place on a platter and keep warm while frying the remaining fritters.

◙ Serve the fritters hot or at room temperature with Sriracha sauce or lime or lemon juice.

Makes about 24 fritters

Grilled Spicy Fish Pâté in Banana Leaf

These spicy fish pâté parcels are a typical portable lunch in Asia. Wrapped in banana leaves,
the pâté is infused with a distinctive floral aroma and taste. Frozen banana leaves may be found
in Asian and Latin American markets; aluminum foil may be substituted.

SPICE PASTE

2	lemongrass stalks, tender heart section only, chopped
6	candlenuts, soaked in water for 10 minutes, or blanched almonds
1	piece fresh ginger, ½ inch (12 mm) long, peeled
2	shallots, quartered
4	cloves garlic
8	fresh small red chili peppers, seeded and coarsely chopped
	About 3 tablespoons water
2	teaspoons ground coriander
¼	teaspoon ground turmeric
2	tablespoons vegetable oil
¾	cup (6 fl oz/180 ml) coconut cream
1	teaspoon salt
1½	teaspoons sugar
	Dash of ground white pepper

1½	lb (750 g) whitefish fillets, preferably Spanish or king mackerel, cut into 1-inch (2.5-cm) dice
6	kaffir lime leaves, cut into hairlike slivers, or shredded zest of 1 lime
24	pieces banana leaf, each 6 inches (15 cm) square
1	bunch basil, stemmed and leaves separated
	Fresh red chili pepper slivers

◙ To make the spice paste, combine the lemongrass, candlenuts or almonds, ginger, shallots, garlic and chilies in a blender. Add the water as needed to facilitate the blending and blend to a smooth paste. Add the coriander and turmeric and blend to combine.

◙ In a wok over medium heat, warm the vegetable oil. Add the spice paste and fry, stirring frequently, until fragrant and the oil takes on a red hue, about 3 minutes. Stir in the coconut cream, salt, sugar and white pepper and simmer until the mixture forms a fragrant thick cream, 3–5 minutes. Remove from the heat and let cool.

◙ Place the fish in a food processor fitted with the metal blade and process to a smooth paste. Add the spice paste and half of the kaffir lime leaf slivers or regular lime zest and pulse just until the fish absorbs the spice paste.

◙ To form the parcels, you must first soften the banana leaves: Bring a saucepan filled with water to a boil. Working with 1 piece of leaf at a time and using tongs, dip the leaf into the boiling water for a few seconds. Lift it out, drain well and place, shiny side down, on a work surface so that the grain runs horizontally to you. Place a few basil leaves in the midsection of the leaf. Spread 3 tablespoons of the fish mixture down the middle (along the grain), forming a flat log about 1½ inches (4 cm) wide by 4 inches (10 cm) long. Scatter a few of the remaining lime leaf slivers or lime zest shreds and slivers of red chili on top. Fold the bottom and top edges over the filling, overlapping in the middle. Press down and flatten the ends; seal both ends with toothpicks to form flat parcels. Repeat with the remaining leaves and filling. The parcels may be formed several hours in advance and refrigerated.

◙ Prepare a fire in a charcoal grill. When the coals are ash white, position the grill rack 3–4 inches (7.5–10 cm) from the coals and place the parcels on it. Grill, turning once, until the parcels feel firm when pressed, about 3 minutes per side.

◙ Serve the parcels hot, warm or at room temperature. Remove the leaf to eat.

Makes 24 parcels

Crispy Green Onion Pancakes

These flaky flat breads can be found in street stalls throughout northern China and in Taiwan. Although the bread requires patience and labor, it is such a delectable treat that it is well worth the effort.

3 cups (15 oz/470 g) all-purpose (plain) flour, plus extra as needed
1 cup (8 fl oz/250 ml) boiling water
¼ cup (2 fl oz/60 ml) cold water
About 4 teaspoons Asian sesame oil
1 teaspoon coarse salt, or more to taste
2 tablespoons chopped green (spring) onion
¼ cup (2 fl oz/60 ml) peanut oil, or as needed

◙ In a food processor fitted with the metal blade, place the 3 cups (15 oz/470 g) flour. With the processor motor running, pour the boiling water through the feed tube in a slow, steady stream. When the dough starts to pull away from the sides of the work bowl in 5–10 seconds, add the cold water. Continue to process until the dough comes together in a rough ball, about 15 seconds. If the dough is sticky, add a little more flour and continue processing for 30 seconds longer.

◙ Turn out the dough onto a lightly floured work surface. Knead until smooth, soft, elastic and no longer sticky, 1–2 minutes, dusting lightly with flour if needed to reduce stickiness. Gather the dough into a ball, place in a lightly oiled bowl and turn to coat lightly on all sides. Cover the bowl with plastic wrap and let rest for 30 minutes.

◙ Turn out the dough onto a lightly floured surface. Knead only until smooth and no longer sticky, 1–2 minutes. Cut the dough into 4 equal pieces. Roll out 1 piece into a 10–12-inch (25–30-cm) round about ⅛ inch (3 mm) thick. Evenly brush the top with a thin film of about 1 teaspoon sesame oil. Sprinkle ¼ teaspoon of the coarse salt and 1½ teaspoons of the green onion evenly over the

round. Starting from one side, roll up tightly and pinch the ends to seal in the onions. Anchor one end and wind the long roll around it into a flat spiral coil. Tuck the end under and press the coil to flatten slightly. Roll out the coil into a pancake 7–8 inches (18–20 cm) in diameter and about ¼ inch (6 mm) thick. Cover with a kitchen towel. Repeat with the remaining dough.

◙ To fry the pancakes, heat a 9-inch (23-cm) frying pan over medium heat. When hot, add enough of the peanut oil to coat the bottom with a ⅛-inch (3-mm) layer. When the oil is medium-hot, add 1 pancake, cover and fry, shaking the pan occasionally, until the bottom is golden brown and crisp, about 2 minutes. Using a wide spatula, turn the pancake over; if the pan is dry, add a little more oil. Re-cover and continue to fry, shaking the pan occasionally, until the second side is golden brown and crisp, about 2 minutes longer.

◙ Remove the cover, slide the pancake onto a cutting board and cut into wedges. Transfer to a serving dish and serve at once, or keep warm while you fry the remaining pancakes.

Makes 4 pancakes; serves 4

Mu Shu Duck

This variation of the popular mu shu pork is made with the Cantonese barbecued duck available at most Chinese delicatessens. Use only the breast meat from the duck for this simple recipe and reserve the rest for another use. Alternatively, you can marinate and grill a fresh duck breast.

8   Mandarin pancakes *(recipe on page 339)* or frozen spring roll wrappers, thawed

¼   cup (1 oz/30 g) dried lily buds

¼   cup (1 oz/30 g) dried wood ear mushrooms

1   whole barbecued duck breast *(see note above)*

2   tablespoons peanut or corn oil

2   extra-large eggs, beaten

½   teaspoon salt

1   teaspoon peeled and finely minced fresh ginger

1   cup (4 oz/125 g) julienned, peeled carrot

1½   cups (4½ oz/140 g) finely shredded green cabbage or napa cabbage

¼   teaspoon sugar

   Big pinch of ground white pepper

1   tablespoon Chinese rice wine or dry sherry

2   teaspoons soy sauce, or to taste

1   teaspoon Asian sesame oil

2   green (spring) onions, finely slivered

   Fresh cilantro (fresh coriander) leaves for garnish

   Hoisin sauce for serving

◙ If you are making homemade pancakes, prepare them in advance and keep warm.

◙ Place the lily buds and mushrooms in separate small bowls. Add warm water to cover to each bowl and let stand until soft and pliable, about 10 minutes. Drain both bowls. Pinch off and discard the hard tips from the lily buds; set aside. Pinch off and discard the hard centers from the mushrooms. Tightly roll up each mushroom, then cut crosswise into thin slivers. Set the lily buds and mushrooms aside.

◙ Cut the breast meat from the duck bones and discard the bones. Using a paper towel, pat the excess grease from the breast. Cut the breast with the skin into julienned strips about ⅜ inch (1 cm) wide. Set aside.

◙ Place a wok over medium-high heat. When it is hot, add 1 tablespoon of the oil. When the oil is hot, add the eggs and stir to scramble. Cook, stirring, until soft-cooked, 1–2 minutes. Transfer the eggs to a plate, break them up into small morsels and set aside.

◙ Add the remaining 1 tablespoon oil to the wok. When the oil is hot, add the salt, ginger, carrot, cabbage and the reserved lily buds and wood ear mushrooms; stir-fry until the cabbage begins to wilt, about 2 minutes. Add the sugar, white pepper, rice wine or sherry, soy sauce and reserved duck strips; stir-fry until fragrant and thoroughly mixed, about 1 minute. Stir in the sesame oil, then gently fold in the eggs. Transfer the mixture to a warmed platter. Top with the green onions and cilantro leaves.

◙ Place the hoisin sauce in a small serving saucer. Set out the steamer basket or plate of pancakes or a plate of spring roll wrappers.

◙ To eat, smear 1–2 teaspoons hoisin sauce across the middle of a pancake. Spread 2–3 tablespoons filling over the sauce. Fold two opposite sides over and the bottom edge up to contain the filling and eat out of hand.

Serves 8

Baked Barbecued Pork Buns

In China, jingling bells or the slapping of bamboo sticks signals the arrival of street vendors, who deliver to the door a mélange of breakfast foods. One popular choice is buns stuffed with honey-glazed pork nuggets.

FILLING
1   tablespoon hoisin sauce
1   tablespoon dark soy sauce
2   teaspoons oyster sauce
½   cup (4 fl oz/125 ml) water
2   teaspoons cornstarch (cornflour)
1   teaspoon sugar
1   tablespoon peanut or corn oil
1   small yellow onion, diced
2   green (spring) onions, chopped
1   teaspoon grated fresh ginger
1   lb (500 g) Cantonese barbecued
     pork *(recipe on page 338)*, diced
1   teaspoon Asian sesame oil

DOUGH
1   package (2½ teaspoons) active
     dry yeast
3   tablespoons sugar
¼   cup (2 fl oz/60 ml) warm water
     (110°–115°F/43°–46°C)
1   cup (8 fl oz/250 ml) milk, heated
3   tablespoons vegetable oil
1   egg, beaten
3¾   cups (19 oz/595 g) all-purpose
     (plain) flour, plus extra as needed
½   teaspoon salt
2   teaspoons baking powder
16   squares parchment (baking)
     paper, each 4 inches (10 cm)
     square

GLAZE
1   egg, lightly beaten
½   teaspoon sugar
1   tablespoon water

◙ To make the filling, in a small bowl, stir together the 3 sauces, water, cornstarch and sugar until smooth; set aside. Preheat a wok over medium heat and add the oil. When it is hot, add both onions and the ginger and stir-fry until the onions are softened but not browned, about 1 minute. Increase the heat to high, add the pork and toss to mix. Stir the sauce quickly and add to the pork. Bring to a boil and stir until thickened, about 30 seconds. Stir in the sesame oil. Transfer to a bowl, cover and refrigerate until well chilled.

◙ To make the bread dough, in a bowl, stir together the yeast, 1 table-spoon of the sugar and the warm water. Let stand until the yeast bubbles, about 3 minutes. Stir in the warm milk, oil and egg; set aside. In a food processor fitted with the metal blade, combine the flour, salt and the remaining 2 tablespoons sugar. With the motor running, slowly pour in the yeast-milk mixture. Process until the dough forms a rough ball and begins to pull away from the sides of the work bowl, about 15 seconds. If it is sticky, sprinkle in a little flour and process for 30 seconds longer.

◙ Turn out the dough onto a lightly floured work surface and knead until smooth and spongy but resilient, 3–5 minutes. Form into a ball, place in a bowl and cover with plastic wrap.

Let rise until doubled in size, about 2 hours at warm room temperature (or overnight in the refrigerator).

◙ Turn the dough out onto the work surface. Sprinkle with the baking powder and knead until incorporated, about 3 minutes. Cut the dough in half and roll each half into a rope 8 inches (20 cm) long. Cut each rope into 8 pieces. Cover unused pieces with a damp kitchen towel. Roll each piece into a ball. Using a rolling pin, flatten each ball into a round 5 inches (13 cm) in diameter. To fill each bun, place 2 tablespoons filling in the center of a round. Pull the edges so that they come together and then pinch them together securely to enclose the filling. Shape into a smooth domed bun and place, pinched side down, on a parchment square. Set on a baking sheet. Make the remaining buns in the same way and place 2 inches (5 cm) apart on the sheet. Cover with a kitchen towel and let rise in a warm place until doubled, about 30 minutes.

◙ Preheat an oven to 350°F (180°C). To make the glaze, in a bowl, stir together all the ingredients.

◙ Just before baking, brush the buns with the glaze. Bake until golden brown, about 25 minutes. Serve hot or at room temperature.

Makes 16 buns

Pork and Tomato Omelet

In the Far East, egg dishes are enjoyed as snacks as well as featured items on dinner menus.
Serve this meaty Thai omelet with steamed rice (recipe on page 338) and offer both store-bought
Sriracha sauce (a chili-garlic purée) and the chili fish sauce presented here for dipping.

OMELET
4 eggs
¼ cup (¾ oz/20 g) finely sliced shallots or green (spring) onions
1 tablespoon Thai fish sauce
½ lb (250 g) ground (minced) pork
1 small, firm tomato, seeded and chopped

SAUCE
3 tablespoons Thai fish sauce
1 tablespoon fresh lime juice
4 fresh small green chili peppers, sliced crosswise

About 4 tablespoons (2 fl oz/60 ml) peanut or corn oil
1 tablespoon coarsely chopped fresh cilantro (fresh coriander)

Sriracha sauce for dipping *(see glossary, page 347)*

◙ In a large bowl, beat the eggs with the shallots or green onions, fish sauce and pork, breaking up the pork to mix it in evenly. Stir in the tomato and set aside.

◙ To make the chili fish sauce, in a small bowl, stir together the fish sauce, lime juice and chilies. Divide the sauce among individual dipping saucers and set aside.

◙ Place a wok over medium-high heat. When it is hot, add 1 tablespoon of the oil. When the oil is hot, pour ½ cup (4 fl oz/125 ml) of the egg mixture into the wok, tilting the pan to spread it evenly across the bottom into a 6-inch (15-cm) round. (The edges should sizzle while the middle puffs up in several spots.)

Reduce the heat to medium and fry until the eggs are almost fully set, about 1½ minutes. Using a broad spatula, flip the omelet over and continue to cook until the second side is browned, about 1 minute longer. Turn the omelet out onto a serving plate and keep warm while you fry the remaining egg mixture in 3 more batches, adding oil as needed to prevent sticking.

◙ To serve, divide the Sriracha sauce among individual dipping saucers. Garnish the omelets with the cilantro and serve with the chili fish sauce and Sriracha sauce.

Makes four 6-inch (15-cm) omelets; serves 4

Salads

In most parts of Asia, salads consist of chilled cooked vegetables, meat, fish and/or poultry arranged on large plates and dressed with a simple vinaigrettelike sauce. Various fruits, crunchy nuts and crispy garnishes of fried shallots, garlic and shrimp crackers provide contrasting flavors and textures. When noodles are also included, these exotic salads become substantial one-dish meals.

The range of Asian salad dressings is as diverse as the ingredients. Thin dressings are a blend of savory and tart ingredients combined with peanut or vegetable oil for smoothness. Soy sauce often imparts a savory tone, while vinegar or citrus juice animates the mixture with a pleasant tang. A drizzle of Asian sesame oil adds a nutty touch, and assertive ingredients such as garlic, ginger, green onions and chilies lend a gentle yet bold kick.

There are also thicker dressings made from ground roasted peanuts and sesame seeds. Hearty, luscious and aromatic, these rich blends are specialties of Indonesia, Thailand and Malaysia, and are easy to reproduce in the home kitchen. A good blender is recommended to take over the traditional practice of hand pounding the ingredients in a mortar.

Grilled Beef, Tomato and Mint Salad

In Thai cuisine, a salad is served as just one of several dishes in a meal. This grilled beef salad has as many variations as there are street hawkers who make it. Although they all differ, every version is certain to combine a mixture of sweet, sour, spicy, savory and herby flavors and to swell the air with fragrance.

BEEF

1	lb (500 g) beef tri-tip or flank steak, about 2 inches (5 cm) thick
2	cloves garlic
2	tablespoons finely chopped fresh cilantro (fresh coriander) root and stems
1	teaspoon ground black pepper
1½	teaspoons sugar
2	tablespoons soy sauce
1	tablespoon Thai fish sauce
1	tablespoon peanut or corn oil

VINAIGRETTE

2	cloves garlic, minced
2	fresh small red or green chili peppers, chopped
1½	tablespoons sugar
3	tablespoons Thai fish sauce
5	tablespoons fresh lime juice

SALAD

6	large red-leaf lettuce leaves, shredded
3	small, firm tomatoes, cut into wedges
1	small red (Spanish) onion, sliced
1	small cucumber, peeled and thinly sliced
8	fresh mint leaves, coarsely chopped
4	kaffir lime or other citrus leaves, very finely shredded (optional)
2	tablespoons chopped fresh cilantro (fresh coriander), plus whole leaves for garnish

◉ Place the beef in a bowl. In a mortar, combine the garlic, cilantro, black pepper and sugar and mash to a paste with a pestle. Stir in the soy sauce, fish sauce and oil. Rub the mixture into the beef and let marinate for at least 1 hour at room temperature, or cover and refrigerate for up to 4 hours.

◉ To make the vinaigrette, in the mortar, combine the garlic and chilies and mash to a paste with the pestle. Stir in the sugar, fish sauce and lime juice. Set aside.

◉ Preheat a gas grill to medium-high heat or prepare a fire in a charcoal grill. Place the beef on the grill rack and grill, turning once, until medium-rare, 5–8 minutes on each side. Remove from the heat and let cool. Cut the beef across the grain into very thin slices. Place in a large bowl. Add two-thirds of the vinaigrette and toss well to coat; set aside.

◉ Just before serving, in a large bowl, combine the shredded lettuce, tomatoes, onion, cucumber, chopped mint, lime or citrus leaves (if using) and chopped cilantro. Drizzle with the remaining vinaigrette, toss gently, and divide evenly among 6 individual salad plates. Mound the beef mixture on top. Garnish with cilantro leaves. Serve warm or at room temperature.

Serves 6

Sichuan Grilled Eggplant and Spinach Salad

Traditionally, the eggplant is steamed for this recipe; grilling, however, produces a firmer texture and enhances its natural flavor. Both methods result in a delicious side-dish salad. To assemble a more substantial meal, add shredded poached chicken or julienned grilled red peppers (capsicums).

6   Asian eggplants (aubergines), each about 6 inches (15 cm) long, or 1 large globe eggplant, about 1 lb (500 g)
Peanut oil

DRESSING
2   tablespoons peanut oil
1   piece fresh ginger, 1 inch (2.5 cm) long, peeled and grated
3   cloves garlic, finely minced
½   teaspoon salt
1   teaspoon sugar
¼   cup (2 fl oz/60 ml) dark soy sauce
¼   cup (2 fl oz/60 ml) red wine vinegar or balsamic vinegar
1½   tablespoons Asian sesame oil
1   teaspoon chili oil, or to taste
½   cup (4 fl oz/125 ml) chicken stock

SALAD
1   lb (500 g) fresh spinach, carefully washed and stemmed
1   tablespoon sesame seeds
1   tablespoon chopped green (spring) onion
1   tablespoon chopped fresh cilantro (fresh coriander)

◉ Preheat a gas grill to medium-high heat or prepare a fire in a charcoal grill. If using Asian eggplants, cut lengthwise into slices ¼ inch (6 mm) thick. If using globe eggplant, cut crosswise into slices ¼ inch (6 mm) thick. Lightly score the flesh with a large crosshatch pattern. Brush lightly on both sides with peanut oil. Place the slices on the hot grill and grill, turning once, until the slices are tender, spongy and have light grill marks, about 4 minutes. Transfer to a plate to cool, then cut into strips ¼ inch (6 mm) wide by 2 inches (5 cm) long. Transfer to a bowl, cover and refrigerate.

◉ To make the dressing, in a small saucepan over medium heat, warm the 2 tablespoons peanut oil. When hot, add the ginger and garlic and sauté gently until fragrant but not browned, about 1 minute. Stir in the salt, sugar, soy sauce, vinegar, sesame oil and chili oil; simmer for 15 seconds. Stir in the chicken stock. Remove from the heat and let cool.

◉ Arrange the spinach leaves on a platter and set aside.

◉ In a small, dry saucepan over medium heat, toast the sesame seeds until golden and fragrant, about 3 minutes. Set aside.

◉ Add the green onion, cilantro and cooled dressing to the eggplant and toss to mix well. Scatter the eggplant over the spinach, then refrigerate until well chilled. Sprinkle with the toasted sesame seeds just before serving.

Serves 6

Vegetable Salad with Spicy Peanut Dressing

Other vegetables such as broccoli, cauliflower or jicama can be substituted for any called for here.
Garnish with wedges of hard-cooked egg and fried shallot flakes (recipe on page 336).

DRESSING
1   oz (30 g) tamarind pulp
½   cup (4 fl oz/125 ml) boiling water, plus extra as needed
2   fresh small red chili peppers
1   lemongrass stalk, tender heart section only, chopped
1   teaspoon dried shrimp paste, optional
1   piece fresh ginger, 1 inch (2.5 cm) long, peeled and chopped
2   cloves garlic
2   shallots, quartered
1   teaspoon salt
1   cup (8 fl oz/250 ml) coconut milk
1   tablespoon palm or brown sugar
1½   tablespoons Indonesian sweet dark soy sauce (*ketjap manis*)
¼   cup (2½ oz/75 g) chunky peanut butter
1   tablespoon fresh lemon juice

SALAD
4   small red new potatoes
1   lb (500 g) spinach
4   cups (8 oz/250 g) bean sprouts
2   carrots, peeled and sliced
6   oz (185 g) green beans, cut into 2-inch (5-cm) lengths
2   cups (6 oz/185 g) shredded cabbage
½   lb (250 g) asparagus, cut into 3-inch (7.5-cm) lengths
1   English cucumber, peeled and cut into ½-inch (12-mm) cubes

◙ In a small bowl, soak the tamarind pulp in the boiling water for 15 minutes. Mash with the back of a fork to help dissolve the pulp. Pour through a fine-mesh sieve into a bowl, pressing against the pulp to extract as much liquid as possible. Discard the pulp; set the liquid aside.

◙ To make the dressing, seed and coarsely chop the chilies and place in a blender. Add the lemongrass, shrimp paste (if using), ginger, garlic, shallots and salt; process to a smooth paste. Transfer to a saucepan and add the coconut milk, palm or brown sugar, dark soy sauce, tamarind liquid and the peanut butter. Bring to a boil. Reduce the heat to low and simmer, stirring frequently, until creamy and fragrant, about 15 minutes. Add the lemon juice and cook for 1 minute longer. Set aside. Just before serving, thin with boiling water to the consistency of a salad dressing.

◙ To prepare the salad, bring 2 large pots of water to a boil. Add the potatoes to 1 of the pots and boil until tender, about 20 minutes; drain and let cool, then cut into wedges.

◙ While the potatoes are boiling, parboil the vegetables 1 at a time in the other pot of boiling water, then refresh under cool running water and drain: spinach for 5 seconds, bean sprouts for 10 seconds, carrots for 8 minutes, green beans for 5 minutes, cabbage for 1 minute, and asparagus for 3 minutes. Change and/or replenish boiling water as necessary. Set the vegetables aside.

◙ Arrange the salad ingredients in layers on 6 individual salad plates: Start with a base of cucumber and spinach, some bean sprouts, a scattering of carrot, green beans, cabbage, asparagus and potatoes. Pour the dressing over the vegetables and serve.

Serves 6

Green Mango Salad

*This salad has a unique contrast of textures and flavors. Tiny bits of sautéed pork are
a rich counterpoint to the crunchy bite and sour taste of green mangoes. Since green mangoes
are not always available, tart green apples may be used in their place.*

2 large green mangoes or 3 tart green apples such as Granny Smith
1 tablespoon fresh lime juice
1 tablespoon vegetable oil
¼ lb (125 g) finely chopped pork
1 tablespoon Thai fish sauce
1½ teaspoons sugar
1 fresh small red chili pepper, seeded and chopped
1 teaspoon dried shrimp powder, optional
2 tablespoons chopped dry-roasted peanuts
½ red (Spanish) onion, thinly sliced
1 tablespoon fried shallot flakes *(recipe on page 336),* optional
1 tablespoon fried garlic flakes *(recipe on page 336),* optional

◙ Peel and pit the mangoes or peel and core the apples. Cut into thin half-moon slices and place in a large bowl. Sprinkle with the lime juice, toss gently to mix and set aside.

◙ Place a wok over medium-high heat. When it is hot, add the vegetable oil. When the oil is hot, add the pork and stir-fry, breaking up any lumps, until it is no longer pink, about 1 minute. Stir in the fish sauce, sugar, chili, shrimp powder (if using) and peanuts; mix well. Spoon the mixture onto a paper towel–lined plate and let drain and cool.

◙ Add the cooled pork mixture to the mangoes or apples along with the red onion. Toss gently, cover and chill. Transfer the chilled salad to a serving plate. Sprinkle the fried shallot and/or garlic flakes over the top, if desired, and serve.

Serves 6

Chinese Chicken Salad with Peanut–Sesame Dressing

Cold shredded chicken in a peanut-sesame dressing is a common component of the exquisitely arranged cold appetizer platters served at Chinese banquets. This salad is as popular among Westerners as it is with the Chinese, and many variations of it are offered in casual dining spots throughout the West.

SALAD
2   large whole chicken breasts
2   teaspoons salt
½   lb (250 g) fresh Chinese egg noodles
1½   teaspoons peanut oil
3   tablespoons white or black sesame seeds
¼   cup (1¼ oz/37 g) finely julienned red bell pepper (capsicum)
1   cup (4 oz/125 g) finely julienned, peeled carrot
½   cup (½ oz/15 g) fresh cilantro (fresh coriander) leaves
1   small cucumber, cut into julienne strips 2 inches (5 cm) long

DRESSING
2   teaspoons peanut butter
2   teaspoons Asian sesame paste
2   tablespoons sugar
⅓   cup (3 fl oz/80 ml) dark soy sauce
⅓   cup (3 fl oz/80 ml) Chinese red vinegar or balsamic vinegar
2   tablespoons peanut or corn oil
1   tablespoon Asian sesame oil
½   teaspoon chili oil, or to taste
2   teaspoons minced garlic
1   teaspoon peeled and minced fresh ginger
¼   cup (¾ oz/20 g) chopped green (spring) onion
¼   cup (1 oz/30 g) chopped dry-roasted peanuts

◉ Fill a large saucepan three-fourths full with water and bring to a boil. Add the chicken breasts and return to a boil, skimming off any scum that forms on the surface, then immediately reduce the heat to low. Simmer, uncovered, until tender, 20–25 minutes. Drain and let cool.

◉ Remove the skin from the chicken breasts, bone the breasts and hand shred the meat with the grain into strips about ½ inch (12 mm) thick and 2 inches (5 cm) long.

◉ Refill the large saucepan three-fourths full with water. Bring to a boil over high heat and add the salt. Gently pull the strands of noodles apart, then drop them into the boiling water, stirring to separate the strands. When the water comes to a second boil, boil for 1 minute longer. Pour the noodles into a colander and rinse thoroughly with cold running water. Drain thoroughly and transfer to a large bowl. Toss with the peanut oil to keep the noodles from sticking together. Set aside.

◉ If using white sesame seeds, toast them in a small, dry frying pan over medium heat until golden and fragrant, about 3 minutes. If using black sesame seeds, leave them untoasted.

◉ In a large bowl, toss together the chicken, bell pepper, carrot, cilantro and toasted or raw sesame seeds. Arrange the cooked noodles in a wide shallow bowl. Scatter the cucumber over the noodles and top with the chicken mixture. Cover and refrigerate until ready to serve.

◉ To make the dressing, in a small bowl, stir together the peanut butter, sesame paste, sugar, soy sauce and vinegar. In a small saucepan over medium heat, combine the peanut or corn oil, sesame oil and chili oil. When hot, add the garlic, ginger and green onion; sauté gently until fragrant but not browned, about 15 seconds. Stir in the peanut butter-sesame paste mixture and cook until the mixture begins to form a light syrup, about 1 minute. Remove from the heat and let cool to lukewarm.

◉ Pour the warm dressing over the chicken salad and sprinkle with the peanuts. Serve immediately.

Serves 6

Tropical Fruit Salad with Chicken and Shrimp

The Thai concept of mixing tangy fresh fruits and vegetables together in a salad is an old one borrowed from India. In Thailand, this colorful salad is popularly sold by street vendors just as its inspiration is in India. Use your favorite local fruits in place of any called for here.

¼ lb (125 g) cooked bay shrimp (prawns)

1 cup (6 oz/185 g) diced cooked chicken (½-inch/12-mm dice)

VINAIGRETTE

1 fresh small red chili pepper, halved, seeded and thinly sliced

3 tablespoons fresh lime juice

2 tablespoons Thai fish sauce

2 tablespoons sugar

¼ teaspoon salt

½ teaspoon finely minced garlic

SALAD

1 mango, peeled, pitted and diced

1 small sweet pink grapefruit, peeled, all white membrane removed, and sectioned

1 Asian pear, peeled, cored and cut into ¾-inch (2-cm) pieces

1½ cups (9 oz/280 g) melon chunks or balls (¾ inch/2 cm in diameter)

1 cup (6 oz/185 g) peeled and pitted litchis, preferably fresh

2 tablespoons chopped fresh mint

2 tablespoons chopped fresh cilantro (fresh coriander)

2 tablespoons fried shallot flakes *(recipe on page 336)*

1 tablespoon fried garlic flakes *(recipe on page 336)*

¼ cup (1 oz/30 g) chopped dry-roasted peanuts

◙ In a large bowl, toss together the shrimp and chicken. Set aside.

◙ To make the vinaigrette, in a small bowl, combine the chili, lime juice, fish sauce, sugar, salt and garlic; stir well to dissolve the sugar and salt. Pour half of the vinaigrette over the chicken mixture and toss to coat.

◙ Just before serving, combine the mango, grapefruit, pear, melon and litchis in a colander to drain off excess moisture. Add to the chicken mixture along with the remaining vinaigrette and toss gently. Mix in most of the mint, cilantro, and fried shallot and garlic flakes.

◙ Transfer to a shallow serving bowl and garnish with the remaining mint, cilantro, shallots and garlic. Sprinkle with the peanuts and serve hot.

Serves 6

Chopped Beef Salad

This flavorful salad from the northern country is popular throughout Thailand. If raw beef does not suit your taste, you may used cooked minced beef, chicken or pork. The beef makes a tasty summer salad stuffed into hollowed-out cucumber cups or eaten with lettuce leaves. Accompany with rice and an icy beverage.

2 tablespoons long-grain white rice
2 tablespoons Thai fish sauce
¼ cup (2 fl oz/60 ml) fresh lime juice
½ teaspoon sugar
½ teaspoon salt
1 lb (500 g) finely chopped, very fresh lean beef round
4 shallots, finely chopped
2 green (spring) onions, finely chopped
2 lemongrass stalks, tender heart section only, finely minced
1 teaspoon coarsely ground dried red chili pepper
¼ cup (⅓ oz/10 g) chopped fresh mint
3 tablespoons chopped fresh cilantro (fresh coriander) leaves and stems
2 English (hothouse) cucumbers
Fresh mint leaves, cilantro (fresh coriander) leaves or basil leaves for garnish

◉ Heat a dry wok over medium-high heat. Add the rice and toast, stirring frequently, until golden brown, 2–3 minutes. Remove from the heat and let cool. Place in a spice grinder or in a mortar and grind or pulverize with a pestle to the consistency of coarse sand; set aside.

◉ In a bowl, stir together the fish sauce, lime juice, sugar and salt. Add the beef and mix thoroughly. Mix in the toasted rice, shallots, green onions, lemongrass, ground chili, chopped mint and chopped cilantro. Taste and adjust the seasonings, if necessary. Cover and refrigerate until well chilled, about 2 hours.

◉ Peel the cucumbers and cut cross-wise into 1-inch (2.5-cm) sections. Using a melon baller, scoop out the seeds to form each cucumber section into a cup. Spoon the beef mixture into the cups and arrange on a platter. Alternatively, slice the peeled cucumbers crosswise ¼ inch (6 mm) thick. Shape the beef mixture into a mound on a serving plate and surround with the cucumber slices. Garnish the filled cups with the mint or cilantro leaves or arrange the basil leaves over the mound of beef.

Serves 6

Soups, Noodles and Rice

Soups play many roles in Asian cuisines. Indeed, no traditional meal is complete without one. For a family repast, they range from a light meat stock flavored with a few vegetables to hearty full-meal dumpling soups such as Chinese *won ton mein* or the Thai curry noodle combination known as *khao soi*. Lighter soups are ideal for refreshing the palate between bites of a multicourse meal.

Noodle and rice dishes assume equally central roles in the Asian diet. Whether the noodle is made from the more common wheat or rice flour or from mung bean flour, the repertoire of preparations, toppings and sauces is limitless. Although only a handful of the possibilities are included in this book, what is presented reflects the variety of styles found in every corner of the region. To expand one's horizon of the noodle world beyond the well-known Chinese crisp panfried wheat noodles, try a taste of Thai sweet-and-sour noodles or Malaysian stir-fried rice noodles with shellfish.

The wealth of Asian rice dishes is represented here by *nasi goreng,* the classic Indonesian fried rice topped with a fried egg, and by an ideal picnic package of fragrant lotus leaf–wrapped rice.

Chinese Rice Porridge

For many families in Asia, a typical day begins with a bowl of jook, or rice porridge. Oftentimes, vendors with pots suspended from the ends of bamboo poles haul the hot meal right to the front door. Although rice porridge comes from humble beginnings, today it is served with a variety of exotic toppings, ranging from sliced raw fish (as here) to thousand-year eggs, or bite-size balls of ground fish or meat.

PORRIDGE

½	cup (3½ oz/105 g) long-grain white rice (or equal amounts of long-grain and glutinous rice)
½	teaspoon salt
1	tablespoon peanut oil
4	cups (32 fl oz/1 l) water
4	cups (32 fl oz/1 l) chicken stock

TOPPING

¼	lb (125 g) good-quality tuna, striped bass or sea bass
1½	teaspoons peeled and finely slivered fresh ginger
2	teaspoons light soy sauce
	Big pinch of ground white pepper
1	teaspoon Asian sesame oil
1	tablespoon chopped green (spring) onion
2	tablespoons coarsely chopped fresh cilantro (fresh coriander)

◉ To make the porridge, rinse the rice with cold water until the rinse water runs clear. Drain. Put the rice in a large saucepan and stir in the salt and oil. Add the water and chicken stock. Bring to a boil over high heat and stir the rice to loosen the grains from the bottom of the pan. Set the cover ajar and boil gently for 5 minutes. Cover, reduce the heat to low and simmer, stirring occasionally, until the rice is soft and is the consistency of porridge, about 1½ hours. Keep warm.

◉ To prepare the fish topping, wrap the fish in plastic wrap and place in the freezer to freeze partially, about 1 hour. Cut the fish into thin slivers and arrange on a serving plate. In a bowl, mix together the ginger, soy sauce, pepper and sesame oil; pour over the fish. Sprinkle the green onion and cilantro over the top.

◉ To serve, ladle the hot porridge into warmed soup bowls. To eat, pick up a few slices of fish, onions and cilantro and set them on top of each serving of porridge. Serve hot.

Serves 6–8

Wonton Noodle Soup

*Although this ubiquitous Chinese soup is served in every conceivable venue from
food stalls to fancy restaurants, the best versions are generally found in the simplest settings.*

NOODLES
Salt
½   lb (250 g) fresh Chinese egg
    noodles
1   tablespoon peanut oil

WONTONS
½   lb (250 g) shrimp (prawns),
    peeled and deveined
1½ teaspoons coarse salt
¾   lb (375 g) medium-grind
    (minced) pork butt
1   tablespoon Chinese rice wine
    or dry sherry
2   teaspoons light soy sauce
1   green (spring) onion, minced
2   tablespoons drained, minced
    canned bamboo shoots
¼   teaspoon sugar
    Big pinch of white pepper
1   teaspoon Asian sesame oil
1   teaspoon cornstarch (cornflour)
60 wonton wrappers
1   egg white, lightly beaten

SOUP
6   cups (48 fl oz/1.5 l) chicken
    stock
¼   teaspoon sugar
    Light soy sauce to taste
1   tablespoon Asian sesame oil
    Salt
1   lb (500 g) bok choy, cut into
    2-inch (5-cm) lengths
1   green (spring) onion, chopped

◎ Bring a large pot three-fourths full of water to a boil and salt it lightly. Gently pull the strands of noodles apart, then drop them into the boiling water, stirring to separate the strands. Bring to a second boil and cook for 1 minute longer. Pour the noodles into a colander and rinse thoroughly with cold running water. Drain well and transfer to a large bowl. Toss with the oil to keep the strands from sticking together.

◎ To prepare the wontons, rinse the shrimp with cold water. Drain. Place in a bowl, add 1 teaspoon of the salt and toss well; set aside for 10 minutes. Rinse the shrimp in cold water again; drain thoroughly, pat dry and chop coarsely.

◎ In a bowl, mix together the remaining ½ teaspoon salt, the shrimp, pork, wine or sherry, soy sauce, green onion, bamboo shoots, sugar, white pepper, sesame oil and cornstarch.

◎ To wrap the dumplings, work with 1 wrapper at a time, keeping unused wrappers covered with a kitchen towel. Place 1 heaping teaspoon of filling in the center of a wrapper. Moisten the wrapper edges with water and fold in half to form a triangle, enclosing the filling. Bring the two long ends up and over to meet and slightly overlap over the top of the filling. Moisten where the edges overlap with egg white and press together to seal. Set on a baking sheet and cover with another kitchen towel. Continue to form dumplings until all the filling has been used. Set aside 3 dozen dumplings for this dish; wrap the remainder and any unused wrappers in plastic wrap and freeze for up to 2 months.

◎ To assemble the soup, in a saucepan, heat the chicken stock and season with the sugar, soy sauce and sesame oil. At the same time, bring a large pot three-fourths full of water to a boil, salt lightly and add the bok choy. Boil for 1 minute; then, using a slotted spoon or tongs, transfer to a bowl and set aside. When the stock is hot, drop in the noodles for a few seconds to reheat. Using the spoon or tongs, scoop out the noodles and divide them among 6 warmed deep soup bowls; keep warm.

◎ Drop 3 dozen wonton dumplings into the boiling water. Cook until they float to the top, about 3 minutes. Using the spoon, scoop out the dumplings and place approximately 6 dumplings in each bowl. Top with the bok choy and ladle over the hot stock. Garnish with the green onion and serve hot.

Serves 6

TOM KHA GAI – THAILAND

Thai Coconut Chicken Soup

A signature dish of Thailand, this simple soup also works beautifully with a Western menu. In winter, its herbal flavors of galangal, lemongrass and kaffir lime warm the body; in summer, its characteristic lightness makes it pleasingly refreshing.

8 kaffir lime leaves or the zest of 1 regular lime

2 cans (13½ fl oz/425 ml each) coconut milk

2 cups (16 fl oz/500 ml) chicken stock

6 fresh or 4 dried galangal slices *(see glossary, page 343)*, each about 1 inch (2.5 cm) in diameter

4 lemongrass stalks, cut into 2-inch (5-cm) lengths and crushed

4 fresh small green chili peppers, halved

1 tablespoon Thai roasted chili paste *(nam prik pao)*

1 whole chicken breast, boned, skinned and cut into ½-inch (12-mm) cubes

½ cup (2½ oz/75 g) drained, canned whole straw mushrooms

½ cup (2½ oz/75 g) drained, canned sliced bamboo shoots

¼ cup (2 fl oz/60 ml) Thai fish sauce

Juice of 2 limes (about 6 tablespoons/3 fl oz/90 ml)

¼ cup (¼ oz/7 g) fresh cilantro (fresh coriander) leaves

◙ Place 4 of the lime leaves or half of the zest in a large saucepan. Add the coconut milk, chicken stock, galangal, lemongrass and chilies. Bring to a boil, then reduce the heat to low and simmer for 20 minutes. Strain the stock through a fine-mesh sieve into a clean saucepan. Discard the contents of the sieve.

◙ Bring the strained stock to a boil. Reduce the heat to medium so that it boils gently. Add the remaining 4 kaffir lime leaves or the remaining half of the zest, roasted chili paste, chicken, mushrooms, bamboo shoots and fish sauce. Boil gently until the chicken is cooked throughout, about 3 minutes.

◙ Stir in the lime juice and cilantro leaves. Ladle into warmed soup bowls and serve hot.

Serves 6–8

Chicken Soup with Potato Patties

This aromatic Indonesian soup is traditionally served with an array of garnishes—blanched bean sprouts, wedges of hard-cooked egg, noodles, sprigs of Chinese celery and crisp fried shallot flakes are some of the customary additions. Prepare as many of the garnishes as you like.

STOCK
1   chicken, 2½ lb (1.25 kg), cut up
3   leafy celery tops
1   yellow onion, quartered
2   cinnamon sticks
2   cardamom pods

SPICE PASTE
3   lemongrass stalks, tender heart
      section only, coarsely chopped
4   fresh or 2 dried galangal slices,
      about 1 inch (2.5 cm) in diameter;
      soak dried slices in water for 30
      minutes, then drain and chop
1   yellow onion, coarsely chopped
4   cloves garlic
6   candlenuts or blanched almonds
1   piece fresh ginger, 1½ inches (4 cm)
      long, peeled and coarsely chopped
2   tablespoons ground coriander
1   teaspoon freshly ground pepper
1   teaspoon ground turmeric
2   teaspoons sugar
1   teaspoon salt
      About 3 tablespoons water
2   tablespoons peanut or corn oil

PATTIES
1   lb (500 g) baking potatoes,
      peeled and boiled until tender
1   green (spring) onion, finely
      chopped
½   teaspoon salt
1   egg, lightly beaten
      Vegetable oil for frying

◙ To make the stock, place the chicken in a large stockpot and add water to cover. Bring to a boil over high heat, skimming off any scum. Add the celery tops, onion, cinnamon and cardamom. Reduce the heat to low, cover partially and simmer until the chicken is opaque throughout, about 40 minutes. Transfer the breasts to a plate and let cool. Continue simmering the stock for 20 minutes longer to concentrate the flavor.

◙ Let the stock cool, then strain through a sieve into a bowl. Let stand until the fat rises to the surface. Using a large spoon, skim off the fat and discard. You should have about 8 cups (64 fl oz/2 l).

◙ Skin and bone the chicken breasts and hand shred the meat with the grain; set aside. Reserve the remaining chicken pieces for another use.

◙ To make the spice paste, in a blender, combine the lemongrass, galangal, onion, garlic, candlenuts or almonds, ginger, coriander, pepper, turmeric, sugar and salt. Add water as needed to facilitate blending and blend to a smooth paste.

◙ In a large saucepan over medium heat, warm the oil. Stir in the spice paste and cook, stirring frequently, until well combined and fragrant,

about 5 minutes. Add the strained chicken stock and simmer for 15 minutes to infuse the stock fully with the paste. Taste and adjust the seasonings, if necessary. Keep warm.

◙ To make the potato patties, combine all the ingredients, except the oil, in a bowl. Using a potato masher or fork, mash the potatoes thoroughly, mixing well. Form into twelve 1-inch (2.5-cm) balls and flatten each into a patty 1½ inches (4 cm) in diameter.

◙ In a deep frying pan, pour in oil to a depth of 1 inch (2.5 cm) and heat to 375°F (190°C) on a deep-frying thermometer. Add the patties, a few at a time, and fry until golden brown on the underside, about 3 minutes. Turn over and continue to fry until golden brown on the second side, about 1 minute longer. Transfer to paper towels to drain. Keep warm while you fry the remaining patties.

◙ To serve, bring the stock to a simmer. Distribute the shredded chicken evenly among 6 warmed soup bowls and ladle the hot stock on top. Garnish each bowl with 2 potato patties and any of the traditional garnishes (see note above). Serve hot.

Serves 6

Spicy Lamb Soup

This spicy Anglo-Indian hawker soup evolved from colonial India's mulligatawny soup. It is popular hawker fare in Malaysia and Singapore, where it is served with fried papadams (page 336). Garnish with chopped celery leaves or fresh cilantro (fresh coriander) leaves and fried shallot flakes.

SPICE PASTE

1	piece fresh ginger, 1 inch (2.5 cm) long, peeled and coarsely chopped
6	cloves garlic
6	shallots, about ½ lb (250 g), halved
1½	teaspoons ground fennel
1½	teaspoons ground cumin
1	tablespoon ground coriander
	About 3 tablespoons water

SOUP

1½	lb (750 g) meaty lamb bones for stock
3	qt (3 l) water or meat stock
2	tablespoons ghee *(see glossary, page 343)* or vegetable oil
2	leeks, including 1 inch (2.5 cm) of the tender green tops, carefully rinsed and sliced
1	teaspoon curry powder
2	cardamom pods, bruised
2	whole star anise
1	cinnamon stick
4	whole cloves
1	large carrot, peeled and thickly sliced
2	teaspoons sugar
1½	teaspoons salt
1	large tomato, cut into large wedges
	Fresh lime juice to taste, optional

◙ To make the spice paste, in a blender, combine the ginger, garlic, shallots, fennel, cumin and coriander. Blend to a smooth paste, adding the water as needed to facilitate blending. Set aside.

◙ To make the soup, preheat an oven to 450°F (230°C).

◙ Remove any meat from the lamb bones, cut into 1-inch (2.5-cm) cubes and set aside. Place the bones in a roasting pan and roast, turning occasionally, until browned, about 20 minutes. Transfer the bones to a plate and set aside.

◙ Pour off the fat from the roasting pan and place the pan over medium heat. When the pan is hot, add 2 cups (16 fl oz/500 ml) of the water or stock and deglaze the pan by stirring to dislodge any browned bits from the pan bottom. Set aside.

◙ In a large stockpot over medium heat, melt the ghee or heat the vegetable oil. Add the leeks and sauté until golden, about 1 minute. Add the spice paste and curry powder and sauté until fragrant, about 1 minute. Add the roasted bones, reserved meat, the liquid from the roasting pan and the remaining 2½ qt (2.5 l) of water or stock. Wrap the cardamom, star anise, cinnamon and cloves in a piece of cheesecloth (muslin), tie securely with kitchen string and add to the pot. Bring to a boil, reduce the heat to low and simmer, uncovered, for 30 minutes. Add the carrot and continue to simmer until the meat is tender, about 30 minutes longer. Season with the sugar and salt and stir in the tomato.

◙ Discard the cheesecloth-wrapped spices and the bones and ladle the soup into warmed bowls. Add lime juice to taste, if desired, and serve hot.

Serves 8

Hanoi Beef and Noodle Soup

Because it is light, hot and refreshing, the broth used to make pho *is often enjoyed as a morning consommé in Vietnam. It also makes a satisfying late-night snack. The best versions of* pho *are available in street stalls or coffee shops that specialize in the soup.*

BROTH
3 lb (1.5 kg) oxtails, chopped into sections
3 lb (1.5 kg) beef shanks
3½ qt (3.5 l) water
3 pieces fresh ginger, each 1 inch (2.5 cm) long, unpeeled
1 large yellow onion, unpeeled and cut in half
4 shallots, unpeeled
1 lb (500 g) Chinese radishes, cut into 2-inch (5-cm) chunks
3 carrots, unpeeled, cut into chunks
4 whole star anise
6 whole cloves
2 cinnamon sticks
¼ cup (2 fl oz/60 ml) Vietnamese fish sauce
Salt

BEEF, RICE NOODLES AND ACCOMPANIMENTS
½ lb (250 g) beef round, in one piece and at least 2 inches (5 cm) thick
1 lb (500 g) dried flat rice stick noodles, ¼ inch (6 mm) wide
1 large yellow onion
2 green (spring) onions
2 fresh small red chili peppers
1 cup (1 oz/30 g) fresh cilantro (fresh coriander) leaves
½ cup (½ oz/15 g) fresh mint leaves
1 lime, cut into 6 wedges

◉ To make the broth, combine the oxtails, beef shanks and water in a large pot and bring to a boil. Meanwhile, preheat a broiler (griller). Place the ginger, onion and shallots on a baking sheet and broil (grill), turning frequently, until browned on all sides, 1–2 minutes. Set aside.

◉ When the water reaches a boil, using a large spoon or a wire skimmer, skim off the scum from the surface, skimming until the liquid is clear of all foam, about 10 minutes. Add the browned vegetables and the radishes, carrots, star anise, cloves and cinnamon to the pot. Reduce the heat to medium-low, cover partially and simmer gently for 3½ hours to concentrate the flavor.

◉ Remove the broth from the heat and let cool. Strain the broth through a sieve into a bowl, discarding the contents of the sieve. Let stand until the fat rises to the surface. Using a large spoon, skim off the fat and discard. Add the fish sauce and salt to taste. (The broth can be made 1 day in advance, covered and refrigerated.) You should have about 8 cups (64 fl oz/2 l).

◉ To prepare the beef, wrap it in plastic wrap and freeze until partially frozen, about 1 hour.

◉ Meanwhile, soak the dried rice noodles: Place them in a large bowl, add warm water to cover and let stand until soft and pliable, about 20 minutes. Drain and set aside.

◉ Cut the beef across the grain into paper-thin slices about 2 inches (5 cm) wide by 3 inches (7.5 cm) long. Set aside.

◉ To serve, bring the broth to a boil. Reduce the heat to low to keep the broth warm. Thinly slice the yellow and green onions and the chilies; set aside.

◉ Bring a large pot three-fourths full of water to a boil. Add the noodles and boil until tender, about 1 minute. Drain and divide the noodles evenly among 6 warmed deep soup bowls.

◉ Top each bowl evenly with the onions, a few slices of the beef and some chili slices. Ladle the hot broth over the top; this will cook the beef. Garnish with the cilantro and mint. Serve with lime wedges.

Serves 6

Sour Fish Soup

Nearly every country in Southeast Asia has its own version of sour fish soup. Loaded with fish, vegetables and fruit, this southern Vietnamese version is herbaceous, spicy, fruity, tangy, sweet and savory. Serve with steamed rice (recipe on page 338) on the side.

FISH

1	whole catfish, striped bass, sea bass or red snapper, 2 lb (1 kg)
1	tablespoon Vietnamese fish sauce
¼	teaspoon freshly ground pepper
1	green (spring) onion, thinly sliced

SOUP

1	tablespoon vegetable oil
2	shallots, thinly sliced
3	lemongrass stalks, cut into 2-inch (5-cm) lengths and crushed
6	cups (48 fl oz/1.5 l) water or chicken stock
2	oz (60 g) tamarind pulp, chopped
1	cup (8 fl oz/250 ml) boiling water
1	cup (6 oz/185 g) diced pineapple
½	cup (2½ oz/75 g) drained, canned sliced bamboo shoots
2	fresh small red chili peppers, seeded and thinly sliced
1	tablespoon sugar
2	tablespoons Vietnamese fish sauce, or to taste
2	small, firm tomatoes, cut into wedges
1	cup (2 oz/60 g) bean sprouts
	Salt and freshly ground pepper
	Fresh cilantro (fresh coriander) sprigs or slivered fresh mint leaves
1	lime, cut into wedges

◙ Fillet the fish and reserve the head, bones and scraps. Cut the fillets into 1-inch (2.5-cm) cubes and place in a bowl with the fish sauce, pepper and green onion. Toss gently to mix, then let marinate at room temperature while you make the soup.

◙ To make the soup, in a large saucepan over medium heat, warm the oil. When the oil is hot, add the shallots, lemongrass, and the fish head, bones and scraps; sauté gently without browning until fragrant, 3–5 minutes. Add the water or chicken stock and bring to a boil. Reduce the heat to low and simmer the stock uncovered for 20 minutes.

◙ Meanwhile, in a small bowl, soak the tamarind pulp in the boiling water for 15 minutes. Mash with the back of a fork to help dissolve the pulp. Pour through a fine-mesh sieve into another small bowl, pressing against the pulp to extract as much flavorful liquid as possible. Discard the pulp and set the liquid aside.

◙ Pour the stock through a fine-mesh sieve into a large saucepan. Discard the contents of the sieve. Bring the stock to a boil. Stir in the tamarind liquid, pineapple, bamboo shoots, chilies, sugar and fish sauce. Reduce the heat to medium and simmer for 1 minute. Add the tomatoes and fish cubes and continue to simmer until the fish turns opaque and feels firm to the touch, 3–5 minutes. Add the bean sprouts and season to taste with salt and pepper.

◙ Ladle the soup into warmed soup bowls and garnish with cilantro or mint. Serve with lime wedges.

Serves 6

Chicken, Shrimp and Bok Choy over Panfried Noodles

There is nothing more enticing than the sizzling sound and the seductive fragrance of noodles panfrying in a wok. At hawker centers, coffee shops and noodle houses throughout Asia, noodles with multiple combinations of meats and vegetables are made to order within moments.

Salt
1   lb (500 g) fresh thin Chinese egg noodles
3   tablespoons peanut oil, or as needed

SAUCE
1   tablespoon cornstarch (cornflour)
1   cup (8 fl oz/250 ml) chicken stock
½   teaspoon sugar
¼   teaspoon ground white pepper
1½ tablespoons soy sauce
1½ teaspoons oyster sauce

TOPPING
1   whole chicken breast, boned and skinned
1   tablespoon peanut oil, or as needed
1   teaspoon peeled and minced fresh ginger
1   teaspoon minced garlic
6   green (spring) onions, cut into 2-inch (5-cm) lengths
½   teaspoon salt
¼   lb (125 g) large shrimp (prawns), peeled and deveined
1   small red bell pepper (capsicum), cut into 1½-inch (4-cm) cubes
¼   lb (125 g) fresh shiitake mushrooms, stemmed and sliced
¾   lb (375 g) baby bok choy, cut into 2-inch (5-cm) lengths
1   teaspoon Asian sesame oil

◙ Bring a large pot three-fourths full with water to a boil and salt it lightly. Gently pull the noodles apart, then drop them into the boiling water, stirring to separate the strands. Bring to a second boil and cook for 1 minute. Pour the noodles into a colander and rinse thoroughly with cold running water. Drain well and toss with 1 tablespoon of oil to keep the strands from sticking together.

◙ Preheat an oven to 200°F (93°C).

◙ Preheat an 8- or 9-inch (20- or 23-cm) frying pan over medium-high heat. When the pan is hot, add ½ tablespoon of the oil. When the oil is hot, spread one-fourth of the noodles evenly over the bottom of the pan, spreading them with a wide spatula to form a pancake. Reduce the heat to medium and cook until the bottom is golden brown, 4–5 minutes. Using the spatula, turn the noodle pancake over and brown the other side, about 3 minutes longer; add more oil if needed to prevent scorching. Transfer to a baking sheet and keep warm while you fry the remaining noodles. Repeat to make a total of 4 noodle cakes.

◙ To make the sauce, in a bowl, combine the cornstarch, chicken stock, sugar, white pepper, soy sauce and oyster sauce. Stir until smooth and set aside.

◙ To make the topping, cut the chicken into ½-inch (12-mm) cubes; set aside. Place a wok over medium-high heat. When the pan is hot, add the 1 tablespoon peanut oil, ginger, garlic, green onions and salt. Sauté until fragrant, about 15 seconds. Increase the heat to high and add the chicken and shrimp. Stir-fry until the chicken is white and the shrimp are pink, about 1½ minutes. Transfer the mixture to a bowl; set aside.

◙ Preheat the wok again over medium-high heat. When the pan is hot, add the bell pepper, mushrooms and bok choy and stir-fry until the mushrooms begin to shrink, about 3 minutes, adding more peanut oil if needed to prevent sticking. Stir the sauce and add to the pan. Bring to a boil, stirring continuously until the sauce is glossy and thick, about 30 seconds. Return the chicken-shrimp mixture to the wok, add the sesame oil and toss together quickly to mix.

◙ Divide the noodle cakes among 4 serving plates. Evenly distribute the topping over each cake and serve hot.

Serves 4

295

Stir-Fried Thai Noodles

Although this dish is traditionally made with flat rice stick noodles, thin dried rice vermicelli can also be used. Dried shrimp and preserved radishes can be difficult to find, but the considerable flavor and texture they provide make them well worth the search.

½ lb (250 g) dried flat rice stick noodles, ¼ inch (6 mm) wide

1 oz (30 g) tamarind pulp, coarsely chopped *(see glossary, page 348)*

½ cup (4 fl oz/125 ml) boiling water

2½ tablespoons vegetable oil, or as needed

8 large fresh shrimp (prawns), peeled, deveined and cut in half lengthwise

1 whole chicken breast, boned, skinned and cut crosswise into slices ¼ inch (6 mm) thick

1½ teaspoons dried small shrimp (prawns), optional

2 tablespoons chopped preserved radish, optional

1 tablespoon chopped garlic

3 tablespoons Thai fish sauce

3 tablespoons fresh lime juice

2 tablespoons sugar

3 eggs

4 green (spring) onions, cut into 1½-inch (4-cm) lengths

1½ cups (3 oz/90 g) bean sprouts

¼ teaspoon red pepper flakes
  Fresh cilantro (fresh coriander) leaves for garnish

2 tablespoons chopped dry-roasted peanuts

1 lime, cut into wedges

◉ In a large bowl, combine the rice stick noodles with warm water to cover. Let stand until soft and pliable, about 20 minutes. Drain and set aside.

◉ Meanwhile, in a small bowl, soak the tamarind pulp in the boiling water for 15 minutes. Mash with the back of a fork to help dissolve the pulp. Pour through a fine-mesh sieve into another small bowl, pressing against the pulp to extract as much flavorful liquid as possible. Discard the pulp and set the liquid aside.

◉ Preheat a nonstick wok over medium-high heat. Add 1 tablespoon of the oil. When the oil is hot, add the shrimp and chicken and stir-fry until the shrimp turn pink and chicken turns white, about 1½ minutes. Transfer to a plate and set aside.

◉ Add the remaining 1½ tablespoons oil to the wok over medium-high heat. Add the dried shrimp and radish (if using) and the garlic; stir-fry until the garlic turns light brown, about 30 seconds. Add the tamarind liquid, fish sauce, lime juice and sugar. Raise the heat to high and cook, stirring, until well mixed and almost syrupy, about 1 minute.

◉ Crack the eggs directly into the sauce and gently scramble them just enough to break up the yolks. Cook until the eggs begin to set, 1–2 minutes, then gently fold them into the sauce. Add the green onions, 1 cup (2 oz/60 g) of the bean sprouts, the red pepper flakes and the drained noodles. Toss gently until the sprouts begin to wilt, about 1 minute.

◉ Return the shrimp-chicken mixture to the wok and stir-fry until the noodles begin to stick together, 2–3 minutes. Transfer to a serving platter and top with the remaining ½ cup (1 oz/30 g) bean sprouts. Garnish with the cilantro leaves and peanuts. Serve with lime wedges.

Serves 4

Red Curry Mussels over Noodles

In Thailand, dishes like this one are commonly ordered in open-air seafood markets, where local vendors cook customers' just-purchased seafood and vegetables in whatever style they request. At home, with premade curry paste on hand, this dish will take only about 10 minutes to prepare.

Salt

1   lb (500 g) thin fresh Chinese egg noodles

2   cans (13½ fl oz/425 ml each) coconut milk, unshaken

2   tablespoons red curry paste *(recipe on page 337),* or to taste

2   teaspoons palm sugar or dark brown sugar

2½   tablespoons Thai fish sauce

2½   lb (1.25 kg) fresh mussels in the shell

8   kaffir lime or other citrus leaves

1   cup (1 oz/30 g) fresh Thai basil leaves or regular basil leaves

4   fresh small red chili peppers, seeded and sliced

Fresh cilantro (fresh coriander) sprigs

◉ Fill a large pot three-fourths full with water, bring to a boil and salt it liberally. Gently pull the strands of noodles apart, then drop them into the boiling water, stirring to separate the strands. Bring to a second boil and cook for 1 minute longer. Pour the noodles into a colander and rinse thoroughly with cold running water. Drain well and transfer to a large bowl.

◉ Do not shake the cans of coconut milk before opening. There should be a thick layer of cream on the top of each. Spoon off ½ cup (4 fl oz/ 125 ml) of the thick cream from the top of each can and place in a wok or heavy pot. Place over medium-high heat and stir until the cream becomes oily and aromatic, about 3 minutes. Add the red curry paste and simmer over medium heat, stirring frequently, until the sharp fragrances mellow, about 3 minutes. Add the palm or brown sugar, fish sauce and the remaining coconut milk; stir well and simmer for 5 minutes longer.

◉ Meanwhile, scrub and debeard the mussels under cold running water. Discard any mussels that do not close to the touch. Bring the coconut milk sauce to a boil and add the mussels, lime or citrus leaves, basil and chilies. Cover and cook, shaking the pan occasionally, until the shells open, about 2 minutes.

◉ Meanwhile, refill the large pot three-fourths full with water and bring to a boil. Drop the reserved noodles into the water for a few seconds to reheat, then drain and divide the noodles among 6 warmed soup bowls.

◉ Ladle the mussels and sauce over the noodles, discarding any mussels that did not open. Garnish with cilantro sprigs and serve hot.

Serves 6

Sweet-and-Sour Crispy Noodles

*One of Thailand's signature creation is a tangle of
crisp lacelike noodles moistened with a piquant sweet-and-sour sauce. Traditionally
reserved for special occasions,* mee grob *is now served at all times of the day.*

½ lb (250 g) crispy fried rice sticks *(recipe on page 336)*

1 lime

1 tablespoon yellow bean sauce

2 tablespoons tomato paste

2 tablespoons Thai fish sauce

¼ cup (2 oz/60 g) firmly packed brown sugar

2 tablespoons peanut or corn oil

1 whole chicken breast, boned, skinned and cut crosswise into slices ¼ inch (6 mm) thick

¼ lb (125 g) medium-sized shrimp (prawns), peeled and deveined

2 cloves garlic, chopped

4 shallots, chopped

1 tablespoon dried small shrimp, optional

2 fresh small red chili peppers, thinly sliced on the diagonal

OPTIONAL GARNISHES

3 cups (6 oz/185 g) bean sprouts

1 lime, cut into wedges

Fresh cilantro (fresh coriander) leaves

◙ Prepare the rice sticks; set aside.

◙ Remove the zest from the lime in fine shreds; set aside. Squeeze the juice from the lime into a small bowl. Add the yellow bean sauce, tomato paste, fish sauce and brown sugar and stir to mix well; set aside.

◙ Place a wok or large frying pan over medium-high heat. When it is hot, add the oil. When the oil is hot, add the chicken and shrimp and stir-fry until they feel firm to the touch, about 1 minute. Remove from the pan and set aside.

◙ Add the garlic, shallots and dried shrimp, if using, to the pan; stir-fry until fragrant, about 30 seconds. Raise the heat to high. Add the lime juice mixture and continue to stir-fry until the mixture turns into a glossy syruplike sauce, about 2 minutes.

◙ Reduce the heat to medium and gently fold in the crispy noodles and the chilies. Try to crush as few noodles as possible. Mix in the reserved shrimp mixture and lime zest. Transfer to a platter, forming the mixture into a mound. If using the bean sprouts and lime wedges, pile them at one end of the platter. Top with cilantro leaves, if desired, and serve hot.

Serves 6–8 as an appetizer

Chiang Mai Curry Noodle Soup

Although this noodle soup from Thailand is delicious served plain, a variety
of crispy, tasty toppings delivers an exciting flavor boost and lively textures.

1   lb (500 g) fresh thin or regular Chinese egg noodles
    Peanut or corn oil for deep-frying
3   cloves garlic, finely chopped
2   cans (13½ fl oz/425 ml each) coconut milk, unshaken
2   tablespoons red curry paste *(recipe on page 337),* or to taste
1½ teaspoons curry powder
½   teaspoon ground turmeric
¾   lb (375 g) chopped chicken meat
4   cups (32 fl oz/1 l) chicken stock
3   tablespoons Thai fish sauce
1   teaspoon palm sugar or brown sugar
¼   cup (¾ oz/20 g) shredded green cabbage
    Juice of 1 lemon

GARNISHES
2   tablespoons fried shallot flakes *(recipe on page 337)*
    Chopped fresh cilantro (fresh coriander)
2   green (spring) onions, thinly sliced
1   lemon, cut into 6 wedges

◉ Bring a large pot three-fourths full of water to a boil. Gently pull the strands of noodles apart, then drop them into the boiling water, stirring to separate the strands. Bring to a second boil and cook for 1 minute longer. Pour the noodles into a colander and rinse thoroughly with cold running water. Drain well, shaking off excess water.

◉ Pour oil to a depth of 2 inches (5 cm) in a small saucepan and heat to 375°F (190°C) on a deep-frying thermometer. Meanwhile, pat dry 1 cup (6 oz/185 g) of the cooked noodles with paper towels. When the oil is hot, add the noodles. Using a pair of long chopsticks or tongs, stir gently to separate the strands and fry until golden brown, about 30 seconds. Lift out the noodles and place on paper towels to drain. Remove the pan from the heat. Crumble the noodles into small chunks and set aside.

◉ Measure out 2 tablespoons of the oil used to fry the noodles and place in a large saucepan over medium heat. Add the garlic and sauté until browned, about 1 minute. Do not shake the cans of coconut milk before opening. There should be a thick layer of cream on top of each. Spoon off ½ cup (4 fl oz/125 ml) of the thick cream from the top of each can and add it to the garlic. Raise the heat to medium-high and cook, stirring frequently, until the cream boils gently. Add the red curry paste, curry powder and turmeric and stir until smooth. Reduce the heat to medium and simmer until the mixture is thick and the oil begins to separate around the edges and rises to the surface, about 5 minutes.

◉ Add the chicken, breaking it up into small pieces. Cook until the chicken becomes white, about 2 minutes. Raise the heat to high. Add the remaining coconut milk, the chicken stock, fish sauce, palm or brown sugar and cabbage and stir well. When the mixture begins to boil, adjust the heat to maintain a gentle boil and continue cooking for 8 minutes longer.

◉ Divide the boiled noodles evenly among 6 warmed deep soup bowls. Stir the lemon juice into the hot soup and ladle equal amounts of the soup over the noodles. Garnish with the crumbled fried noodles, fried shallots, cilantro and green onions. Place a lemon wedge on top of each serving and serve hot.

Serves 6

Stir-Fried Rice Noodles with Shellfish and Bok Choy

A well-seasoned wok and intense high heat are the secret ingredients to this Malaysian favorite. In the home kitchen, a nonstick wok is best for cooking fresh rice noodles, which are particularly delicate and stick together easily. Purchase the noodles at a Chinese market and try to use them the same day.

1	Chinese sausage
2	tablespoons dark soy sauce
1½	tablespoons light soy sauce
1	tablespoon oyster sauce
½	teaspoon sugar
⅛	teaspoon ground white pepper
2	lb (1 kg) fresh rice noodles, about ½ inch (12 mm) wide
2	tablespoons peanut or corn oil
3	cloves garlic, chopped
2	shallots, thinly sliced
1	small whole chicken breast, boned, skinned and cut crosswise into slices ¼ inch (6 mm) thick
¼	lb (125 g) large shrimp (prawns), peeled and deveined
3	green (spring) onions, cut into 2-inch (5-cm) lengths
2	fresh small red chili peppers, seeded and sliced
¼	lb (125 g) bok choy, trimmed, halved lengthwise and cut into 3-inch (7.5-cm) lengths
2	cups (4 oz/125 g) bean sprouts
8	mussels or clams, shucked
1	extra-large egg

◙ Cut the sausage on the diagonal into thin slices. Place the slices on a heatproof plate and set the plate in a bamboo steaming basket over (not touching) boiling water in a wok or on a rack in a steamer. Cover the basket or steamer and steam until glossy and plump, about 10 minutes. Remove from over the water and let cool. Set aside.

◙ In a bowl, combine the soy sauces, oyster sauce, sugar and white pepper. Stir well and set aside. Gently pull apart and separate the strands of noodles; set aside.

◙ Preheat a wok, preferably nonstick, over medium-high heat. Add the oil. When the oil is hot, add the garlic and sauté until a light golden brown, about 1 minute. Raise the heat to high and add the shallots, chicken, shrimp, green onions, chilies and bok choy. Stir-fry until the ingredients are almost fully cooked, about 1½ minutes.

◙ Add the reserved noodles and sauce mixture to the wok; toss until the noodles are evenly coated. Add the reserved sausage, bean sprouts, and the mussels or clams. Stir-fry until the sprouts begin to wilt, about 1 minute. Push the mixture up the side of the wok and crack the egg directly into the center of the pan. Stir to scramble the egg lightly and let it set slightly, then gently fold the egg into the noodles. Continue tossing until the egg is fully cooked and little bits of scrambled egg intermingle with the noodles. Taste and adjust the seasonings, if necessary. Transfer to a platter and serve hot.

Serves 4

Chicken and Sticky Rice in Lotus Leaf Parcels

Lotus leaves impart an earthy taste and aromatic fragrance to the ingredients
concealed in these country parcels. Aluminum foil may be substituted.

2 cups (14 oz/440 g) glutinous rice
2 cups (16 fl oz/500 ml) water
6 dried lotus leaves
2 Chinese sausages, each cut on the diagonal into thirds

CHICKEN MARINADE
¼ teaspoon sugar
Pinch of ground white pepper
1 teaspoon ginger juice (pressed from ginger in a garlic press)
1 teaspoon Chinese rice wine or dry sherry
1 teaspoon light soy sauce
1 teaspoon cornstarch (cornflour)
1 teaspoon Asian sesame oil
1 lb (500 g) chicken thighs, boned, skinned and cut into ¾-inch (2-cm) cubes
12 small dried Chinese black mushrooms
1½ tablespoons peanut or corn oil
3 green (spring) onions, chopped
1 piece Cantonese barbecued pork *(recipe on page 338),* ¼ lb (125 g), cut into thin slices

RICE SAUCE
½ teaspoon salt
¼ teaspoon sugar
1 tablespoon Chinese rice wine or dry sherry
1 tablespoon dark soy sauce
2 tablespoons oyster sauce
1½ teaspoons Asian sesame oil

◉ Rinse the rice until the water runs clear. Drain. In a heatproof bowl 9 inches (23 cm) in diameter, combine the rice and the water. Let soak for at least 4 hours or preferably overnight.

◉ To prepare the lotus leaves, bring a pot of water to a boil. Remove from the heat and add the lotus leaves. Soak until soft and pliable, at least 2 hours or as long as overnight.

◉ Place a deep bamboo steaming basket (or a steaming rack) in a large wok. Add water to come just below the base of the basket and bring to a boil. Place the sausages on top of the rice, put the bowl in the basket, cover and steam until the rice is tender, 35–40 minutes. Let cool, remove the sausages and set aside. Transfer the rice to a large bowl and set aside.

◉ In a bowl, combine all the marinade ingredients. Add the chicken and toss to mix. Set aside for 30 minutes. Meanwhile, in a bowl, combine the mushrooms with warm water to cover and let soak for 30 minutes.

◉ Remove the mushrooms and squeeze dry. Discard the stems and cut the caps in half; set aside.

◉ Preheat the wok over medium-high heat. Add the oil. When the oil is hot, add the mushrooms, chicken, onions and pork; stir-fry for 2 minutes. Remove from the wok and set aside.

◉ In the same wok, combine all the ingredients for the rice sauce, stir well and place over medium-high heat. Cook, stirring occasionally, until slightly thickened, about 30 seconds. Mix in the rice. Fold in the chicken-mushroom mixture.

◉ To wrap the parcels, drain the lotus leaves and squeeze dry. If they are large, cut in half and trim off the tough portions; leaves must be at least 12 inches (30 cm) in diameter. Place 1 leaf on a flat work surface, smooth side up. Divide the rice mixture into 6 equal portions. Mound 1 portion on the center of the leaf. Put 1 piece of sausage on top. Wrap the lotus leaf into a square parcel by folding in the sides, then the bottom and top. Secure with kitchen string. Repeat to make 6 parcels in all.

◉ Arrange the parcels, folded side down, in a single layer in 2 stacked bamboo steaming baskets or tiered metal steaming racks.

◉ Set the baskets or racks over (not touching) water in a wok or pan and bring the water to a boil over medium-high heat. Cover and steam for 30 minutes. When done, transfer each parcel to a plate, remove the string and make a crisscross cut in the top of the parcel to display the rice mixture. Serve hot.

Makes 6 parcels; serves 6

Chicken, Shrimp and Egg Fried Rice

In the Asian kitchen, leftover rice is never discarded. It is stir-fried with bits of meats and vegetables and turned into a tasty snack, light meal or side dish. A favorite way of serving fried rice in Indonesia is to top it with a crispy fried egg. The yolk is broken and mixed into the rice by the diner.

4	shallots or 1 yellow onion, coarsely chopped
2	cloves garlic
1	teaspoon dried shrimp paste
2	fresh small red chili peppers, seeded
½	teaspoon ground turmeric
2	tablespoons catsup
1	tablespoon Indonesian sweet dark soy sauce *(ketjap manis)*
2	tablespoons light soy sauce
3–4	tablespoons peanut or corn oil
5	cups (25 oz/780 g) cold, cooked white rice
1½	cups (4½ oz/140 g) shredded green cabbage
¾	cup (4 oz/125 g) green peas, blanched for 1 minute and drained
¼	lb (125 g) medium-sized shrimp (prawns), peeled and deveined
1	cup (6 oz/185 g) diced, cooked chicken
4	green (spring) onions, sliced
4	eggs

OPTIONAL GARNISHES
Fried shallot flakes *(recipe on page 336)*
Fried shrimp crackers *(page 336)*

◙ In a mortar or mini food processor, combine the shallots or onion, garlic, shrimp paste, chilies and turmeric and mash with a pestle or grind to a paste; set aside. In a bowl, mix together the catsup and dark and light soy sauces; set aside.

◙ Place a wok over medium-high heat. When it is hot, add 2 tablespoons of the oil. When the oil is hot, add the spice paste and fry, stirring continuously, for 2 minutes.

◙ Raise the heat to high. Crumble the cold rice between your palms into the wok. Using a wok spatula, toss and gently flatten any clumps of rice until the grains are separated. Add the catsup mixture and stir-fry until all the rice grains are evenly coated. Add the cabbage, peas, shrimp and chicken; stir and toss until the shrimp turns pink, 2–3 minutes. Divide the rice among 4 individual plates and garnish with the green onions. Cover loosely to keep warm.

◙ Reheat the wok over medium-high heat. When it is hot, add ½ tablespoon of the oil. When the oil is hot and almost smoking, crack 1 egg directly into the oil. Fry until the edges are blistered and crisp and the whites are almost set, about 1 minute. Using a slotted spatula, turn the egg over and fry for a few seconds longer to brown. Transfer the fried egg to the top of 1 plate of rice. Repeat with the remaining oil and eggs. If desired, sprinkle with the fried shallots and garnish with the shrimp crackers. Serve hot.

Serves 4

Main Dishes

The tasty dishes offered by Asian street-hawkers have long provided a way of satisfying hunger pangs with a quick snack, a meal in one dish or a dinner on the run—a comfortable option for grabbing a bite on your own. With food courts sprouting up in many places in Southeast Asia, families, friends and business associates are now sharing family-style meals at these expanded food-stall operations. Main courses rather than just snacks are becoming customary. A routine rice-plate meal of barbecued chicken with rice, light soup and a side vegetable is now enjoyed alongside several other main dishes. A savory curry, claypot casserole and chili crab are rounded up from various stalls to compose a multicourse menu to be shared by all.

The selection of dishes in this chapter encompasses many ethnic and regional styles. They exemplify the full-scale dining now available at food centers, where the formidable wok and ash-white barbecue grill work full time, and the cauldrons filled with curries bubble for countless hours. Nowhere else can you enjoy an authentic Indian curry, Malaysian barbecue or regional Chinese casserole than on the simply set tables of these Asian cafes.

Grilled Five-Spice Chicken

A popular ready-mixed spice blend, five-spice powder is a combination of star anise, fennel, cassia, Sichuan peppercorns and cloves. In this easy Vietnamese recipe, the aromatic powder flavors barbecued chicken. Accompany with steamed rice (recipe on page 338).

2   small chickens, about 2 lb (1 kg) each

MARINADE
1   piece fresh ginger, about 1 inch (2.5 cm) long, peeled and grated
4   cloves garlic, chopped
2   shallots, chopped
1½ tablespoons brown sugar
½   teaspoon salt
¼   teaspoon freshly ground pepper
½   teaspoon five-spice powder
2   tablespoons Vietnamese or Thai fish sauce
2   tablespoons soy sauce
1   tablespoon dry sherry

Fish sauce and lime dipping sauce *(recipe on page 337)*

◉ Cut each chicken in half through the breast and backbone. Using your palms, press down on the breasts to flatten the halves slightly.

◉ To make the marinade, combine the ginger, garlic, shallots, brown sugar and salt in a mortar, blender or mini food processor. Mash with a pestle or process to a smooth paste. Transfer to a large shallow bowl. Add the pepper, five-spice powder, fish sauce, soy sauce and sherry and stir to mix well. Add the chicken halves and turn to coat thoroughly with the marinade. Cover and let marinate in the refrigerator for a few hours or as long as overnight.

◉ Prepare the dipping sauce; set aside.

◉ Prepare a fire in a charcoal grill. When the coals are ash white, place the chicken halves, bone side down, on the grill rack about 4 inches (10 cm) above the coals and grill for 20 minutes. Turn the chicken over and continue to grill until thoroughly cooked and golden brown with nice grill marks, about 20 minutes longer.

◉ Serve hot with the dipping sauce.

Serves 4

Grilled Beef Ribs and Leeks

Bulgalbi *traditionally calls for grilling marinated beef short ribs on a heavy, dome-shaped metal plate with a ridged surface that is sometimes referred to as a Mongolian grill. Flanken-style-cut short ribs make a delicious Korean barbecue, providing lots of bones to chew around. Cut between the ribs before serving, if you like.*

3 lb (1.5 kg) beef short ribs, cut flanken-style across the rib into slices ⅜ inch (1 cm) thick

MARINADE
¼ cup (¾ oz/20 g) sesame seeds
1 piece fresh ginger, about 1 inch (2.5 cm) long, peeled and finely minced
4 cloves garlic, finely minced
4 green (spring) onions, finely chopped
3 tablespoons firmly packed brown sugar
1 teaspoon freshly ground black pepper
¼ teaspoon red pepper flakes
¼ cup (2 fl oz/60 ml) Japanese soy sauce
2 tablespoons dry sherry or Japanese *mirin*
2 tablespoons Asian sesame oil

1 lb (500 g) leeks
Salt

◙ Trim the excess fat from the beef. Place the beef in a lock-top plastic bag and set aside.

◙ To make the marinade, in a small, dry frying pan over medium heat, toast the sesame seeds until fragrant and golden, 2–3 minutes. Transfer 2 tablespoons of the seeds to a spice grinder or mortar and grind or mash with a pestle to a fine powder. Reserve the remaining 2 tablespoons seeds for garnish. In a bowl, combine the ground seeds, ginger, garlic, green onions, brown sugar, black pepper, red pepper flakes, soy sauce, sherry or *mirin* and sesame oil. Mix well and pour into the bag with the beef. Seal the top closed and turn the bag to coat the meat evenly. Let marinate in the refrigerator for at least 3 hours or preferably overnight.

◙ Trim the leeks, leaving part of the root end and about 1 inch (2.5 cm) of the green tops intact. Cut in half lengthwise and rinse well.

◙ Bring a saucepan three-fourths of water to a boil and salt it lightly. Have ready a bowl of ice water. Add the trimmed leeks to the boiling water

and blanch for 30 seconds. Drain and immediately immerse in the ice water to stop the cooking. Drain again and pat dry.

◙ Prepare a fire in a charcoal grill. Meanwhile, bring the beef ribs to room temperature. When the coals are ash white, remove the ribs from the marinade, reserving the marinade in the bag. Lay the ribs flat on the grill rack about 6 inches (15 cm) above the coals. Grill, turning once, until seared on both sides, 2–3 minutes per side. Transfer the ribs to a platter and sprinkle with the reserved sesame seeds.

◙ Dip the leeks into the marinade and place flat on the grill rack. Grill, turning several times and basting with the marinade, until tender-crisp and browned, about 3 minutes.

◙ Transfer the leeks to the platter with the ribs, garnish with the reserved sesame seeds and serve hot.

Serves 4

Grilled Lemongrass Beef

*In Vietnamese homes, these tangy morsels of seared beef are grilled at the table over a
charcoal brazier. The beef strips can be served as a main dish wrapped in rice paper with vegetables,
noodles and herbs; as a topping for cold noodles; or with a plate of steamed rice.*

1   lb (500 g) beef chuck, rump or
     sirloin, in one piece

MARINADE
1   tablespoon sesame seeds
2   lemongrass stalks, tender heart
     section only, finely chopped
3   shallots, minced
3   cloves garlic
1   fresh small red chili pepper,
     seeded
1   tablespoon sugar
1½   tablespoons fish sauce
¼   teaspoon freshly ground black
     pepper
1½   teaspoons Asian sesame oil
1   tablespoon peanut or
     vegetable oil

     Fish sauce and lime dipping
     sauce *(recipe on page 337)*

◉ Wrap the beef in plastic wrap and place it in the freezer until partially frozen, about 1 hour.

◉ Meanwhile, prepare the marinade: Place the sesame seeds in a small, dry frying pan over medium heat and toast until fragrant and golden, 2–3 minutes. Transfer the seeds to a blender or mini food processor and add the lemongrass, shallots, garlic, chili pepper and sugar. Process to a smooth paste. Pour the paste into a large bowl and stir in the fish sauce, black pepper, sesame oil and peanut or vegetable oil.

◉ Cut the partially frozen beef across the grain into slices about ⅛ inch (3 mm) thick, 2 inches (5 cm) wide and 5–6 inches (13–15 cm) long. Add the slices to the lemongrass marinade and toss to coat. Let marinate for at least 1 hour at room temperature, or cover and refrigerate for up to 4 hours.

◉ Prepare the dipping sauce; set aside.

◉ Prepare a fire in a charcoal grill. When the coals are ash white, lay the beef slices flat on the grill rack about 4 inches (10 cm) above the coals. (Alternatively, preheat a ridged grill pan on the stove top over medium-high heat until hot and spread the beef slices over the hot grill.) Grill, turning once, until cooked through, about 30 seconds on each side.

◉ Transfer the beef slices to a platter and serve with the dipping sauce.

Serves 6

Chicken Braised with Kaffir Lime Leaf

This refreshingly light chicken curry has a complex blend of sour flavors perfectly balanced with sweet ingredients. The three distinct sour flavors—kaffir lime, lemongrass and tamarind—are all widely used by Southeast Asian cooks. Kaffir lime leaves perfume the dish with their lemony aroma. Lemongrass injects a subtle herbaceousness. Tamarind adds a citric sweet-sour flavor.

2 oz (60 g) tamarind pulp, coarsely chopped *(see glossary, page 348)*

1 cup (8 fl oz/250 ml) boiling water

SPICE PASTE

1 piece fresh galangal (about ½ inch/ 12 mm), chopped; or 1 piece dried galangal (about ¼ inch/ 6 mm), soaked in water for 30 minutes then chopped

1 lemongrass stalk, tender heart section only, coarsely chopped

4 shallots or 1 yellow onion, quartered

5 fresh small red chili peppers, seeded

3 cloves garlic, peeled

1 teaspoon ground turmeric
About 3 tablespoons water

CHICKEN

¼ cup (2 fl oz/60 ml) vegetable oil

1 small chicken, about 2 lb (1 kg), cut into serving pieces

1 cup (8 fl oz/250 ml) coconut milk

6 kaffir lime or other citrus leaves or the zest of 1 regular lime

1 teaspoon salt, or to taste

◙ In a small bowl, soak the tamarind pulp in the boiling water for 15 minutes. Mash with the back of a fork to help dissolve the pulp. Pour through a fine-mesh sieve into another small bowl, pressing against the pulp to extract as much flavorful liquid as possible. Discard the pulp and set the tamarind liquid aside.

◙ To make the spice paste, if dried galangal is used, make certain it has become soft and pliable from soaking. Coarsely chop the fresh or rehydrated dried galangal. In a blender, combine the galangal, lemongrass, shallots or onion, chilies, garlic, turmeric and 3 tablespoons water. Blend to a smooth paste, adding more water if needed.

◙ In a wok or large saucepan over medium heat, warm the oil. When the oil is hot, add the spice paste and fry, stirring continuously, until fragrant, thick and creamy, about 3 minutes.

Continue frying, stirring frequently, until the oil separates from the paste, about 5 minutes. Add the chicken pieces and fry, turning often, until fully coated with the spice paste, about 3 minutes. Stir in the reserved tamarind liquid and bring to a boil. Reduce the heat to medium and simmer uncovered, turning occasionally, for 15 minutes. Add the coconut milk, lime or citrus leaves or zest, and salt. Simmer until the chicken is tender when pierced with a fork, about 10 minutes longer.

◙ Taste and adjust the seasonings, if necessary. Serve hot.

Serves 4

Chili Crab

A somewhat messy affair, chili crab is not for the timid or the meticulously neat.
Whole chunks of crab in the shell are stir-fried in sizzling hot oil over high heat and then
coated with a rich and tangy tomato sauce. Forget all formalities and eat with your hands.

1   whole Dungeness crab, 2–2½ lb (1–1.25 kg), preferably live

CHILI SAUCE
5   cloves garlic
1   piece fresh ginger, about 2 inches (5 cm) long, peeled and coarsely chopped
3   fresh small red chili peppers, seeded
3   tablespoons catsup
1   tablespoon mild Sriracha sauce *(see glossary, page 347)*
1   teaspoon yellow bean sauce, optional
1   tablespoon sugar
1   teaspoon salt
1   tablespoon light soy sauce
½   cup (4 fl oz/125 ml) chicken stock

1   tablespoon cornstarch (cornflour)
¼   cup (2 fl oz/60 ml) peanut or corn oil
1   extra-large egg
2   teaspoons fresh lime juice
1   green (spring) onion, chopped
1   lime, cut into wedges

◙ If using a live crab, bring a large pot three-fourths full of water to a boil. Grab the crab by its smallest leg or grip the body with a long pair of tongs and plunge it into the boiling water. Remove the crab when it turns bright orange, about 1 minute. Rinse the crab under cold running water. (If you have purchased the crab precooked, simply rinse briefly under cold running water.)

◙ Turn the crab onto its back and lift up and snap off the V-shaped apron from the "tail." Turn the crab onto its stomach, grip the shell where the apron was and pull the shell off the body. Pull away and discard the feathery gills on both sides of the body. Break off the claws and legs from the body. Using a cleaver or heavy chef's knife, cut the body in half down the middle. Cut each half into 3 pieces. Using a nutcracker, crack the joint and midsection of all the legs and claws. Set aside the prepared crab.

◙ To make the sauce, in a mortar or blender, combine the garlic, ginger and chilies and mash with a pestle or blend to a paste. In a bowl, stir together the catsup, Sriracha sauce, yellow bean sauce (if using), sugar, salt, soy sauce and chicken stock. Set both mixtures aside.

◙ Just before cooking, toss the crab pieces with the cornstarch; set aside. In a wok or large frying pan over medium-high heat, warm the oil. When the oil is hot, add the crab pieces and brown lightly for about 3 minutes. Add the reserved ginger paste and stir-fry, coating the crab with the paste, until fragrant, about 1 minute. Mix in the catsup mixture and cover the wok. Raise the heat to high and simmer briskly for 5 minutes if the crab was live, or 2 minutes if the crab was precooked.

◙ Remove the cover. The sauce should be slightly thickened. Crack the egg directly into the wok and stir to scramble slightly. Add the lime juice and green onion and gently fold them into the sauce just until the egg is set and incorporated with the sauce. There should be specks of scrambled egg peeking through the sauce.

◙ Transfer the crab to a serving dish. Garnish with the lime wedges and serve hot.

Serves 2

318

Spicy Beef in Dry Curry

Indonesian curry sauces vary in thickness. A "dry" curry is a rich, thick, clinging sauce.
A "wet" curry may be as thin as a soup or as smooth and luscious as a cream sauce.

2½ lb (1.25 kg) boneless beef chuck, round or stew meat

1 oz (30 g) tamarind pulp *(see glossary, page 348)*

½ cup (4 fl oz/125 ml) boiling water

SPICE PASTE

1 teaspoon coriander seeds

1 teaspoon cumin seeds

10 dried small red chili peppers, seeded, soaked in lukewarm water for 15 minutes and drained

2 lemongrass stalks, tender heart section only, chopped, or zest of 1 lemon

3 fresh galangal slices, each 1 inch (2.5 cm) in diameter, chopped; or 1½ dried galangal slices, soaked in warm water to soften, drained and chopped

1 piece fresh ginger, 1 inch (2.5 cm) long, peeled and chopped

2 cloves garlic

3 shallots
About 3 tablespoons water

3 tablespoons unsweetened shredded dried coconut

3 tablespoons vegetable oil

2 cinnamon sticks

2 cardamom pods

4 whole star anise

1 can (13½ fl oz/425 ml) coconut milk

4 kaffir lime leaves

2 teaspoons sugar

½ teaspoon salt

◙ Cut the beef into 1½-inch (4-cm) cubes. Set aside.

◙ In a small bowl, soak the tamarind pulp in the boiling water for 15 minutes. Mash with the back of a fork to help dissolve the pulp. Pour through a fine-mesh sieve into another small bowl, pressing against the pulp to extract as much flavorful liquid as possible. Discard the pulp and set the liquid aside.

◙ To make the spice paste, in a small, dry frying pan over medium heat, toast the coriander and cumin seeds until fragrant, 2–3 minutes. Let cool, then transfer to a spice grinder or mortar. Grind or pulverize with a pestle until finely ground. Transfer to a blender or mini food processor and add the rehydrated chilies, lemongrass or lemon zest, galangal, ginger, garlic, shallots and 3 tablespoons water. Blend to a smooth paste, adding more water if needed. Set aside.

◙ In a small, dry frying pan over medium heat, toast the coconut until golden brown, 1–2 minutes. Let cool, then transfer to a spice grinder or mortar. Grind or mash with a pestle as finely as possible.

◙ In a wok over medium heat, warm the oil. When the oil is hot, add the spice paste and fry gently, stirring continuously, until fragrant, thick and creamy, 5–8 minutes. Add the cinnamon, cardamom, star anise, ground coconut, tamarind liquid and beef. Cook, turning often to coat the beef thoroughly with the spice paste, for about 3 minutes. Add the coconut milk and bring to a boil. Reduce the heat to medium and boil gently, uncovered, until the beef is tender, about 45 minutes.

◙ Cut the lime leaves into fine slivers and add to the pot along with the sugar and salt. Continue boiling gently, stirring occasionally, until the sauce reduces, is no longer milky and coats the fork-tender meat with a thin film of oil, about 20 minutes longer. Serve hot.

Serves 4

Crab, Shrimp and Bean Thread Noodle Claypot

This fragrant dish is a popular offering in the seafood market cafes and garden restaurants of Thailand. Once the dish is cooked, the pot is carried straight from the burner to the table sizzling hot, with the savory aromas escaping from under the lid. If a claypot is unavailable, any heavy-bottomed pot may be used.

1   package (7¾ oz/240 g) dried bean thread noodles

1   whole Dungeness crab, 2–3 lb (1-1.5 kg), preferably live

½   lb (250 g) jumbo shrimp (prawns) (16–20 shrimp)

SAUCE

½   teaspoon sugar

2   tablespoons oyster sauce

1   tablespoon dark soy sauce

1   tablespoon Thai fish sauce

1½   tablespoons Chinese rice wine or dry sherry

½   cup (4 fl oz/125 ml) chicken stock

1   teaspoon Asian sesame oil

1   tablespoon vegetable oil

4   slices peeled fresh ginger, each about ½ inch (12 mm) in diameter

3   cloves garlic, chopped

1   fresh small red chili pepper, or to taste, sliced

3   green (spring) onions, cut into 3-inch (7.5-cm) lengths

1   lb (500 g) baby bok choy, 4–5 inches (10–13 cm) long, trimmed but left whole

½   teaspoon freshly ground black pepper
    Fresh cilantro (fresh coriander) leaves

◙ In a large bowl, combine the noodles with warm water to cover and let stand until soft and pliable, about 20 minutes. Drain and set aside.

◙ If using a live crab, bring a large pot three-fourths full of water to a boil. Boil, clean and cut up the crab as directed for chili crab (recipe on page 318); set aside. If using precooked crab, rinse the crab briefly under cold running water, then clean and cut up the crab as directed for chili crab (recipe on page 318); set aside. Peel and devein the shrimp; pat dry and set aside.

◙ To make the sauce, in a small bowl, stir together the sugar, oyster sauce, soy sauce, fish sauce, rice wine, chicken stock and sesame oil. Set aside.

◙ In a 3-qt (3-l) Chinese sand claypot or heavy-bottomed pot over medium-high heat, warm the vegetable oil until hot. Evenly distribute the ginger, garlic, chili, green onions and bok choy over the bottom of the pot. Add the softened bean thread noodles and place the uncooked crab pieces on top. (If using precooked crab, add it later.) Sprinkle with the black pepper and then pour the blended sauce evenly over the top.

◙ Raise the heat to high and bring to a boil. Cover and reduce the heat so the contents boil gently. Cook for 5 minutes. Remove the lid and add the shrimp and the precooked crab, if using, to the pot. Using tongs or long chopsticks, stir to mix the ingredients. Cover and cook until the noodles are soft and clear and the shrimp and crab are bright orange, about 4 minutes longer.

◙ Garnish with cilantro and serve hot.

Serves 4

Desserts

Although the Asian table is not known for its desserts, such light preparations as cut fresh fruits, chilled puréed fruit soups and warm sweet almond or red bean soups are sometimes served at the end of a meal. Conventional Western desserts such as cream-filled pastries or fruit tarts are occasionally enjoyed in the afternoons with coffee or tea.

Chilled fresh melon is a favorite Asian dessert, whether cut into wedges and eaten out of hand, or puréed or finely chopped and served as a cold dessert soup, sometimes with tapioca added. There are several crushed ice desserts as well, in which red beans, seeds, litchis, bits of colorful jelly and even corn are mixed with the ice and covered with flavored sugar syrup.

Sticky rice with mangoes and a coconut shell of tapioca pearls steeped in sweetened coconut milk and ice are among the usual finales in Thailand. And naturally sweet banana fritters are consumed everywhere from Vietnam to Indonesia.

Peking Candied Apples

*Although this is not a traditional hawker dessert, a candied apple stand fits perfectly
into the concept of Asian fast food. Being well organized is the key to the success of this dish.
For a memorable presentation, candy the apples at the table in front of your guests.*

BATTER
¾ cup (4 oz/125 g) all-purpose
    (plain) flour
¼ cup (1 oz/30 g) cornstarch
    (cornflour)
¼ teaspoon salt
1 egg, lightly beaten
    About ¾ cup (6 fl oz/180 ml)
    water

2 Granny Smith or other firm green
    apples
    Juice of 1 small lemon

SYRUP
1 cup (8 oz/250 g) sugar
¼ cup (2 fl oz/60 ml) water
1 tablespoon black or white
    sesame seeds

    Peanut or corn oil for frying

◙ To make the batter, in a bowl, sift together the flour, cornstarch and salt. Stir in the egg and ¾ cup (6 fl oz/180 ml) water, adding more water if needed to achieve the consistency of a thick pancake batter.

◙ Peel, halve and core the apples, then cut each into 8 wedges. Place in a bowl and immediately toss with the lemon juice. Set aside.

◙ To make the sugar syrup, in a small, heavy-bottomed saucepan over medium heat, combine the sugar and water. When the sugar has dissolved, raise the heat to high and boil without stirring. Continue boiling until the mixture changes from large, thick bubbles to a smooth, golden brown syruplike consistency, 8–10 minutes. This is the hard-crack stage (300°–310°F/150°–154°C). To test the sugar syrup, using a small spoon, scoop up a small amount of syrup and drop it into the ice water. It should harden instantly. At this point, the syrup could easily burn, so lower the heat or set the pan in a bowl of ice-cold water to cool it quickly; keep warm while you make the fritters. Stir in the sesame seeds.

◙ Preheat a deep saucepan or wok over medium-high heat. Pour in oil to a depth of 1½ inches (4 cm).

Heat to 375°F (190°C). Oil a serving platter. Fill a deep serving bowl with ice cubes and add water to cover. Set the platter and bowl aside.

◙ When ready to serve, slip the apple wedges into the batter to coat each wedge completely. Using long chopsticks or a slotted spoon, lift out the apple wedges one at a time, allowing the excess batter to drip off into the bowl, and carefully lower into the hot oil. Do not crowd the pan; the wedges must float freely. Deep-fry, keeping the wedges separated and turning often, until golden brown, about 2 minutes. Using a slotted spoon, transfer the wedges to paper towels to drain. When all of the wedges have been fried, dip a few of them in the syrup. Turn them with oiled tongs or chopsticks to coat completely with the syrup. Then remove the wedges and set them on the oiled platter, keeping them separate. Repeat with the remaining wedges.

◙ To serve, bring the platter of caramelized apples and the serving bowl of ice water to the table. Pour the caramelized apple wedges into the ice water. Using chopsticks or a slotted spoon, immediately transfer the hard candied apples from the water to a serving dish. Serve at once.

Serves 6

Fried Banana Fritters

In Indonesia, the goreng pisang *hawker is everyone's favorite "candy man." Banana fritters, hot enough to burn the roof of your mouth, are an inescapable afternoon indulgence. In cafes and restaurants, the fritters are served as dessert often accompanied by vanilla ice cream.*

6   small half-ripe bananas

BATTER

½   cup (2½ oz/75 g) all-purpose (plain) flour

2   tablespoons cornstarch (cornflour)

¼   cup (2 oz/60 g) granulated sugar

¼   teaspoon salt

½   cup (4 fl oz/125 ml) water

Vegetable oil for deep-frying
Confectioners' (icing) sugar
Ground cinnamon

◙ Peel the bananas and cut crosswise into 3-inch (7.5-cm) lengths. Set aside.

◙ To make the batter, in a bowl, sift together the flour, cornstarch, granulated sugar and salt. Gradually add the water, stirring constantly, until the batter is smooth and thick enough to lightly coat the back of a spoon. Set aside.

◙ Preheat a wok or deep saucepan over medium-high heat. Pour in oil to a depth of 1½ inches (4 cm) and heat to 375°F (190°C) on a deep-frying thermometer. Add the bananas to the batter. Using long chopsticks or tongs, lift out the banana pieces one at a time, allowing the excess batter to drip off into the bowl, and carefully lower into the hot oil. Do not crowd the pan; the fruit must float freely. Deep-fry, turning often, until golden brown, about 2 minutes. Transfer to paper towels to drain. Repeat with the remaining banana pieces.

◙ Arrange the bananas on a warmed platter and dust with confectioners' sugar and cinnamon. Serve hot.

Serves 6

Mangoes with Sticky Rice

If you cannot find good-quality mangoes for this dish, nectarines, papayas or peaches can be substituted. This recipe uses sticky rice, which is also known as glutinous rice.

2 cups (14 oz/440 g) glutinous rice

2¼ cups (18 fl oz/560 ml) water

1¼ cups (10 fl oz/310 ml) coconut cream *(see glossary, page 342)*

⅔ cup (5 oz/155 g) sugar

½ teaspoon salt
  Banana leaves, rinsed and patted dry (optional)

2 mangoes, peeled, pitted and thickly sliced, chilled
  Toasted, unsweetened, shredded dried coconut or chopped dry-roasted peanuts for garnish

◙ Rinse the rice thoroughly with water until the rinse water runs clear. Drain. Place the rice in a saucepan and add the 2¼ cups (18 fl oz/560 ml) water. Let soak for at least 2 hours or as long as overnight.

◙ Bring the rice to a boil over high heat. Stir to loosen the grains from the bottom of the pan. Continue to boil until all the water on the surface is absorbed, 3–5 minutes. Cover, reduce the heat to low and simmer for 20 minutes. Remove from the heat and let the rice stand, covered, for at least 10 minutes or up to 40 minutes before stirring. The rice should be plumped, tender and sticky. Transfer to a large bowl and set aside.

◙ In a saucepan, combine the coconut cream, sugar and salt and bring to a boil over high heat. Boil, stirring constantly, until reduced to a thick cream, about 5 minutes. Pour the coconut cream over the rice and gently blend together.

◙ To serve, line each individual dessert plate with a banana leaf, if desired. Mound about ¾ cup (4 oz/125 g) of the sticky rice on each leaf. Arrange mango slices around the mounds. Sprinkle with toasted coconut or peanuts and serve.

Serves 8

Coconut Custard in a Pumpkin Shell

Sweet custard is a popular afternoon tea snack in Asia. In Thailand, it is made with coconut milk and steamed in a small pumpkin or Japanese kabocha squash. Before serving, the dessert is cut into wedges and the creamy squash and custard are eaten together.

1	small pumpkin or kabocha squash, about 3 lb (1.5 kg), or 2 acorn squashes, about 1½ lb (750 g) each
6	eggs
¾	cup (6 oz/185 g) firmly packed brown sugar
¼	teaspoon salt
1¼	cups (10 fl oz/310 ml) coconut milk
	Boiling water, as needed

◙ Cut off a slice 1 inch (2.5 cm) thick from the stem end of the pumpkin, the kabocha squash or the 2 acorn squashes and set aside to use as the lid(s). Scrape out the seeds and the pulp; reserve for another use. Rinse the hollowed-out squash(es) and pat dry.

◙ Place a deep bamboo steaming basket or a steaming rack in a large wok. Add enough water to come just below the base of the basket or rack. If using the basket, remove it and set aside. Bring the water to a boil over high heat.

◙ In a bowl, stir together the eggs, sugar and salt until blended. Add the coconut milk and stir until smooth. Pour the mixture through a fine-mesh sieve into the hollowed-out pumpkin or kabocha squash or divide between the 2 acorn squashes. Cover with the lid(s). If using the steaming basket, place the squash(es) in the basket and set in the wok. If using a steaming rack, place the squash(es) in a heat-proof ceramic dish, such as a soufflé dish, and set on the rack. Cover the basket or wok and steam until the custard is set and a wooden skewer inserted into the center comes out clean, 45–60 minutes; check the water level periodically and add boiling water as needed to maintain the original level.

◙ Remove the basket or dish from the wok. Let the squash(es) cool, then cover and refrigerate overnight.

◙ To serve, remove the lid(s) and cut the large squash into 8 wedges or each acorn squash into 4 wedges. Divide among individual serving plates.

Serves 8

Ginger–Peach Sorbet

The origin of ice cream has been traced back to the ancient Chinese, who mixed ice with sweets, thus inventing water ices, the precursors to modern-day ice creams. Chilled fresh fruit is the most popular traditional dessert in Asia, while ice desserts are favorites among the younger set. This fruit sorbet recipe satisfies both traditionalists and the young.

4 ripe peaches, peeled, pitted and cut into chunks
2 tablespoons fresh lime juice
2 tablespoons sugar
1 egg white
4 pieces sweet stem ginger in syrup or crystallized ginger, chopped

◙ In a food processor fitted with a metal blade, combine the peaches, lime juice and sugar. Process to a smooth purée. Pour the purée into a shallow metal pan. Place the pan in the freezer and freeze until the edges are firm and the center is soft, about 2 hours.

◙ In a large bowl, beat the egg white until almost stiff; set aside. Return the semifrozen peach purée to the food processor and process until it becomes frothy, about 30 seconds. Add the ginger and egg white to the processor and, using on-off pulses, process just long enough to blend in the white, 3–5 seconds.

◙ Pour the mixture into a freezer container, cover tightly and place in the freezer until firm but not frozen solid, 1–2 hours. If it freezes solid, allow it to soften in the refrigerator before serving, about 30 minutes.

Makes about 3 cups (24 oz/750 g); serves 4

BASIC RECIPES

Asian cooks rely on a handful of fundamental recipes when creating their famed hawker fare. Here you will find, in addition to the region's ubiquitous steamed rice and an assortment of toppings and crackers, mandarin pancakes for wrapping savory Chinese mixtures, a classic Vietmanese dipping sauce, a fiery Thai curry paste, and Cantonese barbecued pork, which is used in a variety of preparations from baked buns to stir-fried noodles.

ASIAN TOPPINGS AND ACCOMPANIMENTS

You will find these crisp and tasty toppings and accompaniments served with everything from soups and salads to curries and stir-fries. Although commercially prepared shallot and garlic flakes are available in Asian markets, they cannot compare to the freshly made ones given here.

FRIED PAPADAMS

◉ Indian papadams (below, left) are dried lentil wafers that expand when cooked just as rice stick noodles do, so they can be fried in the same fashion (see recipe, at right). The wafers can be purchased at Asian and Indian markets and come plain or embedded with small bits of chili or peppercorn. Papadams are often served as an accompaniment to Malay, Singaporean and Indonesian dishes.

FRIED SHRIMP CRACKERS

◉ These "crackers" or "chips" (below, top), made from shrimp, fish or melingo nuts, are popular garnishes. They are primarily made in Indonesia, where they are called *krupuk*. The crackers are dehydrated and look like hard, dry chips. They are deep-fried in the same manner as rice stick noodles (at right).

FRIED SHALLOT OR GARLIC FLAKES

8   shallots or garlic cloves, cut cross-
    wise into slices ⅛ inch (3 mm)
    thick
    Peanut or vegetable oil for frying

◉ In a frying pan over medium heat, pour in peanut or vegetable oil to a depth of ½ inch (12 mm). When the oil is moderately hot (about 325°F/165°C), add the shallot or garlic slices. Fry slowly, stirring, just until golden brown, 2–3 minutes. Using a slotted spoon, transfer the slices to paper towels to drain. Let cool, then store the flakes (below, front) in an airtight container at room temperature for up to several weeks.

Makes about ½ cup (1½ oz/45 g)

CRISPY FRIED RICE STICKS

◉ Rice stick noodles come in 1-lb (500-g) packages, often separated into 4 wafers. Holding 1 wafer inside a paper bag to capture any shreds, break it apart into several small portions.

◉ In a wok or saucepan over medium heat, pour in peanut oil to a depth of 2 inches (5 cm). When the oil is hot (about 375°F/190°C), drop in the noodles, 1 portion at a time. As soon as they puff, in just a few seconds, turn them over with long chopsticks or tongs and fry on the other side for a few seconds. Immediately transfer the fried noodles to paper towels to drain. Let cool, then store the sticks (near left) in an airtight container at room temperature for up to 4 days.

FISH SAUCE AND LIME DIPPING SAUCE

NUO'C CHA'M

This dipping sauce is as common on the Vietnamese table as salsa is on the Mexican table. It adds an exciting kick and addictive tang to a wide variety of dishes.

1	clove garlic, finely minced
1	fresh small red chili pepper, seeded and finely minced
¼	cup (2 oz/60 g) sugar
¼	cup (2 fl oz/60 ml) fresh lime juice, including pulp
5	tablespoons Vietnamese or Thai fish sauce
½	cup (4 fl oz/125 ml) water

◉ In a mortar, combine the garlic, chili and sugar and mash with a pestle to form a paste. Add the lime juice and pulp, fish sauce and water and stir to dissolve the sugar.

◉ Strain the sauce into a bowl or jar and use immediately. Or, cover tightly and refrigerate for up to 5 days.

Makes about 1¼ cups (10 fl oz/310 ml)

RED CURRY PASTE

KAENG PHED

Since this curry paste keeps well in the freezer for a few months, make a large batch and pack it in an ice-cube tray to use as needed. To save time, look for prepared curry pastes in most Asian markets.

½	cup (1 oz/30 g) dried red chilies
8	pieces dried kaffir lime rind or 1 tablespoon chopped fresh lime zest
8	fresh or 4 dried galangal slices, each about 1 inch (2.5 cm) in diameter, chopped
6	lemongrass stalks, tender heart section only
1	tablespoon whole coriander seeds or ground coriander
1	tablespoon whole cumin seeds or ground cumin
½	teaspoon whole black peppercorns or ¾ teaspoon ground pepper
½	teaspoon salt
1	teaspoon sweet paprika
6	cloves garlic, chopped
4	shallots, chopped
2	tablespoons chopped fresh cilantro (fresh coriander) roots or stems
1	teaspoon dried shrimp paste or anchovy paste

◉ Cut the chilies in half crosswise, then shake out and discard the seeds. In a small bowl, combine the chilies with warm water to cover. In another small bowl, combine the dried lime rind and dried galangal, if using, and cover with warm water; let soak until soft and pliable, about 30 minutes. Drain the galangal and lime rind, chop them and set aside. Cut the lemongrass crosswise into thin slices; set aside.

◉ If using whole coriander and cumin seeds, toast them in a small, dry frying pan over medium heat, shaking the pan occasionally, until fragrant, about 3 minutes. Let cool and transfer the seeds and whole peppercorns, if using, to a spice grinder or mortar; grind or pulverize with a pestle to a fine powder. Combine the ground spices with the salt and paprika and set aside.

◉ Drain the chilies, reserving about ¼ cup (2 fl oz/60 ml) of the soaking liquid, and place the chilies and soaking liquid in a blender or mini food processor. Add the reconstituted or fresh galangal, lime rind or fresh lime zest, lemongrass, garlic, shallots, cilantro roots or stems, shrimp or anchovy paste and reserved dry spices. Process into as smooth a paste as possible, about 30 seconds. If the mixture remains coarse, transfer it to a mortar and mash with a pestle until smooth.

Makes about 1 cup (8 fl oz/250 ml)

STEAMED RICE
BOK FAN

Most Asian cooks agree that perfectly cooked rice should stick together; under light pressure, however, a clump of rice should crumble into smaller lumps.

2   cups (14 oz/440 g) long-grain white rice
2¼ cups (18 fl oz/560 ml) water

◙ Rinse the rice with cold running water until the rinse water runs clear. Drain well and place in a 2–2½-qt (2–2.5-l) saucepan. Add the water.

◙ Place the pan over high heat and bring to a boil. Stir briefly and continue boiling until the water on the surface is completely absorbed and small pits have formed in the surface. Cover, reduce the heat to very low and cook, undisturbed, for 20 minutes.

◙ When the rice is done, remove the pan from the heat and let it sit, covered, for at least 10 minutes or for up to 40 minutes before serving.

◙ To serve, wet a wooden spoon and use it to fluff up the rice. Serve hot.

Makes 4–5 cups (20–25 oz/625–780 g)

CANTONESE BARBECUED PORK
CHA SIU

Barbecued pork is frequently added to noodles, soups, and main dishes. It also makes a delicious snack or appetizer when dipped in Chinese mustard and toasted sesame seeds. Plan several days in advance to allow time for marinating. Make a big batch, as it freezes well for up to 2 months.

¼   cup (2 fl oz/60 ml) light soy sauce
¼   cup (2 fl oz/60 ml) dark soy sauce
¼   cup (3 oz/90 g) honey
⅓   cup (2½ oz/75 g) sugar
1   teaspoon salt
2   tablespoons Scotch whisky or dry sherry
3   tablespoons hoisin sauce
1   teaspoon peeled and finely grated fresh ginger
½   teaspoon five-spice powder, optional
4   lb (2 kg) boneless country-style pork spareribs, pork butt, loin or tenderloin

HONEY GLAZE
3   tablespoons honey
2   teaspoons light soy sauce
1   teaspoon Asian sesame oil

◙ In a small saucepan, combine the light and dark soy sauces, honey, sugar, salt, whisky or sherry, hoisin sauce, ginger, and the five-spice powder, if using. Heat, stirring, until the sugar dissolves. Remove from the heat and let cool.

◙ Cut the pork into strips about 2 inches (5 cm) wide, 7 inches (18 cm) long and 1½ inches (4 cm) thick. Place in a lock-top plastic bag, add the marinade and seal closed. Massage to coat the meat fully with the marinade. Refrigerate overnight or for up to 3 days. Bring to room temperature before roasting.

◙ Preheat the oven to 450°F (230°C).

◙ Pour boiling water into a roasting pan to a depth of ½ inch (12 mm). Rest a cooling rack slightly larger than the pan on top of it. Drain the pork and set the strips across the rack. Roast for 15 minutes. Turn the strips over and roast until browned and firm to the touch, about 15 minutes longer.

◙ Meanwhile, make the honey glaze: In a small bowl, mix together the honey, soy sauce and sesame oil, stirring well. Brush the strips with the glaze and roast until the edges begin to char, about 1 minute longer. Remove from the oven, cover and let rest for 15 minutes, then cut the strips across the grain into thin slices. Serve warm or cold.

Makes about 3 lb (1.5 kg)

MANDARIN PANCAKES

BAO BING

Mandarin pancakes are crêpelike breads used to wrap stir-fried dishes. Commercially prepared pancakes are available in the frozen-food sections of Chinese food stores.

- 2 cups (10 oz/315 g) all-purpose (plain) flour, plus extra as needed
  Pinch of salt
- 1 cup (8 fl oz/250 ml) boiling water
- 3 tablespoons Asian sesame oil or vegetable oil

◙ In a food processor fitted with the metal blade, combine the 2 cups (10 oz/315 g) flour and salt; pulse once to mix. With the motor running, pour the boiling water through the feed tube in a slow, steady stream. Continue to process until a rough ball forms and the dough pulls away from the sides of the work bowl, 15–20 seconds. If the dough is sticky, sprinkle with more flour and process for 15 seconds longer.

◙ Turn out the dough onto a lightly floured work surface. Knead until smooth and no longer sticky, about 3 minutes. Cover with a damp towel and let rest for at least 30 minutes, or wrap in the towel and refrigerate overnight. Bring to room temperature before continuing.

◙ Return the dough to a lightly floured work surface and knead again until fairly firm, smooth and no longer sticky, about 1 minute. Divide the dough in half. Roll out one-half ¼ inch (6 mm) thick. Using a 3-inch (7.5-cm) round cookie cutter, cut out 10 rounds. Brush half of the rounds with a thin film of sesame or vegetable oil, then cover each oiled round with an unoiled one.

◙ Preheat an ungreased frying pan over medium-low heat for 1 minute. Meanwhile, on a lightly floured board, roll out one "sandwiched round" into a round 8 inches (20 cm) in diameter and place in the pan.

Within 45–60 seconds, the round should puff in the middle and blister on the bottom. Turn it over and continue to cook for about 30 seconds longer. Remove from the heat and immediately pull the layers apart to make 2 pancakes. Stack them, dry side down, and wrap in aluminum foil while preparing the remaining pancakes. Use the pancakes immediately, or refrigerate for up to 2 days or freeze for up to 1 month.

◙ To reheat refrigerated pancakes, fold them in half or into quarters and arrange them in a bamboo steaming basket. Set the steaming basket over (not touching) boiling water in a wok; cover and steam for 3 minutes. Serve directly from the basket. If pancakes are frozen, thaw first at room temperature, then steam for 5 minutes.

Makes twenty 8-inch (20-cm) pancakes

ASIAN: BASIC RECIPES

Glossary

The following glossary defines common ingredients and cooking terms, as well as special cooking equipment, used in Italian, Mexican, and Asian cooking.

Anchovy Fillets
Fished in the waters that surround Italy, the tiny anchovy, a relative of the sardine, adds its intense, briny taste to pizzas and other pizzeria dishes. Imported anchovy fillets canned in olive oil are the best, most widely available choice for the recipes in this book.

Artichokes
These large flower buds of a variety of thistle, also known as globe artichokes, are native to the Mediterranean. When large, the tight cluster of tough, pointed leaves covers pale green inner leaves and a gray-green base; together they make up the heart, which conceals a prickly choke.

TO TRIM ARTICHOKES
For baby artichokes, pull off tough outer leaves. Trim stem even with the base and cut away the fibrous, dark green layer around the base, being careful not to trim the meaty crown that lies beneath. Cut off about 1 inch (2.5 cm) from the top.

For large artichokes, cut off about 2 inches (5 cm) from the top. Cut in half lengthwise and use a small, sharp-edged spoon to remove the fuzzy choke. Remove interior leaves that have prickly tips. To prevent discoloration, rub cut surfaces with a lemon half and immerse trimmed artichokes in a bowl of water containing lemon juice.

Arugula
Also known as rocket, this green leaf vegetable has slender, multiple-lobed leaves and a peppery, slightly bitter flavor. Used raw in salads and *panini* and for topping pizzas.

Avocado
Native to Mexico, the avocado tree bears a pear-shaped fruit with leathery skin that conceals buttery, pale green flesh. Several varieties are commonly available, varying in size, color and texture of skin; the finest flavor and consistency belong to Hass avocados, which are small to moderate in size and have dark, rough skin.

Bamboo Shoots
Crisp, mild-flavored, white to ivory shoots of the bamboo plant; popular ingredient in stir-fries and other dishes. Sold canned in water. Drain and rinse well before use.

Bean Sauce
Chinese condiment made from salted, fermented soybeans. Yellow bean sauce, known in Thailand as *dao jiow* and in Malaysia as *tau cheo,* is a lighter variation of the more common, stronger-flavored brown bean sauce from China.

Bean Sprouts
Crisp, fresh-tasting, ivory-colored sprouts of the mung bean, used in stir-fries and a wide variety of other dishes.

Beans
A staple of the Mexican kitchen. Dried beans should be picked over to remove small stones or fibers or any discolored or misshapen beans. Many need also be soaked in cold water for several hours to rehydrate them, to shorten the cooking time. Some popular varieties used in this book include:

Black Small beans with black skins, smoky flavor and a mealy texture. Sometimes called turtle beans, black beans (2) are common along the Gulf Coast and in southeastern Mexico.

Kidney These kidney-shaped beans (1) have reddish brown skins, a robust flavor and a slightly mealy texture.

Pinto This brown-and-tan speckled variety (4)—its name

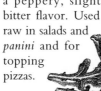

means "painted"—has a rich flavor and mealy texture.

Red Widely available small beans (3) with brownish red skins and slightly sweet flavor.

Bell Peppers
Sweet, bell-shaped red, yellow or green peppers, also known as capsicums, are popular in cantina dishes. Bell peppers must have their indigestible seeds removed before use. Often the peppers are also roasted, which loosens their skins for peeling and enhances their natural sweetness.

TO ROAST AND PEEL A BELL PEPPER
Seed the pepper and place the halves, cut sides down, on a baking sheet. Place under a preheated broiler (griller) until the skins blister and turn a deep brown. Remove from the broiler and place the peppers in a plastic or paper bag. Seal and let steam for 10 minutes. Remove from the bag and peel off the skins.

Bok Choy
This Chinese cabbage variety, which translates literally as "white vegetables," has thick, long white stems fringed with dark green leaves, and is enjoyed for its crisp texture and mild, slightly peppery taste.

Bread
To serve with pizzeria-style meals, or for bread crumbs, choose a good country-style loaf made from unbleached wheat flour, with a firm, coarse crumb; also sometimes labeled

"rustic" or "peasant-style" loaves.

TO MAKE BREAD CRUMBS

When a recipe calls for dried bread crumbs, first make fresh ones. Cut away the crusts and break bread into coarse chunks. Place the chunks in a food processor or blender and process to the desired consistency, usually fine or coarse. To dry the crumbs, spread them in a baking pan and leave in an oven set at its lowest temperature until they feel very dry, 30–60 minutes; do not let them brown. Store in a covered container at room temperature. Fine dried bread crumbs may also be bought.

Capers

The buds of a common Mediterranean bush, capers grow wild throughout Italy. For use as a savory flavoring ingredient, they are preserved in salt or, more commonly, are pickled in salt and vinegar.

Chayote

Pear-shaped member of the squash family with a mild flavor and moist texture reminiscent of cucumbers or zucchini. Although one variety has dark green, prickly skin, most chayotes available outside Mexico have relatively smooth, pale green skin.

Cheeses

ITALIAN

Many different cheeses are produced in Italy. Those used in this book include:

Fontina A creamy, delicate cow's milk cheese noted for its slightly nutty taste. Fontina from the Aosta Valley of northwestern Italy is considered the best.

Goat Generally soft, fresh and creamy, goat's milk cheeses are notable for their mild tang. Sold in small rounds or logs, they are used in antipasti and pizza toppings.

Gorgonzola Dolcelatte Literally "sweet milk Gorgonzola," this is a milder variety of the creamy, pale yellow, blue-veined cheese of Lombardy.

Mascarpone A thick, fresh cream cheese traditionally sold in small tubs. Similar to French crème fraîche or Mexican *crema,* it is used to enrich sauces or desserts, and may also be sweetened and flavored for eating on its own.

Mozzarella An essential pizza topping, this mild, rindless white cheese is traditionally made from water buffalo's milk and sold fresh. Commercially produced cow's milk mozzarella has a firmer consistency and is recommended for the pizza recipes in this book. Fresh mozzarella is sold immersed in water and should be drained before using. Mozzarella may also be flavored and preserved by smoking, giving it a sturdier texture and a deep yellowish-brown color.

Parmesan With a sharp, salty, full flavor acquired during at least 2 years of aging, the best examples of this hard, thick-crusted cow's milk cheese are prized by cooks and diners alike. Although it takes its name from the city of Parma, Parmesan originated midway between that city and Reggio, where the finest variety, Parmigiano-Reggiano,® is produced. Buy in block form, to grate fresh as needed.

Pecorino Sheep's milk cheese, sold fresh or aged. Among its most popular aged forms is pecorino Romano from Rome and its vicinity.

Provolone Pale yellow, fairly firm cheese made from cow's or water buffalo's milk. Its flavor ranges from mild and slightly sweet to strong and tangy.

Ricotta A light, mild and soft fresh cheese traditionally made from sheep's milk, although cow's milk ricotta is more common today. For the best quality, seek out fresh ricotta, found in Italian delicatessens; good ricotta may also be sold in small tubs in most markets.

Taleggio A cow's milk cheese from Lombardy, with a soft, smooth texture and a taste that ranges from slightly piquant to strong, depending upon age.

MEXICAN

While many Mexican cheeses may be found only in ethnic markets, several kinds of more commonly available cheeses serve well as substitutes.

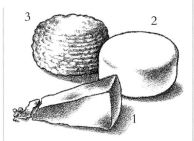

Añejo "Aged" white cheese with a dry, crumbly texture and salty flavor. Grated Romano, Parmesan or feta may be substituted.

Asadero This mild, soft white variety is typically used for melting. Monterey Jack or mozzarella may be substituted.

Cabrales Spanish goat's milk cheese similar in taste to Roquefort. If unavailable, substitute any blue cheese.

Cotija (1) A type of *añejo* cheese.

Manchego The Mexican variety of this classic Spanish cheese (2) is made from cow's milk and has a fine melting consistency, similar to Monterey Jack. Depending on how it is used, Romano, Parmesan, white Cheddar or Monterey Jack may be substituted.

Panela Fresh cheese (3) with a soft, slightly spongy texture. Depending upon the recipe, Monterey Jack, water-packed fresh mozzarella, dry cottage cheese, farmer cheese or dry ricotta may be substituted.

Chili Oil

Made by infusing hot red chili peppers in vegetable or sesame oil, yielding a red, fragrant, spicy seasoning.

Chili Paste, Thai Roasted
Known as *nam prik pao* and available in Southeast Asian markets. Do not confuse with Chinese chili paste.

Chilies
Mexico is the world's largest producer of chilies, with scores if not hundreds of varieties available. Most of a chili's heat resides in its seeds and ribs. For milder flavor, remove both before using. Some of the varieties used in this book are:

Anaheim Fresh, mild to moderately hot green chilies (1), about 6 inches (15 cm) long and 2–2½ inches (5–6 cm) wide. Also called California or long green chilies, and closely related to the New Mexican chili.

Ancho Literally the "wide" chili, this dried form of the poblano, measures up to 5 inches (13 cm) long and 3 inches (7.5 cm) wide. Wrinkled and deep reddish brown, it varies in hotness from mild to moderate, and has a slightly bittersweet taste and aroma reminiscent of prunes.

Árbol This dried, bright red fresh chili, literally a "tree" chili, is very hot. The slender chilies measure about 2½ inches (6 cm) long.

Birds-eye A small red chili used in Asian dishes.

Cayenne Commonly used in its ground dried form, this very hot chili lends subtle heat.

Chipotle Smoked form of the jalapeño, light brown in color, usually packed in a thick sauce called *adobo* or pickled in brine, sometimes found simply dried.

Habanero Measuring about 2 inches (5 cm) in length and up to 1¾ inches (4.5 cm) wide, this fresh or dried chili is one of the hottest available, more than 30 times hotter than the fiery jalapeño. Its flavor is also notable for hints of tropical fruit.

Jalapeño Named for the capital of the Veracruz state, this fresh, fairly small (2–3 inches/5–7.5 cm long and up to 1½ inches/4 cm in diameter), thick-walled, fiery variety (3) is usually sold green,.

Mulato Similar to the *ancho*, this dried chili tends to have a darker color and a fuller, slightly bitter taste.

Pasilla Up to 6 inches (15 cm) long, narrow and notably wrinkled, this dried chili has a rich, spicy flavor with hints of fruit. Also known as the *chile negro*.

Poblano Moderately mild, fresh green—or sometimes ripened red—chili (2). Large and broad in shape—up to 5 inches (13 cm) long and 3 inches (7.5 cm) wide—most commonly stuffed for chiles rellenos or used as a garnish.

Serrano Small, slender fresh green or red chili (4)—up to 2 inches (5 cm) long and about ½ inch (12 mm) wide—is as spicy as the *jalapeño*, though its flavor is notably sharper.

___

TO ROAST AND PEEL
FRESH CHILIES
Roasting fresh chilies develops the flavor, gives a softer texture and enables the thin, indigestible skins to be peeled off. To roast a chili, hold it with tongs or a fork over a gas stove burner set to a medium flame and turn it until its skin is evenly blackened and blistered, 5–10 minutes. Or cook on a dry *comal* or heavy skillet over medium heat, turning occasionally, until evenly blackened, 10–15 minutes. Cover with a damp cloth or seal in a heavy plastic or paper bag for 10–15 minutes. Then hold under a thin stream of cold running water and peel off the skin.

___

Clam Juice
A convenient substitute for fish stock in seafood dishes, this briny, strained liquid from shucked clams may be found in bottles in most food stores.

Coconut
The fruit of the tropical coconut palm. *Coconut milk*—a rich extract made by puréeing the flesh with hot water—is available in both Latin American and Asian markets; do not confuse it with sweetened coconut cream. *Coconut cream* is the thick, extra-rich layer that rises to the top of coconut milk. *Unsweetened*

flakes of dried coconut are sold both in tiny shreds and in wide shards.

To obtain coconut cream, remove top from an unshaken can of coconut milk, scrape off the thick, semi-solid layer of cream, or pour the milk into a glass container and let cream rise to the top. For coconut milk, shake the contents of the can before opening.

To toast coconut, spread on a baking sheet and toast in a 350°F (180°C) oven until lightly golden, about 5 minutes.

___

Corn Husks
The traditional wrapper for tamales, commonly sold in plastic bags, sometimes already trimmed and flattened. Store in a dry place, where they will keep for up to a year. Before use, the leaves must be soaked to make them pliable.

Crema
Used as an enrichment and garnish for both sweet and savory dishes, this Mexican-style cultured cream resembles the crème fraîche of France.

Crème Fraîche
Lightly soured and thickened fresh cream. To make a similar product at home, lightly whip ½ cup (4 fl oz/125 ml) heavy (double) cream; stir in 1 teaspoon sour cream. Cover and let stand at room temperature until thickened, about 12 hours.

Curry Paste, Red
Classic Thai blend of red chilies, garlic, onions, lemongrass, cilantro and galangal. Use store-bought or make your own (see page 337).

Eggplants
Tender, mildly earthy, sweet vegetable-fruits covered with tough, shiny skin, which may

be peeled or left on in grilled or long-cooked dishes. Eggplants vary in color from the familiar purple to red and from yellow to white. The most common variety is the large, purple globe eggplant (above), but many markets also carry the slender, purple Asian variety (Chinese or Japanese eggplant), which is more tender and has fewer, smaller seeds. Also known as aubergine and in Italy as *melanzana*.

Fennel
This bulb vegetable of Mediterranean origin has a mild anise taste and a crisp, refreshing texture. A related variety of the plant produces feathery leaves used as an herb and small crescent-shaped seeds used as a spice.

Fish Sauce
Thai fish sauce *(nam pla)* and Vietnamese fish sauce *(nuoc nam),* both thin, amber liquids, are functionally equivalent to the soy sauce of Chinese cooking, seasoning a wide variety of savory dishes. Although the two types are interchangeable, the Vietnamese variety is milder and more delicate than the Thai.

Galangal
Also called Siamese ginger, *kha* in  Thailand and *lengkuas* or *laos* in Indonesia and Malaysia, this rhizome is related to and resembles ginger, but has a mildly mustardlike, slightly medicinal taste; ginger is not an acceptable substitute. Sold both whole fresh and as dried slices; halve the quantity when using dried. To reconstitute dried galangal, soak the slices in warm water until pliable.

Garlic
This intensely aromatic bulb has helped to define the character of Italian and Mexican cooking. To ensure the best flavor, buy whole heads of dry garlic, separating individual cloves as needed. Do not buy more than you will use in 1 or 2 weeks.

Ghee
One of the most common cooking fats of India, ghee is similar to clarified butter—that is, butter from which the milk solids have been removed. Ghee is slowly simmered to eliminate moisture, a process that lightly browns the fat, giving it a nutlike flavor. Ghee may be purchased ready-made in Asian markets.

Ginger
Spicy-sweet fresh ginger root, actually a rhizome, is a common seasoning in many Asian cuisines. The papery skin is generally removed before use. Pieces of ginger preserved in syrup, usually labeled "stem ginger in syrup," are popular in sweet dishes.

Herbs
A wide variety of fresh and dried herbs add complex character to many dishes. Some popular varieties include:

Basil A sweet, spicy herb used both dried and fresh in pesto and tomato sauces, pizza toppings and calzone fillings. Highly aromatic Thai basil has dark green leaves and purplish stems. Common sweet basil may be substituted

Bay Leaves The dried leaves of the bay laurel tree give pungent, spicy flavor to simmered dishes.

Chives Long, thin, fresh green shoots of the chive plant have a mild flavor that recalls the onion, a close relative. *Garlic chives,* also known as Chinese chives are prized for their distinctive garlic flavor.

Cilantro Also known as fresh coriander or Chinese parsley, this popular Asian herb, which physically resembles flat-leafed (Italian) parsley, has a sharp and somewhat astringent aroma and flavor. An indispensable ingredient in Mexican cooking.

Epazote This Mexican herb has an unfavorable aroma when fresh, but cooked, it lends a pungent dimension of flavor. It is also known as wormseed, Mexican tea and stinkweed. There is no acceptable substitute.

Mint Spearmint and other mints complement the spicy seasonings of Mexican food with their cool sweetness.

Oregano An herb with an aromatic, spicy flavor that intensifies with drying. Also known as wild marjoram.

Parsley Although this popular fresh herb is available in two varieties, Italian cooks prefer flat-leaf parsley, also known as Italian parsley, which has a more pronounced flavor than the curly-leaf type.

Rosemary Used fresh or dried, strong-flavored rosemary frequently scents focaccia, poultry and vegetables.

Sage Fresh or dried, this pungent herb seasons focaccia, beans, meat and poultry.

Thyme Delicately fragrant and clean tasting, this herb is used fresh or dried to flavor a wide variety of savory dishes.

Hoisin Sauce
Thick, savory-sweet Chinese bottled seasoning sauce made from fermented soy beans, variously flavored with vinegar, garlic, chili, sesame oil and other ingredients.

Jicama

This brown-skinned tropical root looks like a large turnip. Its white flesh, however, resembles a radish in texture and a water chestnut in taste.

Kaffir Lime

The leaves and rind of this small, round, gnarled variety of lime indigenous to Southeast Asia—known as *limau perut* in Malaysia and *makrut* in Thailand—are used in curry

pastes and other dishes as a source of intense, citrusy aroma and flavor. The leaves (above) are most commonly dried, but they can also be found fresh or frozen in Asian markets. Domestic citrus leaves or regular lime rind may be substituted.

Lard

A clarified cooking fat rendered from pork, lard adds a signature richness to many Mexican dishes. The best quality lard is sold in specialty butcher shops, although packaged varieties are available in some food stores.

Lemongrass

Stiff, reedlike grass that contributes an aromatic, citruslike flavor to Southeast Asian recipes. If unavailable, similarly cut lemon zest may be used, although it will not provide the authentic flavor.

When a recipe calls for the heart of lemongrass, use only the bottom 4–6 inches (10–15 cm) of the stalk, peeling off tough, outer leaves until you reach an inner purple ring. Chopping or crushing the stalk before using helps release its aromatic oils.

Lentils

Among the green varieties of this small, disk-shaped dried legume, the French Puy lentil, from the town of Le Puy, is considered one of the finest. Pick over lentils carefully to remove impurities or shriveled lentils before cooking.

Lily Buds, Dried

Sold in cellophane bags and also called golden needles and tiger lily buds, these dried flower buds impart a subtle texture and flavor to some Chinese dishes.

Litchis

The small, plump, slightly cylindrical fruits of the litchi tree of southern China. Their brittle brown skins conceal sweet, subtly perfumed, moist white flesh. Most commonly available canned in water or syrup.

Mango

This oval-shaped tropical fruit has sweet yellow-orange flesh, and yellow skin tinged with orange when ripe. A ripe mango will yield slightly to fingertip pressure. Unripe green mangoes have a tartness and crisp character reminiscent of apples. Often used shredded in Southeast Asian dishes.

Masa Harina

A fine flour ground from corn kernels that have been soaked in slaked lime, used to prepare the doughs for corn tortillas and tamales. Prepared masa dough—used for making tortillas and tamales—is available in the refrigerator section of Mexican markets.

Milk, Sweetened Condensed

Made by evaporating 60 percent of the water from whole milk, then sweetening it with sugar, this canned product is a popular ingredient in Mexican desserts.

Mushrooms

With their rich, earthy flavors and meaty textures, mushrooms are regularly featured in Italian and Asian dishes. Some types used in this book include:

Chinese Black, Dried Often sold under its Japanese name, shiitake, this common mushroom gives a hearty, meatlike flavor and texture to recipes. Reconstitute before using.

Cremini Similar in size and shape to common cultivated white mushrooms, this variety has a more pronounced flavor and a rich brown skin concealing creamy tan flesh.

Cultivated Common mushrooms with smooth, white or brown circular caps. White mushrooms come in three sizes, from the smallest, or button, to cup, to the largest, or flat mushrooms.

Shiitake Meaty in flavor and texture, these Asian mush-

rooms have flat, dark brown caps 2–3 inches (5–7.5 cm) in diameter.

Straw, Canned Small, plump brown mushroom, commonly sold canned, with a mild flavor and tender texture. Also known as umbrella mushroom.

Tree Ear Mushrooms, Dried Also known as cloud ear, wood ear and black fungus, and by the Chinese *wun yee* or *muer*. Those labeled tree ears are crinkled, black and about ½ inch (12 mm) in size; cloud ears tend to be slightly larger and two-toned. These are not interchangeable in recipes that rely on size or shape.

Mussels

These bluish black bivalves open to reveal succulent

orange-colored flesh. Before cooking, scrub the shells well under running water and pull away the fibrous threads—known as the "beard"—by which they attach themselves to rocks and piers. Discard any mussels whose shells are open.

Napa Cabbage

Also known as Chinese cabbage, this vegetable is noted for its long, pale green, crinkly textured leaves and mild, sweet taste.

Noodles

A wide variety of noodles are used in Asian cooking. Some types used in this book include:

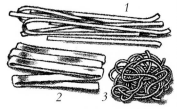

Bean Thread, Dried Thin, transparent noodle also called cellophane, glass, mirror or transparent noodles, as well as their Chinese name, *sai fun*. Also sometimes called bean thread vermicelli.

Egg Noodles, Fresh Chinese Light, thin noodles (3) freshly made from wheat flour and egg, sold in the refrigerator cases of Asian markets.

Rice Noodles, Fresh Whether thick or thin, wide or narrow, these noodles (2) made from rice flour and water are used in Chinese and Southeast Asian dishes.

Rice Sticks, Dried Made from rice flour, these range in shape from wiry threads (sometimes called rice vermicelli) to flat ribbons (1) measuring ¼ inch (6 mm) wide or wider. Soak until soft and pliable.

Nuts

A wide variety of nuts figure in both savory and sweet dishes. Some featured in this book include:

Almonds Popular oval nuts with a mellow, sweet flavor.

Candlenuts Similar in shape to hazelnuts, these small, white,

waxy nuts— *buah keras* in Malaysia and Indonesia—are used primarily as a thickening agent for spice pastes. Blanched almonds or unsalted macadamia or Brazil nuts may be substituted.

Hazelnuts Spherical nuts, also known as filberts, with a special affinity for chocolate. Often used in Italian sweets.

Peanuts, Dry-Roasted Most peanuts sold in the West have been cooked in oil. For authentic Asian taste, use nuts labeled dry-roasted.

Pine Nuts Often referred to by their Italian name, *pinoli,* these small, ivory nuts, the seeds of a species of pine tree, have a rich, resinous flavor that enhances pesto sauce and pizza toppings.

Walnuts These distinctively crinkled nuts have a rich taste and a crisp texture that complement savory and sweet dishes. The most familiar variety is the English walnut. The American black walnut, usually sold as shelled pieces, has a stronger flavor.

Oils

Oils used in this book include:

Olive Oil Extra-virgin olive oil, extracted from olives on the first pressing without use of heat or chemicals, is valued for its distinctive fruity flavor. Products labeled pure olive oil are less aromatic and flavorful and may be used for general cooking purposes.

Peanut Oil An all-purpose cooking oil that possesses a hint of the nut's richness.

Vegetable Oil Refers to many kinds of all-purpose flavorless oils pressed from vegetables or seeds, including corn oil or safflower oil.

Olives

In Italy, particularly in the southerly regions with harsher soil, olive trees thrive. Ripe black and underripe green olives in varied sizes are cured in combinations of salt, seasonings, brines, oils and vinegars to produce a wide range of piquant and pungent results. Greek Kalamatas are ripe olives that have been cured in brine and are packed in vinegar. Moroccan olives are ripe fruits that have first been dried in the sun, then packed in oil.

Onions

The most commonly used types include *green onions,* also known as spring onions and scallions, a variety that is harvested immature, with both its small white bulb and its long dark-green leaves; *red onions,* a mild, sweet variety with purplish red skin and red-tinged white flesh; *white onions,* a white-fleshed variety with a sweet, mild flavor that is the most commonly used onion in Mexican kitchens; and *yellow onions,* the familiar white-fleshed, stronger-flavored variety with dry, yellowish brown skins.

Oranges, Blood

A variety of orange with deep red flesh that has a stronger flavor than regular oranges, which may be substituted.

Oyster Sauce

Popular bottled Chinese seasoning made by blending steamed oysters with soy sauce and salt. A frequent sauce ingredient in stir-fries.

Palm Sugar

Also known as jaggery and coconut sugar, it is derived from boiling down the sap of various varieties of palm tree. It has a coarse, sticky texture and is sold in logs or tubs.

Pancetta

This unsmoked bacon is cured simply with salt and pepper. Available in Italian delicatessens and specialty-food stores, it may be sold flat, although it is commonly available sliced from a large sausage-shaped roll.

Papaya

Prized for its sweet, exotic-tasting flesh, many sizes, shapes and colors of this tropical fruit are grown in Mexico. Remove the seeds before using. Also known as pawpaw.

Pasta

Italy's best-known staple, pasta is a common addition to the menus of many pizzerias. Among the scores of pasta shapes and varieties available, three of the most common, used in this book, are:

Lasagna Broad, flat noodles with straight or ruffled edges, usually layered with cheese, sauce and other ingredients, then baked.

Linguine Literally, "little tongues," describing the shape in cross section of these long, slightly flattened strands.

Orecchiette Bite-sized pasta shaped like "ears."

Pear, Asian
Variety of pear developed by crossbreeding pears and apples, combining the mild flavor of the former with the crispness of the latter.

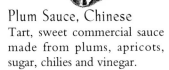

Pizza Peel
This wide, flat wooden spatula, with a square, thin-edged wooden blade is a useful tool for sliding pizzas into and out of the oven.

Plum Sauce, Chinese
Tart, sweet commercial sauce made from plums, apricots, sugar, chilies and vinegar.

Prosciutto
A specialty of Parma, this raw ham is cured by dry-salting for 1 month, then air-drying in curing sheds for 6 months or longer. Used as an ingredient, it is also served as an antipasto, cut into tissue-thin slices that highlight its deep pink color and intense flavor.

Quinoa
This ancient grain, available in health food stores, is rich in nutrients, and has an earthy, pleasantly sour taste.

Radicchio
The most common variety of this type of chicory has small reddish purple leaves with creamy white ribs, formed into a sphere. Used in pizza toppings or served raw in salads. Also called red chicory.

Radish, Chinese
White, cylindrical, stout and mild, commonly used in simmered dishes and soups. Available fresh or preserved in brine for use as a pungent salty seasoning.

Rice
For much of Asia, rice is the daily staple. The two common varieties used in this book are:

Glutinous Also known as sticky or sweet rice, this short-grain variety sticks together when cooked.

Long-Grain White The most common type of Asian rice, with long, slender grains that cook to a fluffy consistency.

Rice Flour
Both long-grain and glutinous rice are ground for flour. The former, called simply rice flour or rice powder, is used for making rice noodles and other savory dishes, as well as some sweets. The latter is known as sweet rice flour and is used for sweets.

Rice Wine
Chinese rice wine has a deep golden color, a heady aroma and a sweet, nutty taste; dry sherry may be substituted. *Mirin,* a Japanese sweet cooking wine offers a mild syrupy flavor.

Salt
Coarse-grained salt adds a robust crunch to focaccia toppings and other pizzeria dishes. Choose from *sea salt,* which is extracted by evaporation from seawater and has a more pronounced flavor than regular table salt, and *kosher salt,* a flaked variety that contains no additives and has a somewhat milder flavor than regular table salt.

Sausages
Fresh and dried sausages are frequently used for topping pizzas, as well as for ingredients in robust dishes.

Italian Sweet Sausages These have a mild flavor and may be seasoned with fennel seed or orange zest. Many innovative fresh sausages are available today, including those made from chicken or duck, which may be substituted for sweet pork sausage.

Chinese Sausage Called *lop cheung* in Cantonese, slender, aromatic, dried pork sausages, sold in linked pairs in plastic packages or hanging from strings in meat markets.

Chorizo A spicy Mexican fresh pork sausage, traditionally seasoned with chilies and garlic. Available ground or as fresh whole sausages. If unavailable, substitute fresh Cajun andouille or Polish kielbasa.

Mortadella A specialty of Bologna, this wide, mottled pork sausage has a mildly spicy flavor and a fine texture that make it a suitable ingredient in pizza toppings and other pizzeria recipes.

Sesame Oil, Asian
Used almost exclusively as a seasoning, it has a full, rich flavor derived from toasted sesame seeds.

Sesame Seeds
These tiny seeds, available both white and black, are generally added to sauces or used for sprinkling as a garnish.

Shallots
These small cousins of the onion have a papery brown skin, purple-tinged flesh and a flavor resembling both sweet onion and garlic.

Shortening, Vegetable
In baked goods, this solid vegetable fat may be used in place of or along with butter or lard, to "shorten" the flour—that is, to make it flaky and tender.

Shrimp
Before cooking, fresh shrimp (prawns) are usually peeled

and their thin, veinlike intestinal tracts removed.

TO PEEL AND DEVEIN FRESH SHRIMP
Use your thumbs to split open the thin shell between the legs, then carefully peel it away. With a small, sharp

knife, make a shallow slit along the back to expose the veinlike, usually dark intestinal tract. Using the tip of the knife or your fingers, lift up and pull out the vein.

Shrimp, Dried
Tiny dried shrimp (prawns), either whole or ground into a powder, used as a seasoning to give a subtly salty, briny taste to Asian dishes.

Shrimp Paste, Dried
A thick Southeast Asian seasoning of salted and fermented shrimp (prawns), ranging in color from light brown to purplish black, sold in blocks or packed in small plastic tubs. Anchovy paste makes a good substitute.

Soy Sauce
A dark liquid typically made from a fermented and aged mixture of soybeans, wheat, salt and water, soy sauce is a common seasoning in Asia.

Dark Soy Sauce Also known as medium soy sauce, this Chinese variety has caramel added, producing a darker color, sweeter flavor and thicker texture.

Indonesian Sweet Dark (Ketjap Manis) Dark, sweet soy sauce commonly used in Indonesian cooking. If unavailable, it can be approximated by simmering ½ cup (125 ml) soy sauce with 2 tablespoons each of molasses and dark brown sugar until the sugar dissolves.

Japanese Japanese soy sauces have a milder, sweeter, less salty taste than Chinese ones.

Light Also referred to as thin or regular soy sauce, this common Chinese variety is fairly thin and light in flavor.

Spices
For the best flavor, grind whole spices with a mortar and pestle or spice grinder just before using.

Cardamom Sweet and aromatic, these small, round seeds come enclosed inside a husklike pod.

Cinnamon This sweet spice is the aromatic bark of an evergreen tree, sold as dried strips—cinnamon sticks—or ground.

Cloves An aromatic East African spice, used whole or ground.

Coriander Spicy sweet, these small seeds of the coriander plant—also the source of the herb known as cilantro—may be used whole (1) or ground.

(1)   *(2)*   *(3)*

Cumin Strong, dusky and aromatic, this Middle Eastern spice flavors Mexican dishes and is sold ground or as small, crescent-shaped seeds (3).

Curry Powder Commercial blend of spices traditionally used in Indian and other Asian curries. Includes coriander seeds, cumin, chili powder, fenugreek and turmeric, along with such additions as cardamom, cinnamon, cloves, allspice, fennel seeds, ginger and tamarind.

Five-Spice A popular Chinese ground reddish seasoning.

Paprika Available in sweet, mild and hot versions, this powdered red spice is derived from dried paprika peppers.

Pepper For the best flavor, purchase this common spice as whole peppercorns, to be ground or crushed as needed. Black peppercorns, pungent in flavor, derive from underripe pepper berries. Milder white peppercorns are fully ripened and the husks are removed before drying.

Saffron This golden-orange, exotically perfumed spice is the dried stigmas of a species of crocus. Sold in whole threads or powdered.

Star Anise Resembling an eight-pointed star, this small, brown seedpod contributes an aniselike flavor (2).

Turmeric This dried powder ground from a rhizome related to ginger contributes yellow color and mellow flavor.

Spinach
Popular in Italy for almost a thousand years, spinach figures in soups, pasta doughs and salads and as a filling for antipasti and calzone.

TO PREPARE SPINACH
For the best results, select smaller, more tender leaves. To remove the tough stems and ribs from mature leaves, fold each leaf in half with its

glossier side in, then grasp the stem and pull it toward the leaf tip, peeling it and any prominent ribs away from the leaf. Place spinach leaves in a sink or basin filled with cold water. Swish vigorously in the water to remove dirt. Then lift them out, drain the sink, and rinse it thoroughly. Repeat until no grit remains.

Squash, Summer
In addition to the familiar *zucchini* (courgette), small, edible-skinned summer squashes include the slightly sweet yellow *crookneck,* which has a bulbous flower end and a slender, curving stem end; the green or golden *straightneck;* and the round, flat *pattypan,* distinguished by its scalloped edge and pale green color.

Sriracha Sauce
Commercial, all-purpose Thai chili sauce, resembling an

orange-red catsup, used in cooking and as a condiment. Available hot or mild.

Tamarind Pulp

Dried pulp prepared from the pods of the tamarind tree, which adds a mild, sweet-tart flavor—without the sourness of lemon—to Southeast Asian recipes. Dissolve tamarind in boiling water and strain the resulting liquid before using.

Tomatillos

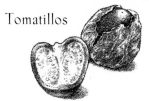

Also called *tomates verdes,* and sometimes mistakenly referred to as green tomatoes, small green tomatillos are actually related to the Cape gooseberry and have a distinctive sharp, fruity flavor. Fresh tomatillos are usually sold still encased in their brown papery husks. Peel off the husks by hand before the tomatillos are cut. Canned tomatillos may be found in most well-stocked markets.

Tomatoes

This vegetable-fruit originated in Peru, traveling northward to southern Mexico before Columbus's voyage to the New World. Making their way to Italy in the mid-16th century, tomatoes were not popular in Italian kitchens until the 18th century. For the best flavor, use sun-ripened tomatoes in season, whether *large red tomatoes, plum (Roma)* tomatoes or small red or yellow *cherry tomatoes.* Out of season, plum

tomatoes—whether fresh or canned—offer the best flavor.

Ripe tomatoes are also dried in the sun and preserved in olive oil or packaged dry; the former remain pliant, ready to add to cooked dishes, while the latter require reconstituting by soaking them in cool water.

Tortilla Press

Made of cast iron or heavy-duty aluminum, this device consists of two flat, circular plates connected by a hinge with a handle that presses them together. A ball of corn masa, placed between the plates and compressed, is formed into a flat tortilla.

Vanilla

The dried aromatic pod of a variety of orchid, the vanilla bean is a popular flavoring in Mexican desserts. Although its most common form is that of an alcohol-based extract (essence), the pod and the tiny seeds within it also impart vanilla flavor.

Vinegars

The term *vinegar* refers to any alcoholic liquid caused to ferment a second time by certain strains of yeast, turning it highly acidic. Vinegars highlight the qualities of the liquid from which they are made. *Red wine vinegar* has a more robust flavor than vinegar produced from white wine. *Balsamic vinegar,* a specialty of Modena for centuries, is made from reduced grape juice and is aged and blended for many years in a succession of casks.

The result is a tart-sweet, intensely aromatic vinegar. *Chinese red vinegar* is a flavorful red vinegar made from rice and used primarily as a dip or in sauces.

Wok

This half-spherical cooking pan made of heavy milled steel is the traditional vessel for stir-frying. Its shape and material conduct heat evenly and efficiently as small pieces of food

are briskly stirred and tossed inside it, using a long-handled wok spatula or long chopsticks.

Wrappers

All kinds of Asian snacks, appetizers and dumplings are enclosed in edible wrappers. The most common types of wrappers, used in this book, are:

Leaves
Fragrant, generously sized leaves are sometimes used as natural wrappers—and subtle flavoring agents—for steamed Asian dishes. Large banana leaves are usually sold frozen in large pieces to be cut into smaller sizes as needed for wrapping. Dried lotus leaves (right)

are sold whole, and must be reconstituted before using.

Rice Paper Ultrathin, brittle, semitransparent, paperlike sheets dried from a dough of rice flour and water, commonly sold in large rounds varying in size from 6½–14 inches (16.5–35 cm). They must be softened in water before use.

Spring Roll Paper-thin noodle wrappers for spring rolls. Sold in 1-pound (500-g) packages containing 2½ to 3 dozen square or circular wrappers.

Wonton Thin, square noodle wrappers measuring about 3½ inches (9 cm) across.

Zucchini

A squash native to the New World, the slender, cylindrical green zucchini (also known as courgette) long ago found its way into Italian kitchens. Seek out smaller squashes, which have a finer texture and tinier seeds than more mature specimens. Italian cooks who grow

zucchini in their own gardens take care to save the delicate blossoms, using them in pasta sauces or stuffing them for an antipasto.

INDEX

INDEX

INDEX